DELTA SIX
SOLDIER SURGEON

RICHARD L. SNIDER, M.D.

HERITAGE BOOKS, INC.

HERITAGE BOOKS
AN IMPRINT OF HERITAGE BOOKS, INC.

S2384-A4105HB

Books, CDs, and more – Worldwide

For our listing of thousands of titles see our websites
at
www.WillowBendBooks.com
and
www.HeritageBooks.com

Published 2003 by
HERITAGE BOOKS, INC.

Map, "Operations Area 25th Division" by SP4 Harry R. Caddick,
combat artist, for *Thunder, The Voice of Tropic Lightning*, an authorized
publication of the 25th Infantry Division

International Standard Book Number: **0-7884-2384-3**

DEDICATION

*This book is dedicated to the memory of
my three soldiers who were killed in action:*

*PFC John Grimmenstein,
SP/4 Steven Segura,
and PFC Everette Briggs.*

*I also wish to remember
the nameless Chinese baby whom I could not save
and all those who never returned
from America's struggle in South Vietnam.
They will ever be in my thoughts and prayers.*

CONTENTS

ILLUSTRATIONS

ACKNOWLEDGMENTS

I would like to thank the people at Heritage Books for their help: Corinne Will for selecting the manuscript for publication, Leslie Wolfinger, my first editor and Roxanne Carlson, my final editor, for their expertise and encouragement.

My daughters Beth, Tracy and Catie and son Rick never tired in their support and helpful criticism throughout the long years of listening to my ramblings about my experiences in Vietnam. My daughter Tracy was instrumental in designing the book cover as well as solving my many computer problems.

My wife Margy always has been and still is my inspiration in anything I do. She unflaggingly edited the many early versions of the manuscript and helped me write down the tangled thoughts stuck in my mind. She still is able to finish my sentences for me.

Any and all inaccuracies in this manuscript are mine, and I take full responsibility for all the material in this book.

PREFACE

In 1967, the war in South Vietnam continued to boil over the comfortable confines enjoyed early on by the then not-too-interested American public. That same year, President Lyndon Johnson decided to make victory there his personal concern, and he ordered the number of United States troops in South Vietnam's war zone to be increased to over five-hundred-thousand men. The Selective Service System became the busiest since World War II. Unfortunately, that draft also included the likes of me, as my years in college and medical school extended my eligibility from age eighteen to twenty-seven. Consequently, I was plucked from my surgical training to become inexorably immersed in that dreadful war.

Over thirty-three years have passed since my return from Vietnam, but that elapsed time has not, in any way, blunted the sharp and cutting memories I incurred there during a single intense year. The relative innocence I enjoyed as a surgical resident was forever erased by the senseless carnage of war I witnessed during that bellwether year. I still agonize over the tragic deaths of three men who were killed while serving under my command, and over the death of a small Chinese baby I was unable to save from a horrible war wound.

The Vietnam War was not the altogether monstrous carnage by crazed American soldiers depicted so often in our news media and movies. My observation was that most of the soldiers who served there did so with remarkable courage and unexpected consideration. In order to honor my dead soldiers, the little Chinese baby, and all those who died there, please let me tell you what happened during the 364 days, twelve hours, and fifteen minutes I spent in the American War in South Vietnam.

My memories, of course, are no longer as fresh as they once were, and may be altered by what I want to remember, rather than what really happened. My dreams are yet just as real, horrifying, and haunting as when I first returned from that horrible war in South Vietnam. These thirty-three years have proven that forgetting will not ever be possible for me. Remembering is the only way for me to deal with what happened that awful year. This is my story. Many of the names have been changed for privacy but the events remain very real.

Dr. Richard L. Snider, M.D.
rls23@georgetown.edu

About the Author

Rick Snider is a retired general and vascular surgeon who divides his time between his Cumberland home in the beautiful mountains of Western Maryland where he practiced for over twenty-five years and his warm weather home in Pentwater, Michigan on the shores of the big lake.

Since retirement, Dr. Snider and his wife Margy have spent two or three months each year volunteering in Pago Pago, American Samoa or on the Navajo Nation in Chinle, Arizona. Together they have raised four children and now immensely enjoy the freedom retirement allows to pursue new adventures.

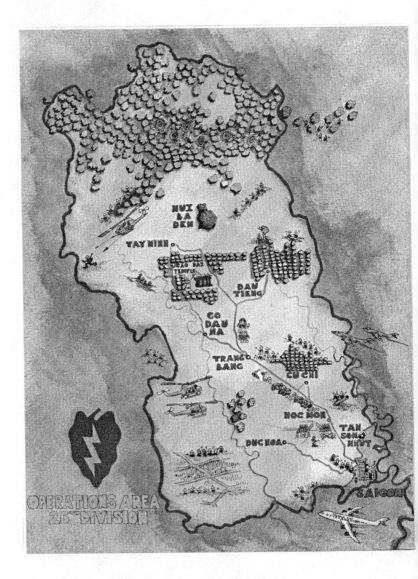

Map of Operations of the 25th Infantry Division
by SP4 Harry R. Caddick. Courtesy of the magazine,
Thunder, the Voice of Tropic Lightning. Vol. 1, No. 1, Fall, 1968

PROLOGUE

The cool breezes coming through the open side doors of the Huey Dust-Off helicopter were delightfully refreshing, making the oppressive heat on the ground below just an unpleasant memory. The pilot had been chatting on the radio most of the thirty-minute flight, but only a few of his escaping words were intelligible to me. Three flight crew members and the two other passengers were along on that morning's ride. As one of the passengers, I was not paying much attention to the pilot's babble. A two-word phrase stood out to me, however, and the pilot repeated the couplet often. Leaning forward, but not loosening the death grip I had on my seat, I asked, "What's this 'Delta Six'? You seem to say it over and over." "That's you, sir!" the pilot answered, shouting over the roar of the engine. At the exact moment he was speaking to me, he popped the chopper over a row of palm trees and back down again. The trees were lining a dike separating one of the many rice paddies we whizzed over that beautiful, crisp morning. Startled and nauseated by the helicopter's sudden upward lurch, I held onto my seat even more tightly. The pilot continued to speak as though he hadn't been fazed at all by the violent up and down motion we had just experienced. Having to angle his head slightly backward to speak to me, he kept his sunglassed eyes rigidly fixed on the landscape speeding by at one hundred miles per hour. "We are heading to Company D," he shouted. "The letter D is 'Delta' in the Army alphabet. You are the new commander, designated by the number 'Six'. The C.O. of the company is called the 'Delta Six'." Slightly flattered by his explanation, but a little embarrassed also, I sat back to enjoy the remainder of my rare and pleasant flight, which was, indeed, a cool respite from the war raging below in the searing tropical heat.

How I found myself tree-topping along in a helicopter at a hundred mph was not an unfamiliar story for those times. Like so many others, I was in the Army. The date was 12 October 1968. Creeping communism was going on below in Vietnam, and we half million American military troops were there to stop it. This was the dreaded war in Vietnam, and I was right in the thick of it. What had been started by "Uncle" Ho Chi Minh many years ago had somehow lasted to now surround and engulf my life!

GETTING THERE

In July of 1966 I entered the first of a five year surgical training program at Yale University's Graduate School of Medicine in New Haven, Connecticut. A few months into my internship year, I realized I was on President Johnson's list of the five-hundred thousand because personal "Greetings from Uncle Sam" found their way into my mailbox! What soon followed was to become the single most memorable chapter in the book of my life, the year I spent in Vietnam at age twenty-seven.

The "Greetings" letter I received from the Department of the Army ordered me to report to the local Army Induction Center in New Haven for a preliminary physical examination. As a result, I was soon sitting naked on a cold bench at seven o'clock in the morning, with about one hundred other shivering, blue bodies. A freckled faced, red-headed seventeen-year-old next to me asked, "Does your mom know you signed up?" Forcing a smile I told him she did and inquired if his mom knew he had. He said yes, but she wasn't happy. Then, as if on cue, we simultaneously turned our heads to the front in hopes of preserving our anonymity and regaining some of our lost dignity. A far off order was shouted and the shivering horde of young men stood to endure what was to become a mass hernia examination. With a gloved index finger, the examining doctor impaled each man's right inguinal area. As the doctor's ice cold finger probed our warm groins, everybody jumped, I more than others. I was abhorred to see the doctor using the same glove for all one hundred examinations! Equally egregious to me was the fact that he never checked our other side for a hernia! I was getting worked up; what kind of medicine is this anyway? Not in a military uniform, the doctor was more than likely a civilian, hired for the task. Calming down, my cold numbed brain told me anyone with a hernia would have spoken up to keep from being drafted. I had to accept the old adage that there are three ways of doing things, "The Right Way, the Wrong Way, and the Army Way."

The parade of naked recruits then walked along, following a white line on the wooden floor, until a piece of red tape signaled a stop. A small plastic jug was thrust into my hand and the technician ordered me to "pee!" Always a bashful urinator, the line behind had to halt for what seemed an eternity while I strained. My prayers were answered when a few drops appeared in the cup! The medic seemed satisfied, and the line moved forward once again. Proceeding through many stations including blood drawing, blood pressure checks, eye charts, manual exams of abdomens and auscultation of hearts, the ordeal continued. Following this dehumanizing process, the examining doctor addressed us for the first time. He thanked us for our patience, and, as an aside, ordered any doctors present to take one step forward. Embarrassed by being singled out, three of us arose. The doctor announced we should have spoken up, and he would have done our examinations in private. Just a little late, I thought.

Internship year didn't allow me much time to dwell on the Army obligations that lay ahead. I was surprised to learn the Army wanted to delay my entry until I had completed my first surgical residency year, but, having no idea why, I chose not to think about it. Remembering an ancient Chinese proverb, "Heaven is high and the Emperor is far away," I decided not to worry about something so distant. There were much more important surgical things to consider. Who knew, perhaps the war in Vietnam would be over by that time, and I hoped that it would.

Finding myself buried in an all consuming training process, I thought little about my upcoming Army obligation, and I had little time to read or listen to accounts detailing the war. My wife Margy was not as naive as I, and she understood, right from the start, all the implications of our situation. In May of my internship year, we were blessed with the birth of our daughter, Beth Ann. My wife quit her job as a Visiting Nurse to take care of the new baby. Her income would be sorely missed, as Yale-New Haven Hospital paid surgical residents precious little, and money was tight. Following the invitation of my in-laws to stay with them, my wife and baby daughter would spend the year I was to be overseas, in Ridgewood, New Jersey. As my first year of residency wound down, there was no sign of the war's ending, dashing my previous hopes. After two years of marriage and surgical training requiring me to stay in the hospital every other night and every other weekend, I had really only spent one year with my wife! On top of that, the Army was now demanding I go away for the next year, which left only one year out of three to spend with Margy and now, Beth Ann. This was the pits, and forecast the hardships ahead for the three of us!

Having completed my first year of surgical residency, the time had come for me to report to Fort Sam Houston, in San Antonio, Texas. Six weeks of "doctor basic training" in the Army's Medical Corps lay ahead. I was fortunate to have my small family accompany me, and that time we spent together in Texas turned out to be very precious. Since we needed somewhere to live, we rented a small car and set out to find a place to call home. A nice garden apartment on the outskirts of town filled the bill and we settled in. Scarcely furnished, the two-level duplex had nice grounds and a swimming pool to boot. Margy soon worked her special magic turning this desperately bare apartment into a comfortable home.

Two of the things I remember about that apartment were the sidewalk and the grass. A local daily paper was delivered early each morning. One day the delivery boy missed our stoop, and the paper landed on the grass. In my bare feet and still in my pajamas at seven o'clock that morning, I stepped onto the sidewalk to retrieve the paper. Even at that early hour, the Texas sun was so hot that the sidewalk scorched my feet. Seeking relief, I jumped to the grass. What I thought to be grass were actually hundreds of miniature cactus plants with tiny thorny bristles. My poor feet had gone out of the frying pan into the fire. Once back in the apartment, the anger and frustration I felt at that instant was cooled by my young daughter's laughter. My antics tickled her, and soon my wife and I joined in the hilarity of the moment.

Basic training was a tedious process filled with classroom sessions covering the basics at first, such as Army protocol, instructions on how to wear our uniforms, whom and when we were to salute, and many other very boring things about military life. Those classroom sessions soon deepened into the care of war wounds, the tropical diseases found in Vietnam, and how to treat them, the Army version of public health in Vietnam, i.e. how to make a latrine, how to inspect kitchens and food, and the caloric needs of a fighting man. Interspersed with the classroom sessions were outside activities such as learning to march, close order drill with the attention posture, how to about face, parade rest, and salute each other. I was surprised to learn that when harassed, I didn't really know my right from my left, and I found I did need the marching practice. Despite my early clumsy efforts, I gradually learned how to do all that was required of me, and I was ever thankful that I did not have to suffer through the more severe enlisted man's basic training. After a while, I found myself enjoying the daily noontime marching, especially when the Army Band and Drum Corps accompanied us.

To intensify the training, our group was taken to Camp Bullis, in a very rural part of Bexar County, Texas. The camp's name was quickly changed to "Camp Bullshit," although we were not the first class to so name this training ground. Passing the entrance gate that read "Army Training Center," I suspected a new and frightening world was awaiting my yet untested spirit. After unloading from the buses, we all took seats on bleachers on the edge of a newly mown field. Facing the bleachers was a podium from which introductory remarks were delivered by a tough looking NCO sporting a crew cut. He used four letter words very effectively, heightening our curiosity about what was to go on at this camp. I certainly had heard words like these before, but never during a formal lecture. He specifically warned those of us who were headed for Vietnam to harden ourselves to the sudden violence that was a way of life there and to keep on our toes to avoid becoming a victim in that war. He told us never pick up a US twenty dollar bill on a jungle trail because it was, more than likely, booby trapped. His warnings continued about the dangers found in a war zone. Mistakes were often fatal to rookies and this was our "Heads Up!" At the end of his profane remarks, the Army, in its infinite wisdom, if not masochism, exploded a large charge of gunpowder right next to the bleachers where we were sitting, right next to my seat. The unexpected explosion, or perhaps reflexes, caused many to fly from their seats in sheer panic. Several landed on the ground and began to run away with the resultant confusion. The lecturing Sergeant chuckled, mocking our fright and demonstrating his grace under pressure. With a sneering voice he advised us to "settle down and take your seats." In a loud condescending voice, he reiterated his point that war was full of sudden violence and that we'd better get used to it. This demonstration left me with doubt of how I could ever be able to steel myself to take such abuse and why the hell I had to anyway.

Splitting up into small groups, we were taken to various stations set up by the camp's cadre. Although Infantry Officers were in command of our training at Camp Bullis, most of our contact was with tough old NCOs, who loved nothing better than to terrify their doctor officer students. We doctors were duck soup for these guys, and they delighted in watching the results of the tortures they inflicted. The NCOs were quite gratified to watch superior officers obeying THEIR orders for a change, and they issued a lot of orders. The ridicule they imposed on us made me try to be sensitive to the feelings of those I would give orders to, and I was grateful for the humility I learned from the Camp Bullis NCOs.

As physicians in the Army, we were to oversee the public health measures instituted for the well being of the troops. We started by learning about the latrine. Civil engineers taught us how human excrement was handled in Vietnam, from the bigger cities to the rural battle camps. Using the latrines at the camp was a new experience for a good many, and I was never happier to have been a Boy Scout than I was then. Mess hall operations and the basics of feeding an army were taught with emphasis on cleanliness as it related to disease transmission. In Vietnam, the Army purified drinking water with iodine pills. Iodine is a more powerful antibacterial than chlorine. The water in Vietnam was loaded with bacteria and viruses, rendering the better tasting chlorine method less effective. The water provided at Camp Bullis had been treated with iodine to get us used to it. The taste was horrible, lingering in my mouth for hours after even a small sip, so I went thirsty most of the time.

Portable packaged food was distributed for the group to sample. I especially liked the "C rations" with desserts such as cut up fruit and small vanilla cakes that came in cans. The C ration kits had a can opener in them, dubbed a "P 36." This was an ingenious little instrument composed of a sharp curved blade that would fold against a metal shield when not in use. This instrument could cut through anything; so most GIs carried one on their dog-tag chains. Food from a portable field kitchen made up the first evening's meal. This meal served a dual purpose: feeding us and teaching us how to use mess kits. Once again, Boy Scout training lent an edge. Upon entering the "chow" line, the mess kit components were dipped in boiling water to cleanse them. I felt right at home using the plate, pan and pot, as well as the utensils. I liked Army chow and still do. My only complaint was that there was never any alkaline relief.

Seasoning with peppers and onions was overdone, I guess to hide the actual taste, and heartburn was a common complaint. Usually, a glass of milk could put out the fire, but the Army usually supplied the acidic "bug juice" instead. This juice was like Kool Aid, and had none of the acid neutralizing properties of milk. I soon learned to keep Tums or other antacids on hand when I had to eat Army chow.

Once at midnight, we were taken to the Night Map Reading Course. Earlier that afternoon, the Day Map Reading Course had been presented. Map reading, coordinate determination, and the use of the standard Army compass were intensely covered. To my surprise, the material was understandable and I enjoyed the instructions. I was eager to try out my newly learned skills. Of course, that particular night was pitch black and overcast. No moon or stars were out to lend light to the upcoming exercise. Supplied with maps, compasses, and flashlights, we were divided into groups of four. The object of this exercise was to proceed to a prescribed location, two miles distant, where our arrival would be noted and timed by the camp staff. The return to the starting point would have to be by a different route. Only the compass, the map, and the flashlight could be used to guide us. To liven up this midnight jaunt, machine gun emplacements would fire at the travelers if they passed too close. If the course were plotted correctly, there would be no machine gun fire and no problems. The terrain was hilly and was surrounded by fields full of prickly pear cacti, armadillos, and grazing Black Angus cattle. Believing in what I had been taught at the map reading course earlier, I had faith in my ability to plot a course. Three others and I set out fearlessly into that black night armed with our compasses and maps.

Speaking in hushed tones to avoid giving away our position to the machine gunners, we gradually picked our way over the initial two-mile course. Arriving at the first stop, I was gratified to learn that our group was one of the first to reach the midway point. With pumped up confidence, we started back by way of the new course for the finish line. After walking for about fifteen minutes, I was confident that we were on course and would probably be one of the first groups to make it back. My pride was shattered by the noise and flash of machine gun fire! The night turned into day with the light of the machine gun firing blanks. The gun was directly in front of us, and mercifully, the blasts ceased after a few moments. The fright of being fired upon left me speechless, and the audible laughter from the machine gunners erased any confidence I had left. Not only had I been shot at, I now knew I was lost and way off course also.

Walking and looking at my map at the same time, I bumped into something that felt ungiving, like a tree. Puzzled, I felt softness and noted black fur! Slowly, a massive dark face turned in my direction and mooed a bovine laugh that hurt as much as the machine gunner's! Walking backwards from that large cow in dumbfounded awe, I stepped on an armadillo that erupted from under my boot squealing as it darted away into the grass. What a night! Would it never end? Running appeared to be a logical way to end this ordeal and run we four did. A down hill direction was the easiest course to take, and to our surprise, we soon crossed the finish line! We had been the first group to get back. The sergeant in charge of the finish line was very pleased that we had completed the course in near record time. He attributed our speed to his own expert instructions he had given us in that afternoon's class. He didn't realize that our speed was due to a blind dash in panic, not careful plotting. If he did, he wouldn't have been so smug. I kept quiet, and enjoyed, albeit undeservedly, his self-gratifying praise. Secretly, I promised myself if I became lost again, I would just run downhill and forget the compass. The next morning, rumors circulated that several of the night map course participants had to be retrieved by helicopters. I was happy we had been spared the embarrassment of needing to be rescued, although only pure luck had saved us from that fate.

The next morning we went to the rifle range after eating breakfast at the crack of dawn. The rifle issued that day was the older .308-caliber M-14 model. This had been the standard Army weapon for many years, but, after the Vietnam War began, the Army switched to the smaller .223-caliber M-16. To simulate combat conditions, we fired from foxholes. Each of us was given several clips of ammunition to fire at the standard targets positioned a hundred yards away. I enjoyed shooting the rifle, but a huge bruise rose on my right shoulder that night. I had a very sore shoulder the next day, which proved that, unlike the M-16, the M-14 recoiled with quite a wallop! The smaller M-16 rifle was to prove less traumatic to my shoulder when next I was to fire an Army weapon in Vietnam.

After leaving the rifle range, the next stop was at an old Army barracks building where our group was exposed to "tear gas." This exercise would also help acquaint us with the government-issue gas mask. In groups of ten we were positioned inside a building with the doors and windows closed. C-2 Gas, the military name for the chlorinated tear gas, was sprayed in the midst of our group. The object was to place the gas mask on the face while not breathing and without panicking. Once the mask had been properly positioned, breathing could finally be resumed without choking and gagging on the irritating fumes. Tear gas was aptly named as the slightest exposure to even tightly closed eyes caused a torrent of tears to flow. Then, one at a time, the mask wearers had to remove their masks in the gas filled room, recite their name, rank, and serial number, and then run out of the room to the relief of outdoor air. In order to find my way out through the closed door, I had to open my eyes for a brief look, which caused severe pain in my eyes, which, in turn, caused me to breathe in. Just that tiny reactive inhalation burned my lungs beyond what I thought I could stand. I reached the outside and took in huge breaths of pure air. After a few moments of agony, my respirations no longer brought pain and my eyes began to recover. Others were not as lucky as I, and they gagged and vomited. The pitiful vomiting of the affected soldiers conjured up snickers and frank laughter by some of the supervising NCOs.

I was flabbergasted that anyone could laugh at another's misfortune. This ridicule by the NCOs was but a small component of the big picture of hate that is inculcated into a man at the time of war. This learned hate would infuriate a peaceful man, allowing him to kill another human being. I saw a lot of this derisive behavior later in Vietnam, and the world's history is full of examples of the same kind of wartime hate. Although a giant step going from laughing at vomiting men in Camp Bullis to soldiers being able to kill comfortably, there is a definite connection. In Vietnam, the enemy troops were called dehumanizing names like "Gooks" and "Slopes" much like the epithets "Dirty Jap" and "Krauts" used often during World War Two. When a soldier thinks of an enemy as something less than human, killing becomes much easier, and the remorse for such actions is lessened for a while at least.

My most memorable experience of Camp Bullis was the "Infiltration Course." The course simulated wartime battle conditions and is a long standing Army basic training tradition. Not exempt by benefit of rank or Medical Corps status, all doctors were subject to the "acid test" the ordeal provided. Going through this course was the last stop on our basic training sojourn and had to be the most stressful. Barbed wire had been strung over a field that measured about fifty yards long by thirty yards wide. The ground surface was dotted with shallow pits which held explosive charges set to explode when someone crawled near. The explosions could elevate the crawling person several inches off the ground, demonstrating in a small way the magnitude of the danger existing on a battlefield. Thirty-six inches above the ground were real live .30 caliber bullets fired from two machine guns at the far end of the course. If a person stood up abruptly under this intense fire, his body would be literally stitched through with bullets before the soldier firing the gun would see him!

Entering at one end, the participant would have to crawl the fifty yards to the finish line under the barbed wire, all the while enduring the explosions on either side as well as the machine gun firing tracer bullets overhead! The NCOs warned about losing our bearings and ending up circling around hopelessly, prolonging the time spent under those frightening conditions. Our instructors also warned us to guard against accidentally sliding into one of the explosion pits, which could be lethal. We were told the supervisors hated to do all the paper work necessitated by such a tragedy. Additionally, we were advised there were to be two crawls made through this maze, one in daylight and one after dark. After our group had heard the explanation of the upcoming ordeal, an eerie silence fell over the usually jocular men around me, and I felt fear dry my mouth. "Did I hear right?" I thought, "One mistake and I could be killed!" Also intimated by the explanation was the old Army dictum that if we did exactly what we were told to do, we would all end up safe and sound, and everyone knew that was pure baloney.

Standing by the entrance smoking cigarettes and laughing at popular anti-Army jokes, many were ignoring what was about to happen. The merriment came to an abrupt stop when the machine guns opened up. Bullets slammed into the dirt wall with sickening thuds and flying sand next to where we were standing. This was my first appreciation of the horrible sounds the war would generate, a sobering and chilling moment, to say the least. I had little time to contemplate this martial harbinger. The sergeant blew his whistle, and our group reluctantly began crawling, four at a time, under the barbed wire, around the exploding pits, with the bullets whizzing close overhead all the while. I found myself talking out loud to no one in particular. Explosions, coming from the shallow pits as I passed, deafened and jarred me at irregular intervals. Flying grime stuck to my sweating body, and I left a smooth trail in the dirt behind me that hot Texas evening. As I carefully stood, having crossed the finish line, I looked back to watch my buddies crawling along at a fast pace. They looked like real soldiers, which I extrapolated to myself. My morale soared. I was beginning to feel like a soldier. The basic training was working for me. To my surprise, no one refused to go, no one stood up, and, most amazing, no one had died! One thing was left. I had to steel myself and crawl under the wire once more, only this time in the dark of night! Two hours had to pass for the sun to go down before the second run could take place. There was no more joking or laughter as we queued up waiting to go again. The whistle finally blew and once again, "into the breach!" As I emerged at the other side, I was quickly ushered into an awaiting bus, which took me back to Fort Sam and my family. The brief but memorable "Basic Training" was now over. The bus ride home was very quiet. Kindled by the infiltration course experience, unsettling visions of what was to come filled my mind. They didn't leave until I saw my wife and child later that night.

The remaining days at Fort Sam flew by. Each Friday we were given multiple vaccinations for exotic diseases I had never seen, but had only read about. Those painful injections kept me from swimming in the pool because my inoculations would contaminate the water for the other swimmers. After Camp Bullis, the routine of class lectures, noontime marches and inspections was much more tolerable. In fact, the training was becoming old hat. I was ready to leave and get on with my upcoming year. There wasn't much more I felt I could learn about saluting, and I was anxious to get my family out of the Texas heat.

Finally, the day came when I was released from Fort Sam Houston and given two weeks leave, including travel time, before I had to report to my next duty station. That station was Travis Air Force Base in San Francisco. From there I was to be transported to the Army replacement center in Long Binh, in the Republic of South Vietnam! With only two weeks left to be with my family, we three scrambled back to New Jersey and my in-law's house. I took my family with me and said good-bye to my parents in nearby Montclair. My father was confident things were going to be all right, but my mother was worried. She laughed her feelings off by saying,

"Mothers always worry." I would spend those last few days in America nervously awaiting my future in Vietnam, the likes of which I could never contemplate. The time was now early August, 1968.

Having crammed uniforms and all my personal belongings into an olive drab duffel bag made of stiff canvas, I left for Kennedy Airport in New York. The day I left was beautiful, full of sunshine and singing birds. The trip across Manhattan's usually crowded streets was a breeze. I didn't even have any trouble finding a parking space at the airport and all too quickly, I was walking down a long corridor to my plane. Turning around as I walked, I waved good-bye to my wife and daughter. I couldn't help wondering if I would ever see them again and I remember the looks on their faces as they waived back. My daughter had an innocent smile on her face, which contrasted with the forced brave smile on my wife's face that couldn't quite mask her underlying fear.

ON TO VIETNAM

In San Francisco, I hooked up with Bob Dragon and his wife. Bob and I had spent the two previous years together as interns and residents in Yale-New Haven Hospital. Wanting to sit together on our upcoming flight to Vietnam, we had made plans to meet in San Francisco. I waited in the lobby while Bob said good-bye to his wife upstairs in his hotel, then we took a cab to Travis Air Force Base, arriving in the departure area at eleven P.M. The plane was scheduled to depart at one A.M., giving us two hours to kill. The airport terminal was buzzing with soldiers, airmen, and naval personnel all milling about with the same anxious faces. The resultant din violated the usual nighttime quiet and midnight seemed like noon.

Everyone was justifiably nervous about leaving for Vietnam, and I was no exception. The heat of the August night coupled with all those frenetic men filled the terminal with the odor of sweat. I saw enlisted men and officers of many ranks in that sweltering place, from privates to lieutenant colonels. A loud speaker disinterestedly announced that our flight was going to be delayed for several more hours. Bob and I joined a group of doctors sitting on the floor. I recognized many of them from my days at Fort Sam. Propped up on our duffel bags we tried to talk over the din with raised voices. This only made the noise worse as everyone else did the same. My head was throbbing in the heat and the smoke-filled air burned my eyes.

After a while, the noise level lessened, allowing some conversation. There were questions about where we were from, what our specialties were, and what we had heard about the situation at our destination. Rumors flourished and were embellished as they were passed on. Interruptions from the loud speaker gave us the latest news about our plane. Soon enough, the plane was ready and we were given boarding instructions. Colonels and above boarded first, followed by the lesser ranks in descending order. Captains were boarded relatively early and sat in a group. Those troop transport ships I had seen in old newsreels from the Second World War scared me about this trip, but I was pleasantly surprised to find myself seated in a very modern passenger jetliner. The flight was complete with pleasant stewardesses and good food. Messages from a very friendly pilot came over the loudspeaker assuring a comfortable, but long flight.

The avuncular pilot announced the flight plan was to land next in Anchorage, Alaska, where the plane would be refueled. Then we would continue on to Yakota Air force Base in Japan. From there, six, or so, hours in the air would take us to the Replacement Depot in Long Binh, South Vietnam. All in all, we would be in the air for about twenty-four hours! As we sped down the tarmac and became airborne, I began to relax. My sweat-drenched uniform began to dry in the air-conditioned cabin, and I was soon overcome by sleep. Asleep for about two hours, I was awakened by the Captain's voice over the loudspeaker, but I only heard the last of his message. He had explained that our flight had somehow missed the Anchorage, Alaska stop, and we were now headed straight for Japan. He assured us the plane had plenty of fuel to carry us to Japan, as long as the tail winds held up! Looking around, almost everyone else on board was sound asleep. If they didn't worry, neither should I, and I fell sound asleep again.

After six hours, I awoke, stretched my aching limbs, and realized I was famished. The cabin was filled with the delicious smells of coffee and food, which is probably what awakened me. The stewardesses were busy serving breakfast to a planeload of hungry soldiers. The aromas and the beginning excited conversations awoke the remaining soldiers as if a breakfast bell had rung. To make the wait for food go faster, I went to the lavatory to brush my teeth and shave. Returning to my seat refreshed, I was greeted by a smiling stewardess with a piping hot plate of bacon, eggs, hot coffee and a roll. I didn't know that I was that hungry as I quickly bolted down my meal. My spirits had been revived by the meal and a new dose of caffeine was coursing through my veins.

I am still amused by the memory of a single conversation I overheard on the plane. The young enlisted man sitting several rows in front of me was talking loudly to the soldier next to him and found that he was from Los Angles. The young soldier said to his new friend, "Los Angeles, huh. Do you know Bill Smith? He's from LA." The reply came back, "No, but LA is pretty big." That question and answer broke me up, and it still does. Looking around the plane, I found the cabin was mostly filled with young men who had been unlucky enough to have been drafted in President Johnson's build up. The average age of the fighting man in Vietnam was nineteen, the youngest average age recorded for American soldiers in any war. World War II soldiers averaged twenty-six years, probably because so many were needed at once that older men had to be called. Spread out over twice as many years and needing far fewer men each year, the Vietnam draft quota rarely left the eighteen-year-old level. After being drafted, a year was spent in training making the average soldier nineteen upon arrival in Vietnam. Although only nineteen, the men aged quickly.

Sleeping helped the hours on the plane pass quickly, and land was seen on the horizon. The pilot announced this was Japan, and Mount Fujiyama loomed into view. Unlike Alaska, we did find Japan! The touchdown at Yakota Air Base was smooth and cheers went up from the passengers, but I'll never know why. My best guess was that this was a relief after the Alaska mess up. Emerging from the plane I was quickly engulfed by the hot and very humid air of a Japanese summer. Herded into a very large hangar with the other passengers, I was advised to make myself as comfortable as possible. Our connecting plane was delayed on its return from Vietnam, and possibly twenty hours would pass before we would be airborne again. "Hurry up and wait!" That Army motto certainly applied to us. A very disgruntled bunch of soldiers settled into another long delay on yet another concrete floor. The heat and smells were rank in that hangar, and, making matters worse, no one was allowed outside to walk around, because of a designated "Restricted Area." There were only two bathrooms, causing tempers to flare when long lines to use them developed. Sitting on my duffel bag, I passed those long hours as best I could. Sustenance was supplied by several vending machines that offered crackers, candy bars, and soda pop. The hard floor and loud conversations made sleeping impossible. Time passed very slowly that day, but fortunately the plane arrived two hours short of the twenty expected.

The next step of the journey was via another large passenger jet as before. After boarding, most of us were soon asleep again, and instead of breakfast aromas awakening us, loud speakers roared the terse message, "Next stop, Vietnam!" The pilot announced that we would soon be landing at Ben Hoa Airstrip, but his voice was stern now. He also advised, "Hang on!" for he was going to drop from thirty-five thousand feet almost straight down to the runway to avoid artillery fire. His following wisecrack, "There's a war on, you know!" was met with boos from the awakening passengers. True to the pilot's word, my introduction to South Vietnam was almost a free fall down through the clouds ending in a very abrupt landing. My stomach was still at thirty-five thousand feet as I rose out of my seat and prepared to deplane. The plane doors opened, and I was startled by loud cheers as I exited. The 365-day veterans waiting to board our "Freedom Bird" for their long awaited trip back to the "World" were cheering uncontrollably as far as my eyes could see. Shouts of, "Short!" rang out as I passed by the waiting men. Euphoric in freshly pressed khaki uniforms, their smiling tanned faces portrayed just the opposite of how I felt and looked. Pale in comparison, and very disheveled, I felt embarrassed as I walked past them. There was precious little for me to smile about at that moment. This was all their show. Three hundred sixty-five more days would have to pass before my time to shine would come. I was impatient to get on with my tour so I could begin my own count-down. Someday I too would yell "Short" and be euphoric just like them.

As I walked off the runway I noted a large sign which read "Welcome to Vietnam!" Alongside was a smaller sign that demanded, "Pave Vietnam!" Looking around, I saw Ben Hoa airport was filled with fighting men, carrying weapons, and looking like men who had seen combat. Although they appeared stern, as I passed them most smiled and that was certainly not what I had expected. I thought combat GIs would have a constant scowl on their faces and would never smile. The focused and piercing eyes of these men spoke volumes about their combat experience, but there was a decided friendliness in their appearance. Wherever I would go in Vietnam over the next twelve months, I was always surprised to find these tough, combat-hardened soldiers paradoxically smiling.

Walking along, following every one else, I couldn't help thinking that I would have to stay over here in the "Swamp" for the next whole year unless I became wounded, killed, or so sick that I would die if I were left in-country. Early on as this was, I began to look forward to the day of my DEROS, "Date Expected to Return from Over Seas." Obviously there was an in-country vernacular used by GIs in Vietnam, and I wanted to learn it as quickly as possible so as not to appear like such a rookie.

Realizing newly-arrived soldiers would need help in adjusting to their new life, the Army took steps to help mollify the drastic change. The Army wanted energetic, willing participants, and not a bunch of sluggish and depressed soldiers. Slogans meant to encourage were ubiquitous, hanging on walls, positioned on desktops, or spoken at the many pep talks. I can only remember two of those slogans: "All journeys, no matter how long, begin with the first step" and "When the going gets tough, the tough get going," but there were many more.

The long walk from the plane ended with my being loaded onto a big Army truck, which took me and others to Long Binh, nicknamed the "Repo Depot." Many welcoming speeches were delivered to us, and then we were broken up into groups by rank and military specialty. I was surprised to see all the doctors present in my group, but I soon figured out why. August had to be the month most doctors arrived in country as academic residential years were over in June and basic training took six weeks. August was the month, therefore, that most new Army doctors arrived in Vietnam.

The talks we received were repetitive and, at times, inane. I was very relieved to have finished for the day after six hours of indoctrination. I and the other doctors were then fed an evening meal, packed into stuffy barracks, and told to get a good night's sleep. That night I heard my first sounds of the real war. Loud noises intermittently and abruptly interrupted the night's silence, and each was different. I heard the rapid staccato of machine gun fire, the chop-chop-chop of helicopter rotors, and the explosions of artillery from dusk to dawn. Even though Long Binh was right next door to Saigon, the war was very much in evidence.

Awakened early the next morning from a fitful sleep, I ate breakfast and resumed the in-processing steps. I was informed that I was assigned to the 25th Infantry Division's headquarters and would be going to Cu Chi, a base about sixty miles northwest from where I was. The 25th Infantry Division was nicknamed "Tropic Lightning." I was instructed to look for a large truck with the Taro Leaf and Lightning Streak insignia of the 25th Infantry painted on its doors. When the truck arrived, I climbed up onto its open back and found myself in the midst of a group soldiers. I sat down next to another Army captain who smiled politely when I faced him. He had a Medical Corps caduceus on his lapel and a small black cigar clenched tightly in his teeth. He looked more like a rugged character from a motion picture than a real life doctor. Continuing to smile, he said in a soft southern drawl, "Ain't this some shit!" I instinctively responded, "Yeah, it sure is." We talked for a while as we waited on the back of the truck. He told me he was a partially trained surgeon too and was drafted from his first year of surgical residency at the University of North Carolina in Chapel Hill. We had probably bumped into each other at Fort Sam, but we had never spoken. Thrown together halfway around the world on the back of a truck, we struck up a friendship. Duncan Morton was his name, and we were both headed to our new life as doctors with the 25th Infantry Division at Cu Chi.

CU CHI
AND
THE 25TH INFANTRY DIVISION

The ride to Cu Chi in the back of that truck was a bumpy and dusty one. To me our truck driver looked like a kid who liked to race hot rods, and the ride that day made me think my guess had been correct. As the truck jerked forward and stopped suddenly, I slid all over the smooth bed in the back because it was hard to find anything to hold on to. Corners were especially demanding, and I ended up in a ball of people after each one. A minor miracle, no one fell out or got hurt. As we neared the base, rutted dirt roads turned into smooth macadam and led to the very busy main gate of the huge base camp. There were several soldiers guarding this gate, and the traffic was heavy both ways. The closest guard we passed looked imposing in his well-ironed jungle fatigues which were nicely faded indicating he had been in-country a while. A black band circled around a well-muscled arm that read "MP" in large white letters. "New meat," he remarked as he signaled our truck to proceed on through the gate and into the camp. Seeing that there were two captains in the back of the truck, he snapped to attention and gave a smart salute. Almost apologetically, he said, "Welcome!" as we passed by. I wasn't sure if he was trying to stifle a smile, or he was just sneering, but his face was definitely contorted in a very unusual manner as we passed.

Our truck turned onto a macadam road with dividing white lines down the center, the main road of the base. We passed what looked like suburban blocks complete with single story houses which had recently been painted brown. Some of the well-manicured lawns around these buildings were bordered with white painted bricks that glistened in the tropical sunshine. Soldiers in jungle fatigues were everywhere, scurrying around like rush hour in New York City. Duncan and I stood out like sore thumbs in our khaki uniforms, which were more than wrinkled after sleeping in them off and on for over forty-eight hours. The truck stopped in front of one of the brown buildings, which read "25th Medical Battalion Headquarters." Jumping down from the back of the truck, I had to jump aside to miss getting hit by my duffel bag which was tossed from the back of the truck as it began to speed away. Dragging my bag behind me, I made my way into the air-conditioned building with Duncan right behind.

Coming out of an office to greet us was Major Rogers. Not a doctor, he was a Medical Service Corps officer, an administrator of medical affairs. He was grinning broadly, and seemed genuinely pleased to see us. Major Rogers, whom we later learned had the nickname, "Buck," invited us inside to meet the colonel. The colonel was the head of the Medical Battalion. His name was Lieutenant Colonel George Hensel, and he told us he was an allergist back in the States, but he only did administration work here in Vietnam. Lieutenant Colonel Hensel also greeted us warmly and was very solicitous of our comfort. He was a career Army officer, a "lifer," and he had a fatalistic attitude about his being in Vietnam. We listened to him ramble on about duty, honor, country, and the good life for doctors in Cu Chi. There was little doubt that Lieutenant Colonel Hensel was comforting himself as well as us with his comments, but his prattle was friendly and reassuring. He promised clean living quarters and fresh clothes to wear. He also promised a place to take a shower so we could freshen up from our long trip. Thoughts of that shower and a place to call home were overwhelming and I found myself relaxing a bit. The Colonel promised a tour of the compound later on that day, and he dismissed us. I left the air-conditioned office and went back out into the oppressive heat.

An open top jeep was to take us to our barracks, and our gear was stuffed into the small space behind the rear seats. I sat in one of the back seats, and several other soldiers climbed aboard also. After traveling for a block, the jeep rounded a corner, and, as if in slow motion, rolled over! In a heartbeat, I found myself pinned beneath that jeep in a shallow water ditch that lined the edge of the road. Although I couldn't turn my head to see, several others were also pinned in that ditch. I could hear cursing and I tried to push the jeep over. The light jeep began to rock back and forth as I grunted with my efforts. The driver had been lucky enough to jump clear as the jeep overturned, and I could hear him excitedly calling for help. My face was partly under some water in the bottom of the ditch, and I could taste toothpaste! The driver had managed to get some soldiers who had been walking by to help, and they quickly righted the jeep. That whole episode lasted only a few minutes. Amazing! Nobody got hurt. I was now soaked with foul smelling ditch water, but I was thankful I was not hurt. This incident taught me a fear for the untrustworthy Army jeep that I would never lose. There were so many ways to get hurt in Vietnam. Duncan smiled and exclaimed another, "Ain't that some shit?" while I thought to myself, "Welcome to Vietnam!"

My new home in Cu Chi was better than I imagined. The barracks I was to stay in had just been built and still smelled of new wood and fresh paint. Duncan was my roommate, and he was also pleased with the new digs. There were two standard Army cots along each wall, and footlockers, olive drab of course, by each cot. Screening inside the louvered sideboards kept out the plentiful mosquitoes and other insects, and there was a screen door that snapped shut with a spring. Breezes flowed easily through the billet, making the inside usually cool. A single light dangled from the ceiling and had a pull string to light it. Outside the walls of the barracks were sand bags and sand-filled metal barrels for protection from enemy fire. I was impressed with the protection afforded by my new quarters and I felt secure. Outside, the yards were laced with boardwalks that led every which way. During rains, the grounds of trimmed grass were quickly turned into mini-swamps and that's when those walkways came in very handy.

After I stowed my gear, I found a towel and headed to take a long-awaited shower. About fifty yards away via the boardwalk, the shower and sink area was in a screened-in shack on a platform six feet off the ground. Sideboards came up about waist-high for privacy, and there was a corrugated tin roof overhead. Shower heads derived their water from several fifty-five-gallon drums, soldered together and painted black to absorb heat from the intense tropical sun. The water became very hot after a long sunny day and the best showers were to be had later in the day. Morning showers, or showers on a cloudy day, on the other hand, could be very cold! The water from the shower and the sinks drained through the widely spaced floorboards into a roadside ditch system. Tracing the path my shower water took that day, I spied the very ditch I had landed in when the jeep overturned. No wonder the water had tasted like toothpaste!

The Cu Chi human waste disposal system was maintained by the Army Corps of Engineers, who took into consideration the tropical climate, the low level of the land and the high water table. To dispose of urine, the Army devised a system of tubes made of iron pipes sticking just so high out of the ground at strategic locations. These "piss tubes" had oil in them to float on top of the urine to remove the odor. The urine itself filtered into the soil below. Most of the tube sites were out in the open, offering no protection for the bashful. Being very bashful, I never really got used to the Army's form of public urination. Females on the bases were rare and they were given special consideration. Facilities for women were usually found only near larger hospitals where female Army nurses lived and worked.

Management of solid waste was through another method. Wooden sheds were fashioned with six openings or more, and beneath each of these openings were open fifty-five-gallon drums. These drums were filled with used motor oil, which was burned at regular intervals. The smell of the burning oil wasn't pleasant, and those odors permeated Army base camp air. The Vietnamese handled their own waste with total indifference. Men, women, and children used any field or curb to relieve themselves, and that practice had to account for the contaminated ground water. I was to find that whether in the country or in the big cities, all the world was a Vietnamese toilet. Understanding why there was rampant hepatitis, parasite infestation, and typhoid fever wasn't hard in this land without any public health conscience. A responsible government-run system of waste management would have rid this country of a lot of disease and suffering. The Army tried to construct and maintain a system for them, but it never really worked. If the system broke down, there was no one to fix it. The war, with its uncontrolled violence, didn't help the public sewer system, and the system gradually fell into hopeless disrepair.

On a much lighter note, Headquarters Company of the 25th Medical Battalion was a very pleasant place. The lawns grew profusely in this sunny, wet climate, and they were always kept neat and trim. "Hooches," the Army's nickname for living quarters, were

Typical "hooch" in Cu Chi Headquarters of the 25th Infantry Division

Duncan Morton standing in front of the
heavily sandbagged infirmary at Cu Chi

Duncan and I in conversation

newly painted and the surrounding areas were kept free of litter as if always awaiting an Army inspection. The base soldiers seemed unusually happy and went about their business with pleasant determination. Compared to what I had seen in Long Binh, the men of the 25th Infantry Division base camp were several cuts above the norm in appearance and civility. The mess hall was spotless and good smells abounded most of the day. I thought the food served there was excellent, and there was always plenty of it.

Vietnamese women were brought in each morning to do cleaning, laundry, and even boot shining for the base camp troops. These "mama-sans" worked very hard and were well paid for their endeavors. Americans in Vietnam were making a heretofore unheard-of middle class by employing the local uneducated natives. Used to working under the hot sun in the rice paddies for little recompense, the exposure these women had to middle class Americans by working for them was very enlightening. The locals marveled at the radios, televisions, clothes, soda pop, foods and the general amenities of their occidental employers. Just as the presence of our troops had inexorably changed the way of life for the Filipinos, the Japanese, and the Koreans, so also had we done for the Vietnamese. After seeing how the Americans lived, the old, unattractive life they once knew would never again satisfy the Vietnamese people. This exposure probably did more to fend off Communism's stark grasp in the future, than did all the fighting. As a result of the mama-san's work the soldiers of the base camp looked sharp in freshly washed and ironed uniforms and shined boots, lending great élan to their otherwise isolated existence. Looking good made one feel good, and so did the knowledge that clean sheets, towels, and laundry were available each day. Were it not for the Vietnamese women's work force, cleanliness and the resultant benefits would have been woefully lacking.

There was a ball field in our company area that was used often for games of football, volleyball, and baseball. There always seemed to be some kind of contest on that field, and these daily sports lent an air of peace to the scene. Watching all the peaceful and pleasant activities happening around me, imagining a war was going on was sometimes difficult. Headquarters Company even had an Officers' Club complete with rattan furniture and a well-stocked bar. Also in the company area was an NCO Club. The only one around, this NCO Club was a very popular spot. Comparable in size, the two clubs had been built on stilts of woven bamboo with thatched roofs. Each had a small stage for entertainment and an old-fashioned jukebox. That first night in Cu Chi, I sipped a Canadian Club Manhattan and felt pretty good about all the unexpected comforts I had found in my new home. Mellow from the alcohol, I suggested to Duncan that maybe this war zone wasn't so bad after all. He smiled and with wisdom beyond his years, he cautioned me to "Wait until tomorrow."

The next day Duncan and I met the other doctors in the company. With the two of us, there would be six doctors available to tackle the task of the company's medical operations. In general, the doctors of the 25th Medical Battalion in Cu Chi were to hold sick call seven days a week for anyone wishing to be seen, and to care for the war wounded who would not require a formal operation. Most war wounds were relatively minor, requiring surgery that could be done under local anesthesia and were cared for at our facility. One block away was the large 12th Evacuation Hospital. This Army field hospital would take care of most major injuries requiring general anesthesia in a fully equipped operating room. The "Evac" hospital had a sufficient compliment of fully trained surgeons, including orthopedic surgeons, and several operating rooms that were the state of the art for that time. This evacuation hospital was made up of several buildings that housed the operating rooms, hospital wards for the post-operative cases awaiting transfer out of the country, and a large receiving area for the freshly wounded soldiers. Head wounds, or any other kind of injury that required other specialists not found in Cu Chi, were stabilized at the 12th Evac and sent out as soon as possible to the nearest facility that could handle the specific injury. The military plan for evacuation had been meticulously conceived and in 1968 the wounded soldier got the care he needed rapidly, and often would find himself back in the United States, near his hometown, before he could realize what was happening. Many soldiers remembered getting wounded, being operated upon, and waking up stateside. Some recovered on their way home. The 12th Evac Hospital was the place where a lot of the more critically injured soldiers of the 25th Infantry Division started their journey home in the Army's evacuation system.

For less serious wounds, the injured 25th Division soldier was transported to our facility, where he would have the appropriate surgical procedure performed under local anesthesia. He would then spend his recovery period on our ward and would probably be returned to his former unit when he was deemed in shape for active combat duty. Triage of war wounds usually began where the injury occurred, and was performed by trained combat medics. On the battle field, often under dangerous enemy fire, these brave medics treated the wounds as best they could, then sent the wounded man by stretcher to a close-by Battalion Surgeon, who had been stationed with the fighting unit in the field. The Battalion Surgeon did what he could in the field, and then called in a "Dust Off" helicopter to take the soldier to the 25th Med aid station, or the Evac Hospital. Sometimes, the medic at the injury site called in the Dust Off or sent his wounded patient by the nearest non-medical helicopter to the closest treatment facility. Triage of wounded would occur on the battlefield, in the air by the Dust Off medics, or in the admitting areas of either the aid station or the Evac Hospital. Triage would send the more seriously wounded to the hospital and all the rest to us. This system worked very well, although, at times, patients were traded back and forth up and down the street between the hospital and our aid station as misjudged wounds demanded. In my two and a half month stay at Cu Chi, misjudgment rarely happened, attesting to the field and the Dust Off medics' acumen in evaluating wound severity.

The six doctors that manned the 25th Infantry's aid station in August 1968 were made up of four General Medical Officers (GMOs) and two partially trained surgeons, namely Duncan and myself. One doctor would have to be available every night to handle any patients coming into the aid station. That made our night call every sixth night; a piece of cake compared to being on call every other night in my surgical residency. However, in a multiple casualty situation, with many wounded to care for all at once, the off-call doctors understood they would be called on to help. Duncan and I were willing to help in any way we could, and we were especially eager to do the surgery. Being a workaholic, I wanted to be busy all the time, and I knew that would make the time pass more quickly.

Sick call was held each morning, including Sunday, and each doctor saw twenty to thirty patients. Our patients were from the many military units on and off the base. I saw Marines, Navy Riverine Force personnel, Airmen, and South Vietnamese soldiers, as well as civilians. Foreign nationals came from many countries, and there were many local Vietnamese to be seen. The presenting ailments ranged across the whole spectrum of human diseases, far more than had been seen by us in the United States. Tropical diseases were common, but there were also cases of appendicitis, gall bladder attacks, angina pectoris, and psychological problems galore. I had to bone up on things like the different kinds of malaria, snakebites mostly from cobras and kraits, poliomyelitis that vaccinations had eradicated in the United States many years ago, and many other things that a surgical resident from America had never seen. The aid station had a few text books on tropical diseases which were somewhat helpful, but, most of what I learned about these unfamiliar maladies, I learned from other doctors who had been in Vietnam longer, who had, in turn, learned from their predecessors. This was an accepted way of teaching and learning in medicine, but unfortunately, the doctors who had finally become most familiar with these exotic diseases, left because their tours were over. I did have access to experts I could phone for advice when treating unfamiliar diseases, and transferring sick patients was strongly encouraged. Sick soldiers could end up back in the States or any facility in between, like the Subic Bay Naval Hospital in the Philippines, Camp Zama in Japan, or the Third Field Hospital in Saigon for their treatment. The ultimate thrust was to get critically ill soldiers to the large facilities in the continental United States where they could receive expert care from the appropriate specialists. This was all well and good, but our other patients who happened not to be American soldiers needed specialized care also. In these cases we had to do the best we could with what we had.

War injuries came in spurts, as battles were joined in the villages and countryside around us. For a while I felt that there was no fighting around Cu Chi at all, just malaria and gonorrhea. After the first few quiet days, I unfortunately found out the real business of the 25th Infantry. The savagery of war was a shock for me to witness. My first night on call, dark clouds rolled in, and the weather turned from hot and sunny to a very cold rain in just a few short minutes. The artillery batteries around the perimeter of the base began firing a lot that evening. This was the first time I could recall hearing them fire at all. The sounds and the concussions produced by the outgoing howitzer shells created a sinister atmosphere. I never got used to the feel and sounds of the artillery. I was uncomfortable at those times and was embarrassed by the flinching I did. The tinnitus I experience today was started by the artillery fire I endured in Vietnam. The concussive booms echoed every few minutes and, at times, were more frequent than that. I overheard the corpsmen talking in hushed tones among themselves about a firefight that had been going on. The fight involved the First of the Wolfhounds, a famous fighting battalion of the 25th Division and was close by. The 25th Division was made up of many battalions; some were infantry, some were mechanized infantry complete with armored personnel carriers (APCs) and tanks. Other battalions were made up of engineers, artillery units and, of course, the medical battalion. Many of the infantry battalions in the 25th Division had a proud history of fierce fighting in battles from the Second World War, through Korea, and here in Vietnam. The most famous of these were the First of the 27th and the Second of the 27th, referred to by the adopted name, "The Wolfhounds." The Wolfhounds were, at this very time, engaged with the enemy, explaining the artillery fire and the subsequent commotion at the aid station. I would soon learn that the increased artillery missions meant a fight close by, and that wounded would soon be knocking at our door. Sergeant Jiminez was the NCO in charge that night. He was a fully trained medic and had worked in many Army hospitals in the States and in his homeland of Puerto Rico. Busy positioning stretchers on sawhorses and placing them in long rows, he obviously expected a lot of casualties. When I asked him if he felt we would get wounded soon, he answered, "Yes Sir, beau coup!" French idioms were commonly used by the Vietnamese and subsequently picked up by the GIs. There was a whole language of expressions used by soldiers in Vietnam, which were all new to me. We heard from the radioman next door at the Dust Off helicopter headquarters that beau coup VC were in the one area and the Wolfhounds were after them "like flies on a carcass."

The pleasant day had given away to a wet, cold, and dark night. The Dust Off helicopter outside the aid station started its whining engine. Whirring sounds became flapping sounds, and the clumsy looking land bound machine took off with powerful grace. The big red crosses on the side doors of the Dust Off helicopter stood out against a bright white background, easily seen on the ground by friend and foe alike. Several of the aid station medics nervously lit cigarettes to have one quick smoke before the anticipated action. Sergeant Jiminez was a picture of confidence, which I guessed was probably because of his months of experience in Vietnam. He was the senior medic at the aid station, and I stuck close to him hoping he would point me in the right direction when the fertilizer hit the ventilator. My mouth was getting dry and I had heartburn from the "bug juice" I drank with my dinner. Sucking on a Tums tablet, I waited to be baptized.

A medic ran from the helipad through the large opened barn doors at the front of the aid station. "Six KIAs!" he shouted loudly, as he made his way over towards me. "Don't go out there yet, Sir," he said to me. "Let my guys put them in the dead shed for you first." The soldiers had been killed in action and would have to be washed off and disarmed before I could examine them. Knowing I was new at this, the aid station medic explained to me, "These darned grunts have grenades hanging everywhere and if you pick one up, it may go off. We don't want any more of our guys dying now, do we?" I nodded okay, but so far had not clue one what he was talking about. I knew "KIAs" meant Killed In Action. The Army expected medical units to carefully examine each and every body in great detail for the cause of death, and, even more importantly, to be sure of the exact identify of the bodies. Even body parts were carefully analyzed and sent to Graves Registration for preserving. After my medic was sure there was no danger, I went out to see what was going on. A 25th Divvy chopper, not the Dust Off that had left a while ago, had landed on our pad. This was a fighting chopper, and I had never seen one this close. The two side door machine guns on the helicopter were unmanned and pointing towards the ground. They lent a menacing atmosphere to the scene, and my medic's warning about danger rang in my ears. Stern-looking soldiers wearing flak jackets and side arms were pulling bodies of slain soldiers out from the bloodied interior of the Huey helicopter. The bodies were hidden in ponchos wrapped around them, but bloody limbs sticking out here and there left little doubt that there were dead bodies under those waterproof covers. Every fighting soldier was issued a poncho along with the rest of his gear. These raincoats were light in weight, olive drab or camouflaged, and were pullovers with a hood that would fit over a steel helmet. I had one and it worked well keeping me dry. This night, ponchos were used as a soldier's shroud. Watching the bodies being off-loaded in the pouring rain was an eerie sight. The rain was coming down so hard I couldn't hear what the men were saying above the roar of the falling water.

Our medics and the soldiers from the helicopter were carrying the bodies of their fallen buddies into the "dead shed," a wooden building with two levels of shelves lining the walls to hold the bodies. Each body was positioned in its perch where a medic hosed away the mud and blood covering the wounds, allowing me to be able to identify the cause of death in each case. The medics then went over each body, expertly removing grenades and live ammunition. Alongside the dead shed was a hole surrounded by sandbags in which the medics could throw grenades if they had become activated in this process. A standard practice at the time, soldiers buttoned grenades to their blouses in such a way that pulling the grenade from the shirt released the activating pin. This way the infantrymen could pull and throw the grenade with only one hand. When activated, the grenade's explosive charge was set to go off after thirty seconds. This delay was necessary to allow time for the grenade to reach the enemy before exploding. Medics were keenly aware of grenades and carefully unpinned them from the shirts of dead soldiers. If a pin came out, activating the grenade during this process, the medics would yell, "fire in the hole," and toss the grenade into the sandbagged pit while everyone hit the dirt. The sound of metal hitting the floor and smoke coming from the fuse were sure indications of an impending catastrophe. If the medic were lucky, he would have a few seconds to find the smoking grenade and toss it into the sandbag pit, rendering the explosion less deadly. If the medic failed to find the grenade in a few seconds he could jump out of the shed letting the dead bodies absorb the exploding fragments. This initial examination of KIAs obviously was a tense time for the medics. I gave them a wide berth on that rainy night and in the future.

The medics signaled me to view the bodies. In I went and saw my first KIAs. In fact, I will never forget the first corpse I saw that night. He was very young-looking with a freckled face, red hair, and blue eyes, paled in death. Most of his chest had been shot away. There was a hole so big where his heart had been, I could put my whole hand through it. The smell of the dead bodies in those sheds was very characteristic and easily recognized. The mixtures of varying amounts of old blood, perspiration and Vietnamese mud present in the dead shed resulted in a sickening, almost sweet smell. The mud had the odor of a sewer, and when mixed with human blood, torn flesh and sweat, well there's just no way to miss it, or to ever forget it. I examined the other five bodies and found assorted gunshot and fragmentation injuries that were obviously fatal to their

doomed owners. One poor guy had most of his head blown off and
brain tissue was oozing out onto the bunk. The medic must have
noticed my discomfort and, trying to be nice, remarked that the
smell was always worse when it rained. A feeling of nausea was
building in me in that shed, but, mercifully, it began to leave when I
got outside. The damp breeze carried the unpleasant odor away, and
the cold rain hitting my face quickly revived me.

The corpsman readied the death certificates for me to sign, and
he pointed that I had to sign my name eleven times for each dead
soldier. Army regulations clearly stated carbon copies would not do.
Just as I finished signing all the death certificates, a medic shouted
"WIAs!" which stood for Wounded In Action. The whirring, flapping noise of the Dust Off chopper landing outside filled the triage
area. Papers from the sergeant's desk flew around in the sudden
gusts of helicopter rotor wind that burst through the open doors of
the aid station. Medics with stretchers hurried to the chopper to off-
load the wounded onto the hard canvas litters. Although made of
stiff canvas, these collapsible, dark brown Army stretchers were
fairly comfortable to lie on. They were lightweight and very sturdy.
The best quality these stretchers possessed was the way they could
be easily washed free of the mud and blood they acquired from the
wounded soldiers they carried.

Once inside, the stretchers with the wounded on them were returned to their waiting sawhorses. The stretchers were placed about
ten feet apart in two lines to leave ample space between patients for
the doctors and medics to work. Within a few moments that night,
there were five wounded soldiers lined up on the stretchers in the
triage area of the large aid station building. Constructed like a metal
barn, the building had a high roof and a bare concrete floor. Drains
were situated every ten feet or so in the floor to facilitate drainage of
the hose water used to clean up the area after each use. Fluorescent
lights hung from the ceiling every few feet affording ample light for
the work below. At the other end of this building, away from the
two large sliding doors opening onto the helipad, were two modest-
sized operating rooms and sick call offices. Being the NCOIC (Non-
Commissioned Officer in Charge), Sergeant Jiminez had his office
there also. The whole place was air-conditioned! This building and
the medics made for a very efficient system of evaluating and treating mass casualties. Up to thirty wounded could be accommodated
at any one time, which often was the case.

Fortunately, the wounded my first night were not too seriously injured, although any wound was serious to the soldier who had it. There was one T&T GSW (through and through gunshot wound) of the shoulder, and the rest were fragmentation wounds in various locations. Wounded combat soldiers who were lucky enough to survive firefights with the enemy were usually very talkative. The adrenaline rush these men exhibited was something to witness. Their chatter helped hide the fear they had for what they had just been through, and what I was going to do to them. Although I never heard anyone express this feeling in words, these soldiers were obviously jubilant just to still be alive! They usually shut up when I approached, but they couldn't help smiling. I certainly didn't mind their excited conversations. After all, they had survived a very close call with death and they deserved to be listened to. Our medics encouraged them to talk about what happened, and they listened intently and respectfully to the stories they heard.

I would assess the wounds, and then I could instruct the medics how to care for them. Army medics such as these were given special training in wound debridement and surgical care back in the States and they were eager to help out. Vietnam fragmentation wounds were dirty. They had been contaminated by the mud, vegetation, and clothing particles that got dragged into the wound by the flying metal of the explosion. Rocket-propelled grenades (RPGs), hand grenades, land mines, etc., caused death by exploding, and sending metal chards from their casings hurling through the air in all directions. To prevent wound infections later, these fragments had to be meticulously sought and removed, including the surrounding damaged tissue injured by the flying pieces. X-rays helped find the metal pieces hidden in the flesh and muscles of the victims. Then, using one-percent Xylocaine for local anesthesia, the medics, or a doctor, dug out the fragments, cut away the surrounding damaged tissue, and left the wounds open. Suturing these wounds at the time of debridement would lead to significant and frequent wound infections resulting in a longer recovery time. The plan was not to suture the wounds for three to four days from the time of injury. Each day after the injury, a doctor would carefully inspect the wounds. After three days, if the wounds were judged to be free of any signs of infection, they were sutured closed. This process was called "delayed primary closure," or DPC, and it seemed to work very well.

Through and through gunshot wounds were also handled with wide debridement and subsequent delayed primary closure. The .30-caliber bullet fired from the high-powered AK-47, used by the Viet Cong and North Vietnamese Army, caused a lot of damage when passing through human flesh. The tissue damage caused by the shock waves the speeding bullet's energy imparted to the tissue was more severe than could be imagined. After being shot with an AK-47, or any other high-velocity weapon, the tissue around the bullet's path would be rendered inviable, i.e., the surrounding tissue was killed by the shock energy of the missile. Tissue damaged in such a manner could look deceivingly normal, and often the only clue the tissue was non-viable would be the lack of bleeding in the area. The tissue around the bullet track, therefore, had to be cut away until normal bleeding was seen. If dead tissue were left behind, serious infection could be the result. Remarkably, a lot of tissue had to be removed, and the dissection had to be more aggressive than not. The soldier with the T&TGSW that night had been shot through the deltoid muscle, the major muscle of his right shoulder. No significant blood vessels or nerves had been hit, and X-rays showed the bones were intact.

While the medics tended to the fragment wounds on the others, I picked the soldier with the shoulder wound to work on myself. Using a lot of local anesthetic to control the pain, I vigorously washed his wound with Betadine solution and then I widely removed the subcutaneous fat and muscle from the bullet's path. When the dissection got back to good bleeding tissue in all corners of the wound, I was finished cutting. The wound was about four inches long, two inches deep and two inches wide. The soldier talked to anyone who would listen while I was working on him. When I was finished, he declared he was "fine!" He could move his injured shoulder all around and wanted to go back to his company. I explained to him that the mobility he enjoyed now was due to the anesthetic, and he was going to have a lot of pain even without moving his arm when the Xylocaine wore off. I ordered him to stay in our hospital ward for intravenous antibiotics and pain shots for the next several days, at least. I would have to perform daily wound inspections, and he would need twice-daily dressings to be done by the corpsmen. The medics took my protesting patient for a shower and to his bed in the Quonset hut ward next door.

By the time I finished with my surgery the medics had completed their debridements on the other wounded soldiers. I inspected each wound they had worked on, and found they had done excellent work in every case! I admitted these other soldiers to the ward and after the medics finished cleaning up the work area, we all relaxed. Word from Dust Off Control was that there were no more casualties for us. The fight was over. The enemy broke off the attack as quickly as they began it. We were told that there were no living remnants of the attacking VC force. Sadly, fourteen young Vietnamese men were killed in that fight, men who had been alive short hours ago. The Army brass would brag the body count was twice that of those our side lost that night. I couldn't help thinking twenty young men died for nothing that wet and cold night, and nobody will ever make me change my mind about that. War is senseless! Twenty young men alive at the beginning of that day were no more. For what?

VC stood for Viet Cong. These were local South Vietnam rebels and were different from their counterparts, the North Vietnamese Army soldiers, or NVA. The NVA regulars sometimes joined forces with the VC irregulars, but not often and not tonight. The NVA and VC had elaborate tunnel systems around Cu Chi, complete with mess halls and underground hospitals. The VC could just melt back into their villages after a fight, making it almost impossible to tell them from peaceful villagers during the day. VC and NVA were referred to as "Charley" after the second word in the Army code for the VC, i.e. "Victor Charley." Most grunts depicted their lot in life as "Humping the Boonies, looking for Charley." The soldier didn't care who was shooting at him, VC or NVA, but the Army did. The NVA usually moved in large numbers, but the VC rarely did. If the Army Intelligence people could determine the NVA were doing the shooting, more must be hidden around, then an all-out effort would be undertaken to find them. The United States controlled the roads and highways by day while the enemy roamed more freely at night. There was no doubt that we had the superior force, i.e., men and materiel, but the determination of our enemies foretold their eventual success. Our wounded were admitted to a warm bed after getting all the medical attention they needed, a far cry from the care the enemy soldier got after that fight that night. I shudder to think of how many of the enemy died for want of what our men took for granted. The greatest enemy weapon had to be their determination, which ultimately proved to be better than the sum total of all we brandished for all those years.

The remainder of my first night on call went well. There were a few other minor problems to be handled, but none needed more than a pain pill or two. The medics saw the patients first and screened them for me. The medics were invaluable at this, allowing me a lot more sleep than if I had to see them all myself. The medics worked in eight-to-twelve-hour shifts, depending on the need. I worked each day for about eight hours and took call every sixth night or so. Duncan and I, being the ones with surgical training, were consulted a lot when we were not on call, but we loved it There were many very interesting problems and we often discussed the cases, staying up at night talking about what we had seen that day. The American soldier in Vietnam got good care from the 25th Medical Battalion, and I was beginning to like my part in it.

Working, playing football and volleyball, and exploring the sprawling base occupied a lot of my time those early days. The weather was hot and dry at first, and then, as the weeks went by, the other season began in Vietnam, hot and wet. Rain poured down, seemingly for weeks at a time. Although the daytime temperatures were in the nineties, a chill often settled in at night, and I needed a blanket at times. The raindrops were the largest I had ever seen, and they actually hurt when they hit you. The noise of the rain on the tin roofs was extremely loud, but was soothing when trying to get some sleep those nights. Listening to the rain pound against my roof at night, I thanked God I didn't have to sleep outdoors, and I said a prayer for the men who did.

I was well-fed, clean, and pleased with the work I had to do. There was a never-ending supply of interesting tropical diseases to test my diagnostic acumen, and many exotic medical problems, never seen stateside, to pique my interest. My Army experience in Vietnam broadened my young and very narrow career with challenges unique to the situation, and, for the most part, I enjoyed it. Mail from home finally caught up with me and I soon became busy writing back. As many soldiers in Vietnam did, I bought a small tape recorder in the Post Exchange (PX) and sent voice messages home every week. Listening to those tapes from home gave me many happy moments, but they made me miss my family even more. Missing home was the hardest thing a soldier had to endure when he had time away from his duties and was able to reflect on his situation. I couldn't wait to get letters from the States, especially from my wife, who wrote every day without fail. I would devour those letters, reading them over and over again. I saved all my letters for a while, but Margy wrote every day making the pile of them unmanageable. I threw out a bunch of letters one day only to have them all returned to me with a warning. American soldiers had been ordered to burn all their personal correspondence and were instructed never to just throw them away. I didn't know about this order. Some letters had fallen into the hands of the enemy, and they would send telegrams to the return addresses stating the soldier had been killed in action. I had a hard time believing that explanation at the time, but from then on, I burned my all letters. I dealt with missing my family by saying I was in country for only so many days more, and I could do the remaining time "standing on my head." Thinking back on that, I could never figure out how that consoled me, but the false bravado helped somehow. Besides, my uniforms were beginning to fade nicely, I was tanned, and felt I was beginning to look less like a rookie every day.

SNIPPETS FROM CU CHI

I was in the 25th Cu Chi area from early August to early October in 1968. I had passed my twenty-eighth birthday after a hard day's work by having a drink at the Officers' Club and going to bed early. In addition to that personal note, many other occasions stand out in my memory about my time in Cu Chi. Here are some of the most notable episodes I remember about those days.

The most haunting memory I have of that time is that of a very lonely soldier I saw on sick call one day. He had worked in a motor pool on the Cu Chi base, and had, I imagine, a pretty safe and comfortable existence. He related to me in an uneasy and clumsy manner, that he was having trouble falling asleep. Although this was not an unusual complaint, he seemed more far more depressed to me than the others I had seen with the same problem. I gave him a few Benadryl capsules to use when he had trouble falling asleep. Benadryl is an antihistamine drug often prescribed as a sleeping pill because of its pleasant side effect of drowsiness. I asked him to come back to see me on sick call if he still had any trouble. The very next day he was back saying the pills didn't work. When I suggested he try them for another day or so, he promptly broke down and began to cry uncontrollably. Through his tears he told me how much he hated his life in the Army, and he just couldn't take it any more. He related he was so lonely he couldn't control himself and he was beginning to break down in front of his friends at the motor pool. To add to his problems, the other guys were beginning to make fun of his crying which profoundly embarrassed him. Through wracking sobs, he said he just couldn't make it over here in Vietnam and he needed to go back to the real world. This crying was new to me. I had heard every curse word and every threat, but I had never experienced such deep sorrow on sick call. Wounded GIs often cried with their great pain, but somehow this was different. There were no wounds to cause physical pain, only shattered emotions. I felt this man's mental anguish were equal to the pain of a gunshot wound and needed to be taken very seriously. This patient needed help from a psychiatrist, not me. He was severely depressed, and I wasn't the kind of doctor to handle his illness. Sergeant Jiminez suggested he be seen by our outfit's psychologist since there were no psychiatrists available locally. Arrangements were made for an emergency consultation with the psychologist that afternoon, and I continued seeing the sick call patients.

At dinner that evening, I sought out the psychologist and spoke with him about that patient. Agreeing the patient was depressed, the psychologist didn't feel the man warranted an admission or an emergency visit to a psychiatrist. The patient was to come back the next day for a return visit and seemed happier when he left for his unit. I felt uneasy because I had been so impressed by his crying. I made myself a mental note to follow up with the psychologist the next day.

The next morning I was called from my sick call office in the aid station to see a gunshot wound of the chest! Immediately I recognized the depressed patient from the past two days! He was brought in when his buddies discovered he had shot himself in the chest with his M-16 rifle. With a full clip of twenty rounds, he had placed the rifle on the fully automatic setting and pulled the trigger. Fifteen slugs had pierced his chest before his trigger finger relaxed in death. He had killed himself on his bunk in his hooch right after his roommates had left for work. He had surrounded himself with pictures of his family and homemade placards that read, "Fuck the Army." His hooch-mates were so upset I had to ask my medics to usher them outside so I could work. There was really nothing for me to do but fill out his death certificate. Sergeant Jiminez, the medics, and I were all shaken by this unfortunate episode. The psychologist turned ashen when he saw his dead patient. A self-inflicted gunshot wound seemed so unnecessary with the war going on all around.

That afternoon all of us involved with that patient, including the psychologist, myself, Sergeant Jiminez, and the medics pored over all the details of the past three days' events. Of course, everyone wanted to prevent this type of incident from ever happening again. Although it was fairly common for GIs to complain bitterly about being in the Army and in Vietnam, our patient seemed more upset about being here than most. I resolved not to hesitate to get an immediate visit with a psychiatrist if I even suspected severe depression. Although everyone agreed with me about early consultation with a psychiatrist, there was one problem. Army psychiatrists were hard to find in Vietnam. I was able to locate one in Saigon, and I wrote his name and telephone number down for use in the future. I never recognized another suicide case during my stay in Vietnam, but I was overly careful to admit anyone who went over my personally set limits for anxiety and depression. Maybe I put a lot of soldiers in the ward for a rest they didn't need, but I never regretted it. I will always remember that soldier crying so hard in front of me, and I will always regret not having been able to help him.

A second notable occurrence during my time in Cu Chi was that of an ARVN soldier who had, literally, over one hundred tiny fragment wounds in his legs, from his feet to his thighs. The Army of (South) Vietnam had its own doctors and hospitals. Our Dust Off units picked up many wounded ARVNs for us to care for out of expediency and compassion. Our armed forces tried to treat them the same as we did our own soldiers. My personal policy was to treat all soldiers the same. I took the most seriously wounded soldiers first, regardless if they were American troops, Allied soldiers, ARVNs, or the enemy. Most doctors did the same, and no one ever suffered because of it, friend or foe.

On the particular ARVN soldier, I spent hours digging out the minuscule fragments, many of which went deep into his muscles, i.e., through his skin, through the fat beneath his skin, and finally, through the fascia into the deep muscles of his legs. Being physically impossible to remove every sand-sized particle of foreign body from those many puncture wounds, I stopped trying after many hours. The pieces that were left were too small to feel or find, so each and all of his wounds were widely debrided and dressed. I started him on prophylactic intravenous antibiotics and admitted him to our ward. He was very quiet and frightened. The next morning, Vietnamese interpreters found he had no complaints, and that he actually felt well. The first dressing change and inspection of his wounds the next day showed no signs of infection. I was making the necessary arrangements for returning him to his unit, but my process was slow, hampered by all the usual red tape. On the next day's visit, his legs demonstrated a slight redness to the skin in the spaces between his debrided wounds. There were no signs of pus or any

dead tissue in the wounds themselves. Noting nothing more to debride, I decided to increase his antibiotic dosage. On rounds the following morning, the third day after his injury, he had a fever of 102
degrees! Now an examination of his legs showed swelling and severe pain to the touch! Crepitus, the dreaded sign of gas crunching
in the tissues, was easily elicited. There was no doubt; my patient
had gas gangrene. He would need immediate attention at a larger
facility. Gas gangrene can be caused by any one of several species
of deadly bacteria that chew up the tissues, and give off gases as a
metabolic by-product. This rapidly spreading infection is certain
death when left untreated, and even with the best possible treatment
death occurs most of the time. As the eternal scourge of military
wounds, there is little effective treatment for this gas producing
gangrenous process once it starts. Death usually follows in a few
short hours, and the associated pain is always excruciating. Back in
the United States he possibly would have undergone wide debridement of his legs in a hyperbaric chamber, or, if the process had gone
too far, bilateral amputations would be the next treatment option.

Realizing the gravity of the situation, I called the Vietnamese
hospital in Saigon directly. A Vietnamese doctor suggested the soldier was going to die in any case, so I should just put him in a corner and let him die. There was little doubt in my mind he needed
amputations. The crepitus had not extended above his knees, and
bilateral above-the-knee amputations could result in uninfected surgical margins. Our operating rooms lacked the tools to do major
amputations, putting me in a real bind as how to handle this critically ill patient.

In Vietnam, leg amputations meant an even more compromised
life than in the States. No one could fashion artificial legs, and mobility would depend upon homemade devices and family members.
The Army prosthetists were only stateside because that's where
American amputees were sent. Desperately wanting something to be
done for this poor guy, I carefully wrote down my diagnoses and
recommendations, including my thoughts on the unavoidable amputations. Working closely with the Dust Off pilots as we did, I was
able to convince a crew to fly this patient directly to the ARVN
hospital in Saigon. There, he would at least have a shot at survival
and his physical presence might force action on the part of the
ARVN doctors. The Dust Off helicopter landed outside my aid station, and I carefully loaded my very sick patient on board. He was

resting more comfortably because I had given him a shot of morphine earlier. The injection must have relieved some of his pain, as much of the terror was gone from his eyes. The Dust Off radio operator had already called the ARVN hospital advising them the helicopter would be inbound with my patient which didn't leave them any room for dissent. Standing on the helipad, I watched as the helicopter got smaller and disappeared into the distance. I never heard what happened to that ARVN soldier despite several calls later that day and the next. The Dust Off crew said the Vietnamese doctors did examine him, and they were looking at the notes I sent as well. The patient was eventually taken out of the crew's sight, hopefully to surgery for those amputations. Fortunately, I would never see another case of gas gangrene while in Vietnam. Like so many other patients in Vietnam, I never did learn the final outcome of my patient. Vietnamese patients tended to get lost in the big civilian hospitals. No hospital records were kept, and the hospital staff went home after five P.M. There were very few beds, and most patients slept on rice mats. Care and food were given to patients by their families. There were stories of patients actually starving in those Vietnamese hospitals because there were no family members to care for them. All this helped explain why the Vietnamese liked American doctors and Army hospitals.

Most of the dealings I had with the Vietnamese people were good. The modern medicine the Army doctors dispensed and the way they were treated impressed the local citizens. Vietnamese people waited long hours in long lines to be seen by the American doctors. On several occasions we had to turn people away at the end of a long day. The people didn't mind. They would return the next morning to wait all over again. They often came with their whole families and brought rice to feed them during the long wait. Usually the entire family was examined at one time. Vietnamese called doctors, "Bac Si," a Chinese word that meant, "barefoot doctor." A Bac Si would take care of the sick villagers, but had little formal medical training. Vietnamese Bac Si treatments often left tell-tale bruising from the tissue twisting they did to rid the villager of illness. Most of the Vietnamese patients I saw had the characteristic Bac Si bruising.

"Dai Wi," the Vietnamese words for the military rank of captain, were added to Bac Si to describe Army doctors. Dai Wi Bac Si was the result, and it had a nice ring to it. When they would pass me on the street, these patient, gentle people, men, women, and children, would bow from the hip and say in broken English, "Good Morning, Dai Wi Bac Si." To me, the habit of bowing when formally greeting others was very polite and courteous. I looked forward to seeing these friendly Vietnamese patients, and I returned their bows whenever I could. Interpreters were not always available and the language was definitely a barrier. "Dow ho dow" meant, "Where is the pain?" "Nicht dow" was headache; "dow lum" was abdominal pain; and "dow bung" meant back pain. Knowing this much of the language greatly helped when examining them, and I could usually communicate somewhat when no interpreter was at hand. The full spectrum of tropical diseases plagued these people and I had read little about these diseases, let alone seen any of them. Malaria was rampant, as were things like polio, bubonic plague, venereal disease, hepatitis and intestinal infestations like typhoid fever, amoebiasis and worms of all kinds in every part of the body. If I were able to zero in on the major complaint I was usually able to help. Parasites responded well to our medications, as did malaria, typhoid fever and the amoebic diseases. Polio, hepatitis and other viral diseases were untreatable and would usually run their courses without much residual ill effect.

I remember one woman particularly well for a huge staphylococcal abscess that took up the whole back of her neck. She was very ill with a high fever and shaking chills when I first saw her. I admitted her to our hospital ward for intravenous antibiotics and close observation. I used a new antibiotic, nafcillin, which worked well for her. Nafcillin was for penicillin-resistant staphylococcus aureus, which I surmised she was suffering from. She had been taking pills she bought in a drugstore for over a week. No prescriptions were necessary to obtain antibiotics in South Vietnam, and she had probably been taking penicillin. The staph had most likely become resistant to the penicillin, as it will often do, which explained her continued fever. After the first night on nafcillin, her fever broke and she lost the delirium she had on admission. The next morning the lab reported that the bacteria responsible was indeed a penicillin-resistant staphylococcus, which also confirmed she was on the correct antibiotic.

As was the Vietnamese custom, her sister accompanied her on our ward to help with her care. My patient was about fifty years old, five feet tall, and weighed only ninety-five pounds, about the average size for a Vietnamese woman. Her teeth were blackened by chewing betel nuts. These nuts were very popular with the older Vietnamese, both men and women. Possibly having a narcotic-like effect, these nuts were plentiful in the surrounding shrubs, and most rural farm workers had a mouthful.

I drained her abscess under local anesthesia and widely debrided the surrounding involved tissue. The result of the debridement was a skin defect four inches in diameter that would take months to heal. A skin graft would allow healing in a week to ten days, but I didn't have the tools I needed to perform the graft. A week later, when all signs of infection had cleared, I borrowed a dermatome (a skin graft harvesting machine) from the Evac hospital. With the dermatome, I harvested and grafted a piece of skin from her right leg to the defect on the back of her neck. That old Brown dermatome harvested a perfect graft, and I carefully sutured the harvested skin over the old abscess site. I fashioned a compressive dressing to hold the graft tightly to the receiving wound. Three long days later I anxiously changed the dressing and viewed the result. There is always the worry the graft won't heal because of infection, poor blood supply, motion, or all of the above.

My patient took all of this with courage and dignity, never really fully understanding what I was doing to her. She particularly didn't see why I had "cut" her right leg when there was nothing wrong with it in the first place, but she had faith in the Dai Wi Bac Si and let me do it. Like something from a Hollywood movie, the dressings were teased away from the graft with the entire ward watching with great anticipation. A background Vietnamese conversation was heard in hushed tones as I worked. The patient and her sister watched my every move in a manner that told me they let me get away with the leg thing, but they were not going to allow any more monkey business. My heart was in my mouth as I pulled the last of the bandages from the graft. There was a hush in the room as all eyes fixed on the four-inch graft. After the dried blood was washed away with hydrogen peroxide, one of Mother Nature's miracles was easily seen. The graft had become firmly attached to the old wound site, covering that ugly area with bright new skin! The new skin blanched when I touched it and then quickly refilled with flowing blood, showing that the tiny vessels below had knitted with those in the split-thickness graft. There were no signs of infection. The success was intoxicating to me. That's why I loved surgery. This was no humbug. I was so pleased I couldn't stop smiling for hours. Being only a first-year resident in a five-year surgery program, so far I had only done a few skin grafts back in the U.S. The patient herself could not see the outcome, but her sister was amazed and as pleased as I was. Using a mirror borrowed from another, my patient could now see the result. Tears came down her cheeks as she hugged me. I don't believe I've ever been "paid" as well for anything else. The next day after staying two weeks in the ward, she returned to her village. With black teeth bared in smiles, the two sisters said fond good-byes to the ward medics and GI patients as they left. I gave explicit instructions on how to care for the graft and donor site. They were to return to the aid station in one week to see me. True to my Vietnamese experience, she never returned, which led me to believe she did well and saw no reason to come back.

The busy 25th Infantry Division base camp at Cu Chi usually had thousands of soldiers in its confines at any given time. Grunts in from the field on "stand down" used the day or two allotted for a well-deserved rest. The engineers had constructed a swimming pool only to be used by soldiers in from the field. The pool was naturally very popular and heavily used on the hot days of the Vietnamese dry season. There was an outdoor stage in camp that could seat hundreds of GIs for shows and concerts. Bob Hope usually visited Cu Chi at Christmastime each year and had used this stage for his famous wartime shows. Convening so many soldiers in one place at one time afforded a great target of opportunity for our well-informed enemy. Mortar or rocket attacks could be very effective killing large numbers of soldiers at well-attended shows like Bob Hope's. You could be sure that during the Bob Hope shows, which were televised all over the world, there were at least four soldiers on guard out in the field for every one soldier in the audience. Most of the entertainment on this stage, however, was put on by touring groups from the Philippines, Japan, and Korea, singing the popular songs of the day. During one of these shows I was introduced to Sergeant Robinson, a man whom I was to come in contact with on many occasions in the future.

On a beautiful sunny Sunday afternoon, I was manning the aid station and hadn't seen a patient all day. The war had been quiet for the past few days and, out of boredom, Sergeant Jiminez was play-ing cards with the medics in a back room. The empty stretchers were lined up in neat rows, and the emergency area sparkled with military cleanliness in anticipation of patients. The smell of the anti-septic wintergreen oil used to scrub the floors permeated the air. The pleasant but sometimes overpowering smell of wintergreen al-ways reminded me of candy. As I started to join the card game, a very loud explosion made us all jump. Chairs, cards, and people went flying as the startled medics sought cover. In a single chorus, everyone asked, "What was that?" An excited debate about the cause of the explosion ensued. Loud explosions were routine in Cu Chi, usually invoking opinions as to the cause. Explosions from hostile incoming shells had to be excluded from the similar sounds of outgoing friendly artillery fire. This was usually easily deter-mined by anyone with some experience, but some sounds were im-possible to categorize even by the most expert of listeners. This was such a noise. We soon got an answer, as excited soldiers with bloody wounds rushed through the open doors of the aid station, dragging other wounded soldiers behind them. Their high-pitched voices told of an explosion at the afternoon concert. There were de-scriptions of a small black satchel, probably the bomb, in the space between the first row and the stage. There had been only one explo-sion, which made incoming rounds unlikely because hostile fire usually was more than one. Other doctors had heard the loud explo-sion, and they came running in to help. The wounded were placed on the stretchers. There were no dead as yet. Many had deep shrap-nel wounds, some had burns, and a few had their bones broken dur-ing the scramble to get away. Sergeant Robinson had received a moderate-sized fragmentation wound of his calf. He was in civilian clothes, and was wearing Bermuda shorts so that his calf wound was readily seen. I learned his name from his aid station record, and I focused in on him as my patient that afternoon. The explosion had summoned several doctors that day, leaving me free to take care of the Sergeant. He was twenty years old, slender, and he seemed too quiet. Talking with him, I found he was an MP in Cu Chi, and was trying to enjoy a Sunday afternoon off duty watching the weekly show when the explosion went off. As I worked on him, he opened up more. My modus operandi was to talk to my patient as I washed the wound and injected the local anesthesia. Taking a patient's mind off what I was doing by carrying on a conversation seemed to help, and I talked with Sergeant Robinson as I worked on him. The piece of metal stuck in the flesh of his leg came out with little trouble, leaving a much smaller defect than I thought it would. After debriding the wound, I decided to close it primarily. Waiting three days in such a small, clean wound didn't always seem necessary as in this instance, so I took leave of the Army's policy, used my own judgment, and sutured his wound right then and there. His wound closed nicely, and the patient was pleased when he looked over what I had done.

Although his wound pained him somewhat, he was more troubled by the sudden and totally unexpected violence that peaceful Sunday afternoon. Obviously this act of terrorism was intended to maim and kill the GIs, but also to demoralize and frighten them. It worked! Although no one died, terror was easily seen in the eyes of the victims. That day I made up my mind to avoid large crowds and mass activities while in Vietnam. After all, there was a war going on, and our enemy was smart. The concert had been advertised for a while, giving a hopeful saboteur plenty of time to arrange his surprise attack. Most GIs, like Sergeant Robinson, served their time in combat, kept to themselves, and went home all the wiser for not having placed themselves in harm's way when they didn't have to. Being a military policeman, Sergeant Robinson couldn't always avoid crowds, but he told me he never again went into a crowd as a participant. Getting to know Sergeant Robinson, I was impressed by his gentle nature, and his ability to reduce complex situations into understandable explanations. Over the next several months I saw him on many occasions in Cu Chi and other places. Policemen and doctors are frequent associates in the military and in civilian life. They usually meet in the emergency departments of hospitals where victims of accidents, crimes and altercations are brought in by the police. Sergeant Robinson and I met like this many times. I remembered him from that explosion at the concert. He was small for an MP, but he commanded respect from larger soldiers because of his serious demeanor and his fearlessness. I found it good for me to have someone to talk with outside medical circles. He brought a different perspective to the limited outlook I had, and I enjoyed his company.

The business of the 25th Infantry Division was to destroy the enemy, plain and simple. The VC evaporated during the day and came out in the dark to kill and to terrorize. The NVA regulars were amazingly adept at hiding large numbers of troops and materiel, rarely coming out in force to fight in the open, and only when they chose to. The NVA would attack in small groups, limiting losses, but they would throw in a lot of soldiers when they smelled victory. They loved to annihilate American forces completely for the psychological victory garnered, but avoided long battles whenever possible. Our soldiers had to patrol the countryside looking for hostiles, but they rarely found any concentrations of them. Booby traps lined the jungle trails and GIs would be killed by this unseen and unavenged enemy. After days of not seeing anything and losing men to booby traps, punji sticks, and small ambushes, they were frustrated, angry, and very ready to fight. In order to locate enemy concentrations, some of our soldiers were sent out on patrol for long weeks at a time. The idea of these long patrols was to observe the enemy, but not to engage him, hoping to find the location of the major NVA concentrations so these could be annihilated. Limited radio contact with their home base lent more security to the American patrol missions, and this silence offered more opportunities to discover groups of enemy without being discovered themselves. These GIs would shadow groups of enemy soldiers, trying to find the locations of base camps and plotting frequently traveled enemy supply routes. Being gone so long, and out of close contact with their own, these guys had to be tough. They were often ambushed, and without support, they had to fight for their lives alone, far from any help. These troopers were called LRPs, short for Long Range Patrols. I met many of these intrepid soldiers and their stories were always intense, filled with suspense and fright. One guy hadn't bathed for over a month! Each day they waded through rice paddies to have the water cover their trails. They reported that at night flashlights lit up all over the place, reaffirming the enemy could move at will all night long.

There were never any true front lines in the Vietnam War. Most of the time, the enemy preferred to hide and snipe at the GIs. Every once in a while, when they figured the time was right, they'd hit us with all their might, often inflicting a great deal of death and suffering. Then they would retreat back into the jungles to hide before the American forces could gather in any strength. In their rapid retreat, they had to leave their dead behind, allowing the American forces to brag about a big body count. Ten to one was the usual enemy to GI death ratio. Ho Chi Minh had plenty of soldiers, and he sacrificed them like pawns. I could detect frustration in the eyes of the GI combat commanders as they came up against the enemy's willingness to sacrifice his own soldiers' lives. Here we were, the best army in the world, the best equipped, the best fed, with the best medical care; we owned complete control of the sky, yet we were still slowly losing the war. No wonder the war dragged on so long! If the enemy could continue to hold on with its unending supply of men, we could never win! Hard to understand, I never will know why the politicians took so long to pull out of there. Unfortunately, pride and saving face will always be the driving political force until public opinion allows differently. In 1968, public opinion wasn't ready to back a pullout of Vietnam until five years in the future, when Richard Nixon bit the bullet and began the withdrawal of our forces. Even back in 1968, every day I heard rumors the 25th Infantry Division was going to head back to their home, Schofield Barracks in Hawaii. How sweet the sound of that! Imagine my finishing out my military duties in beautiful Hawaii. The rumors went on to say that the United States was going to supply the South Vietnamese government with weapons and materiel, but not the soldiers. This plan wouldn't take shape for years to come of course, but discussions of returning to Hawaii were always animated and a lot fun at the time.

The 25th's area was very rural in places, with triple-canopy jungle, hundreds of rice paddies and many small bucolic hamlets. Huge rubber plantations with trees planted only a few feet apart gave good cover to the enemy. The most famous of these was the Michelin Plantation near Dau Tieng. Believe it or not, our forces tried to avoid hurting those rubber trees through some kind of occult agreement with the French, and many an enemy owed his life to the no-fire rule for the Michelin plantation.

The enemy was very skilled at digging three-foot-deep pits and lining the bottoms with sharpened bamboo stakes that had been dipped in human excrement. The pits were then covered with leaves and grass cut from the surrounding vegetation for camouflage. Most "point men" (lead man of a patrol) could recognize these faint warning signs of a punji stake pit and would alert the patrol following along behind. At night, many more men fell victim to those dangers, because the warning signs couldn't be seen under the cover of darkness, and a lot of patrols went out at night. A GI who had fallen into a bamboo stake pit had his outer calf impaled with a punji stick. The stick went through and through, i.e. each end of the stick was showing while the mid-portion of it was under six inches of his calf's skin. Medics in the field were reluctant to pull out the stick. Instead, they quickly transported him to our aid station, which took about thirty minutes.

When I first examined that unfortunate soldier that night, the skin of his impaled leg was already a scarlet color. A fever of 101 degrees and shaking chills indicated a serious infection had set in. I soaked his wounds in Betadyne solution to cleanse away as much of the external contamination as possible. Then I injected the skin of his leg overlying the stake with lots of local anesthesia. With a scalpel I made a six-inch-long incision through the overlying skin, down through the subcutaneous fat, fascia and on into the muscle, in order to free the contaminated punji stick from the soldier's leg. After the bamboo stick was removed I could then effectively and vigorously irrigate the resultant wound with a powerful antibiotic solution. Left unsutured, the wound was packed open with Betadyne-soaked gauzes to further ward off infection. I kept the soldier on our ward for careful observation, and I pumped him full of intravenous antibiotics. Thank goodness the injured soldier was nineteen years young and in excellent health. He didn't turn a hair and began to heal rapidly. He really enjoyed his time on our ward often saying, "This beats infantry life all to hell!" Four days later, his wound looked clean and was ready to be sutured. I closed the long, deep gash with wire sutures placed over cotton bolsters, which are the things the dentist puts in your mouth to keep your tongue out of his way. These bolsters were used to prevent the wires from pulling through the skin.

The wound healed nicely and after twelve days, the sutures were removed. Luckily, he was able to walk despite the muscle involvement, but, even so, I put him on "light duty" for another two weeks. The soldier himself was pleased with the outcome. He had seen what his leg looked like that first night, and, for a while, was concerned he might lose the leg. He didn't like the idea that he was well enough to go back to his unit, however, and he wanted to stay in Cu Chi for rehabilitation. Unfortunately, I had to send him back, but with his light duty status, he would be able to avoid patrols for another few weeks. On the bright side, he went back to his outfit two weeks closer to going home and ten pounds fatter.

War was never really a gentleman's game, and occasional barbarity was seen from time to time on both sides, as expected. One night a "Jolly Green Giant" Marine helicopter off-loaded a score of slain "Leathernecks" in a line alongside our helipad. The Marine helicopter crew wasn't familiar with our dead shed, and they laid the corpses in such a way that a crowd of passersby began to gather. Curses and tears were mixed as fellow Marines and GIs viewed the bodies lined up in a ghastly, unintended military formation. My medics knew if KIAs were left out in the open on this busy base, a crowd would quickly gather, and things would soon get ugly. There was no time to change what had already happened, so rather than move the bodies at this time, I thought I'd inspect them where they lay. This way, the bodies would be moved only once, to Graves Registration. On my examination of those slain men, I saw what the angry crowd had already realized. Many of the dead Marines had their hands tied behind their backs, and their fatal wounds were due to single nine-millimeter slugs to the back of each of their heads! The now milling and gawking crowd began to shout heated questions at me as I worked, "Do you see any other wounds? What's that guy's name? I think I know him." The crowd was getting unruly despite my medics pleading, "Please stand back, and let the doctor do his job." MPs finally arrived, and pushing the crowd back, order was quickly restored.

I saw that many of the bodies were missing fingers, all ring fingers, but I had no idea why. The fingers had been cut off, not shot off, making this a deliberate act of savagery, rather than a freak happenstance of war. Perhaps the fingers were taken as a souvenir of battle, like the enemy ears some of our soldiers cut off and wore on strings around their necks, like scalps from days of yore. The bullet wounds in their heads suggested these Marines must have been taken prisoner, tied up, and then summarily executed! I was stunned as I examined the bodies and tried to reconstruct what probably happened. Army Intelligence was called, and soon the macabre scene was crawling with even more people. Investigators were taking photographs and going over the bodies looking for additional evidence. Lights from surrounding ambulances cast an eerie glow to the ashen faces of the dead Marines whose grotesque head wounds gave mute testimony to man's cruelty to man. As the process wound down, the bodies were taken to Graves Registration, cooling the molten rage of the onlookers. The crowd disappeared into the night as quickly as it gathered, and I went back into the aid station to complete my awaiting paperwork.

Later that night, I saw a survivor from that party of Marines in the dispensary. He had been brought in with wounds from that same fight. His wounds were not serious and while I was working on them, he told me what had happened. The medics gathered around his stretcher, mindful of my working, and quietly listened in somber reverence as he began to tell his story. About thirty Marines had been out on patrol looking for Charley that night, as they did so often. When the sun began to set, they went about making their nighttime defensive position (NDP). They posted guards and then began to dig in for the night. A party of NVA had spotted them on the trail earlier, and, keeping out of sight, followed them closely. Before the Marines could secure their perimeter with the usual claymore mines and machine guns, and before they were secure in their foxholes, the NVA attacked. Woefully outnumbered, the Marines put up a good fight, but could only hold out for a short while. Most of the Marines never even got a chance to fire their rifles. Some hand-to-hand combat went on for a while, but the Marines were quickly overwhelmed. My patient, the one telling the story, had been shot through the flesh of his arm, which luckily bled a great deal all over his shirt, making him look like he had been killed rather than just wounded. Realizing the situation was hopeless, he lay back and played dead. From his prone position he could see NVA soldiers dressed in pith helmets and khaki uniforms, binding his buddies' hands behind their backs. Laughing now, the enemy soldiers began to systematically rob the living and dead of money, rings, and watches. Seeing he was about to be robbed next, my patient experienced pure panic! The NVA soldiers took his high school ring from his finger and his brand new Seiko watch from his wrist. All the while he continued to feign death. "My heart was pounding so hard," he said, "I thought for sure they would notice me sweating and blow my shit away! I held my breath for as long as I could, and I tried to remain limp. In an instant, it was over. The NVA soldiers walked away! I guess they were eager to search the other bodies." To his surprise, his ruse had not been discovered so far.

To his horror, through tiny slits in his eyelids, he watched as the Marines with tied hands were executed, one by one, from a single bullet to the back of the head. An NVA officer fired the shots from his Browning nine-millimeter pistol. Very emotional now, and beginning to weep, my patient said the NVA soldiers cut off the ring fingers of the executed Marines, to get the rings they had missed earlier. At the beginning of his story, I had asked one of the medics to give my patient a shot of morphine. The drug was starting to work. The Marine's words were beginning to slur and he was yawning through his story. Finished telling his amazing account of survival, the Marine looked around at the spellbound medics, and in a sobbing voice asked, "Did I do right? I wanted to get up and kill those S.O.B.s, but I didn't know where my rifle was! Oh, I hated just lying there watching that prick shooting my friends, but what could I do?" He was frantic again and sobbing more audibly. Several of the medics said at once, "No! No! You did all you could. You would have just been killed like your buddies! We're glad you're alive; you owe it to your family to stay alive!" The Marine's drug-sodden mind mulled over that response, and forcing a weak smile, whispered, "Yeah, I guess you're right." Relieved by the medics' singular response, the Marine closed his eyes and slept a well-deserved sleep.

I kept him in the ward for several days longer than his arm wound required, but he finally had to return to his unit. What a story! Hard to imagine, the enemy soldiers never noticed he was still alive, but in the excitement of the battle, I'm sure even stranger things have happened. The next day I learned that several of the Marines had managed to slip away from the fight that night and had called for help. Fresh Marines arrived quickly on the scene and completely wiped out that NVA band. No NVA survived that second battle which came as no surprise to anyone who saw the dead Marines. When he heard that news, my Marine patient wanted to go back and try to find the brand-new watch he lost. He didn't, and he never mentioned the watch again. There was, at least, one very lucky Marine that horrible night.

When I left my parents back in the States, my father gave me a solemn piece of advice. Although he had never been in the military himself, he warned, "Never volunteer for anything! That's a good way to get killed." I thought that was sage counsel, and I imagined many dads all over the world had given their sons that same advice for centuries. I took his advice to heart and resolved never to volunteer for anything as long as I was in the Army. One evening in Cu Chi, I found out that the Army's way of asking for a volunteer was

Chi, I found out that the Army's way of asking for a volunteer was to select one. That way, no one could ever refuse. That's what Major "Buck" Rogers did to me one night after dinner in Cu Chi. As the 25th Med Battalion's Executive Officer, the major had received a radio call from the commander of a 25th unit involved in fighting an NVA group that night. Buck told me an American soldier was trapped on a tank that had been hit and completely disabled by a rocket-propelled grenade. The tank was burning in the middle of a rice paddy with the NVA keeping up machine-gun fire from a well-hidden position behind a dike on the opposite side of the tank from the 25th's unit and the trapped soldier. The soldier couldn't get away because his foot was inextricably caught in twisted tank metal on the side away from the enemy fire. To bombard the enemy with any kind of artillery would kill our soldier because the tank was too close to the enemy position. The commander said the burning tank would probably soon blow up from all the ammunition and gas on board, and this would, of course, kill his soldier. Using the tank as cover, the commander said, his own soldiers were able to crawl up to the tank and the trapped soldier, but they were unable to free the soldier's foot.

As I listened in frightened disbelief, Buck went on explaining the situation in more detail. What the combat commander wanted was a doctor to amputate part of the trapped soldier's foot and free him from the burning tank. With his soldier out of harm's way, the enemy behind the dike would be annihilated with artillery fire. Remembering my father's words, I asked Buck if he was asking me to volunteer, hoping I could say an emphatic, "No!" But, alas, Buck said he was ordering me to do this, short and sweet. He said I shouldn't worry, why, I might even get a Silver Star for this! Seeing no way out, I anxiously began to assemble the instruments and local anesthetics I would need.

With my steel helmet on my head, wearing my flak jacket, and with my Colt .45 strapped to my side, I awaited the helicopter to take me to my unavoidable destiny. All of my equipment fit into a small Army rucksack that hung heavily over one of my shoulders. The Dust Off helicopter appeared, landing in front of the aid station. I ducked down to walk under the still twirling rotors and began to climb up into the vibrating helicopter. Just then the crew chief held up his right palm signaling, "Stop!" He was talking into his helmet mouthpiece with his pilot. The next thing I knew, he was motioning me to back away, which I did. In a noisy whirling windstorm, the helicopter took off, leaving me standing there very confused.

Later that same night, I was still standing by in the aid station when Major Rogers strolled up to me. I was sure the tank had exploded and my services were no longer needed, but that was not the case at all. Actually, an orthopedic surgeon from the 12th Evac had gone in my stead. The orthopedic surgeon amputated several toes of the trapped soldier, freeing him from the burning tank and certain death. That orthopedic surgeon did get the Silver Star for his action, and he deserved it. My big chance to become a hero evaporated, but I didn't mind a bit.

One day in mid-October of 1968, I was summoned to come to Lieutenant Colonel Hensel's office. Reporting quickly, I had a premonition something was up, but I had no idea what. Colonel Hensel was a hands-off commander and kept to himself in his headquarters building. Not wasting any time, he saw me right away. His office was always cool, but today I felt downright cold. Colonel Hensel came right to the point. Captain Lewis, the Commander of Company D, 25th Med in Tay Ninh was getting short and was to DEROS in one short week. The colonel wanted me to "get up there tomorrow" so I could learn about my new duties. I was to replace Captain Lewis as the new Commanding Officer of Company D, and my new assignment would commence as soon as I could get up there. Tomorrow, at 0600 hours, a Dust Off helicopter was to ferry me and my stuff to Tay Ninh's base camp, and Company D. Inevitably, doctors were transferred during their year in country, sometimes two or three times. As a partially trained surgeon, I was a likely candidate for command of a medical company. Since treating war wounds called for surgical training, the Army logically preferred someone with surgical training, and I fit the bill. Dr. Lewis was an exception; he was a general medical officer. He was made the CO of Company D six months earlier because there probably weren't any partially trained surgeons around at the time. Colonel Hensel dismissed me with, "Good Luck," and off I went. I ate dinner, packed my duffel bag, had a beer at the Officers' Club, set my alarm for 0500 hours and went to sleep. I was ready for my new adventure.

DELTA SIX - TAY NINH

Leaving on the dot of 0600, the Dust Off helicopter rose twenty feet with its nose down slightly, then raced down the main street of the Cu Chi base, gradually gaining altitude. As if in salute, the artillery battery we flew over belched smoke and fire. The concussion of those explosions shook our helicopter with each blast until we were far enough away to be out of the vibration range. Chief Warrant Officer James Berrigan was our pilot that day. He was an experienced Huey pilot and had flown many life-saving missions as a Dust Off pilot during his six months of South Vietnam duty. Twenty-five years old, a black moustache, white helmet and air force sunglasses lent a swashbuckling air to this dashing figure. He looked every inch the fearless pilot he was, and I was relaxed knowing he was at the helm that beautiful morning. Low-leveling fifty feet above the ground at a speed of one hundred miles per hour, we avoided being sniped at by the enemy. The rice paddies and jungle streaked by just below us, and I had an urge to touch the tips of the water reeds as we passed over them. Approaching a tree line on a rice paddy dike, Berrigan suddenly swooped over without slowing down. He did that often, and each time I felt I left my stomach on the top of one of those palm trees. I could feel the helicopter crew watching my reactions, but, no matter how hard I tried, I couldn't hide my discomfort. Below, I could see many signs of the war. The jungle was dotted with small-fire support bases, bristling with the barrels of the smaller 105-millimeter howitzers sticking out from their sandbagged emplacements. These 105s were the backbone of the Army's artillery because of their light weight and maneuverability. I could see heavily armed GIs walking in long, lazy, single file lines. They were out humping the boonies, looking for Charley. Out in front of each file was the point man, the most experienced and most important member of the patrol in Vietnam. He led the patrol.

Often written on his helmet was the slogan, "God is my point man." Next in line, would come the patrol commander, usually a second lieutenant. In the bright morning sun, I could make out the single black bar on his lapel. The RTO (Radio-Telephone Operator) came right behind the second lieutenant, with the long black radio antenna whipping behind him as he slogged along in the six-inch-deep rice paddy water. The main body of the group, about ten to twenty sweating soldiers, followed about twenty yards behind. That explained why the point man, the RTO, and the second lieutenant were usually the first hit in a VC ambush. They were the first through the bushes and out into the open. Most of the soldiers waved as we whizzed over that morning. GIs appreciated Dust Off helicopters and their crews. They knew the crews would extract their wounded from battles, no matter how much danger, no matter the time of day, and no matter the weather. GIs were quick to buy drinks for Dust Off crews, and they were always treated with respect. Many lives were saved in the long years of fighting in Vietnam by these fearless flying medics.

After about thirty minutes of low-level flying, the helicopter began to rise and leveled off at one thousand feet on its final approach to the Tay Ninh base. As we flew into the Third Brigade area of the 25th Infantry Division, the Black Virgin Mountain loomed into view. Rising 3,400 feet above the landscape, the mountain dominates the surrounding countryside. Located fifty-five miles northwest of Saigon, the mountain was best known by its Vietnamese name, Nui Ba Den. To the north, long reaches of triple-canopy jungle stretched as far as my eyes could see. Immediately below us, the lush tropical jungle was dotted with rice paddies and small villages. Water had seeped into the many B-52 bomb craters studding the green jungle, turning them into long rows of blue pools. Looking at those tiny lakes that morning, I thought that Mother Nature could change even war's ugly scars into something of beauty if given enough time.

The Third Brigade's base camp at Tay Ninh was less than one-third the size of the 25th's Headquarters at Cu Chi. I had never been to the Tay Ninh base camp before, so I took a good look around as I approached from the air. An airstrip long enough to land lumbering C-134s was located in the center of the base. The C-134 could stop on a dime, but needed jet-assisted take-off (JATO) for the short runways of Tay Ninh. As our helicopter flew over the airstrip, a C-134 was beginning its take-off. The JATO tubes on either side of the C-134's fuselage simultaneously shot out flames, pushing and thrusting the heavy plane up into the air just as the end of the runway was nearing. Once airborne, the plane's JATO flames went out, leaving only the steady drone of its straining motors to pull the plane on its way. All kinds of smaller planes and helicopters in orderly fashion lined the single runway. The perimeter of the camp had a raised grassy berm that was covered with intertwined concertina wires. Bunkers with machine guns were evenly spaced along the berm and could fill their section of perimeter with deadly fire from their elevated positions. Every so often along the berm were stationed "quad-fifties." These were jeep-like trucks, rear-mounted with four fifty-caliber machine gun barrels projecting out from slots in a square-shaped thick metal shield. They looked very threatening, even when not firing! In one corner of the base was a large compound, housing the whole gamut of Army artillery pieces. I saw many 105s, several 155s, a few 175s and one eight-incher. I surmised there must be plenty of fire missions for the artillery up here in Tay Ninh. After all the stories I had heard about this being the jumping place from the Ho Chi Minh Trail, I was comforted by the presence of all this artillery firepower. As I got closer to the base camp, I could see men walking along dirt roads, not as sharply dressed, nor walking as intently as I had noticed in Cu Chi. A large red cross on a white background loomed large on the road we were now following, and we quickly landed on a helipad alongside a small "MUST" hospital by that red cross. MUST was the acronym the Army chose for this type of inflatable portable hospital. The buildings were pumped up with air and had all the modern conveniences needed in a small surgical hospital. I have long forgotten what MUST stands for. Across the narrow dirt road from where we landed were the buildings of Company D, 25th Medical Battalion; my new home. CWO Berrigan landed our Dust Off Huey like a feather on a pillow. I stepped out into my new world, squinting my eyes to protect them from the bright sun's glare and the whirling dust from the rotor's wash.

I was sure someone would be there to greet me, but there was no one. My smile was for naught. The Dust Off crew climbed back into the chopper and motioned me to stand back. Berrigan lifted the Huey off with a gust of wind that nearly knocked me down. I had no idea what was going on. The helicopter flew a few feet away then relit in a space that was surrounded by perforated steel plate (PSP). This was the garage for the helicopter, made to protect the Dust Off helicopter from incoming shells. The PSP pieces held dirt between them and were in a three-sided configuration. The "garage" would stop shell fragments and bullets at least on three sides. The open side allowed easier access for the chopper's crew in an emergency. There were a lot of these protective garages for the many helicopters the First Brigade used, scattered around the base. My flight crew walked over to me from the parked helicopter and apologized for nearly knocking me over. They said they were just putting their "baby to bed." Patting me on the back, Berrigan smiled and said he wasn't trying to tick off the new Delta Six. Together, we walked across the street to the long Quonset building that was the aid station of Company D.

Passing through the wide door under the familiar sign of the 25th Med Battalion, I went inside. A crew was mopping the floor with oil of wintergreen solution. That friendly smell greeted me and made me feel at home. The two men doing the mopping were sweating profusely as they worked hard trying to remove the dried blood on the concrete floor from the previous night's casualties. The men were wearing the standard sleeveless aqua blue scrub tops loose outside of their jungle fatigue pants. Their jungle mesh boots were dusty, unlike the spit-shined boots of the medics in Cu Chi. Otherwise, they looked the same. Familiar with the Dust Off crew, the medics said a friendly hello to them, laughing and wisecracking until they spied me. One politely acknowledged me, saying, "Hello, Sir, can I help you?" I replied that I was Captain Snider, and I was looking for their Commanding Officer, Captain Lewis. I was told Captain Lewis was attending the morning Third Brigade briefing with the Brigade Commander, Colonel Bobby Wair, and he should be back any minute now. Realizing the soldier was nervous about having called the Commander Officer of the 25th Infantry Division's Third Brigade "Bobby," I pretended I didn't catch the breach in Army protocol. Berrigan and his crew were hungry, and they suggested I eat breakfast with them in the mess hall. The crew was very familiar with Company D and the Tay Ninh base camp in general, because the Dust Off command in Cu Chi supplied crews for Dau Tieng and Tay Ninh. The crews and helicopters rotated every two weeks in all three base camps, so they were well-known in Tay Ninh, Dau Tieng, as well as Cu Chi.

The mess hall was about fifty yards away from the aid station via a narrow boardwalk. Like Cu Chi, a complicated network of boardwalks led every which way. As in Cu Chi, they were completely unnecessary when it wasn't raining. The day had grown very hot and still, which caused profuse sweating with the slightest exertion. A thermometer outside the aid station had read ninety degrees earlier, and now the temperature was hovering around one hundred degrees, fairly typical for a sunny day in Vietnam. Arriving at the mess hall, breakfast was over for the majority of the company, but several men were lingering over a cup of coffee. The building was "T" shaped and made of clapboards over wooden framing. The upper part of the walls was screening nailed over the frame for coolness. The corrugated tin roof had long low eaves to keep out the cruel sun. The inside was much cooler than I would have expected, but still, just the slightest effort would cause profuse perspiration. Slowly revolving ceiling fans helped make the inside bearable. Old flypaper tapes hung from the uncovered rafters with attached dead flies attesting to their efficiency. Red-checkered tablecloths adorned the tables, which added a little class. Not just a place to eat, this mess hall was the center of fraternization for Company D. Lively conversations and laughter were always heard in Army mess halls, and this one was no exception.

I met "Short Round," the main cook. A short round is an artillery shell that explodes before it reaches its target, and Short Round, the cook, was so named because he had a short temper. He was twenty years old and wise beyond his years. Not the NCOIC of the mess hall, he served under Sergeant Knoerr, whom I would meet later. Short Round was the heart and soul of the mess hall operation in Company D. Everyone appreciated what he did with GI food. Not only could he make it edible, somehow he even made it tasty.

That first morning, I ate scrambled eggs. Both the eggs and milk were powdered and reconstituted by adding iodinated water. Making such combinations edible was the unique genius of Short Round. He was truly the "King of Reconstitution!" I also took a cup of coffee and a piece of toast to go with my ersatz eggs. By now, I was used to the Army-in-Vietnam chow and this morning's fare tasted especially good. In this mess hall area, over coffee, I too was to spend a lot of good times. Here stories were told that shaped a lot of my future reactions. Medical issues were also discussed at the mess hall table and treatment plans formulated.

I knew the Dust Off crew from Cu Chi, and they had "rotated" in Tay Ninh many times before. That first morning, the crew took me under their collective wing, and told me all about life in Company D over a second cup of strong coffee. Captain Lewis was a real mellow guy, they said that morning, as they launched into many detailed stories about the previous Delta Six. Captain Lewis paid little attention to the military side of running the company, letting First Sergeant Rossnagel do all of that stuff. About 80 to 90 men made up the company at any given time, and the morale of the men had been great with Captain Lewis at the head. Berrigan smiled and told me I had a hard act to follow. I nodded in agreement as I listened to the stories unfold. Dr. Lewis was a good friend of Colonel Robert Wair. Almost every night, the colonel and the doctor enjoyed a couple of strong martinis at the 3rd Brigade Officers' club. The Dust Off crew advised me to always try to be on the "good side" of the colonel, and if I knew what was good for me, I'd develop a taste for martinis. Master Sergeant Knoerr introduced himself to me as he walked into the mess hall. The crew all knew him and greeted him like an old friend. He was very courteous, spent a few minutes talking with me, and then excused himself to talk to Short Round. The crew then filled me in on the sergeant.

Sergeant Knoerr ran the Enlisted Men's Club on Company D's ground and it was one of the best in the jungle according to the local grunts. In his club, Sergeant Knoerr made the only bacon, lettuce, and tomato sandwiches this side of San Francisco, but he was the most famous for his spicy pizza! I had no idea there was any pizza in Vietnam and was amazed about the BLTs. Berrigan suggested not asking Sergeant Knoerr how he managed to make pizza and BLTs way out here in Vietnam, as he would always answer, "Don't ask!" Evidently Sergeant Knoerr was very good at "midnight requisitioning" and was very well connected with the covert military procurement system. He was a real humanitarian to the common soldiers and had a heart of gold. He took special, dedicated care of all the enlisted men of the Third Brigade, especially the grunts. Sergeant Knoerr devoted almost all of his time to his EM Club and food procurement, wanting little to do with operating the mess hall. He left that to his right-hand man, Short Round.

I enjoyed the conversation I was having with the pilots this first morning in Tay Ninh. The coffee was good and there was now a very pleasant morning breeze coming in through the screens. While he was talking to me, Berrigan suddenly looked up over me, and said, "Hi, Doc!" Looking up also, I saw an older-looking man in very faded jungle fatigues with an unfiltered Camel cigarette dangling from his lips. With a wheezy voice he replied with, "How's yourself Jim. Is this my replacement?" Smiling, he held out his hand and I shook it. He said to me, "God, I'm glad to see you, what took you so long?" "I got here as quickly as I could," I replied, smiling back. He laughed and coughed a Camel smoker's cough. He got a cup of coffee from the kitchen and sat down across from me at the table with the sticky red-checkered tablecloth. I leaned back on my squeaky chair's legs, settling in to listen to what Captain Art Lewis had to say.

Looking philosophical, he seemed to surprise himself when he said he would be a little sad to leave Tay Ninh. He had liked it here. Before getting his M.D. degree, he had earned a Ph.D. in Entomology. He loved the insects, but disliked the life of a researcher. He eventually chose medicine. The two doctorates explained why he was older than most of the drafted doctors. He was thirty-six, rather than twenty-eight like I was. Drafted from a private family practice back in the States, he was surprised to find that the government wanted an "old fart like me in this goddam war. The only good thing about this place is the bugs!" He was chain-smoking and talking a mile a minute. Listening to him cough and wheeze as he spoke made me feel a little short of breath. My uneasiness left when Art sprang from his chair abruptly, and suggested, "Let's take a tour." So, Doctor Lewis and I went off to see just what Company D of the 25th Medical Battalion was all about.

Situated in a block like piece of real estate in the center of the Third Brigade base at Tay Ninh, the Company D area was about two hundred yards long by one hundred wide. The Company area was surrounded by dusty dirt streets on all four sides and was treeless. Grass was growing here and there, offering the only color to the drab surroundings. The company officers lived along the main street not far from the aid station. A forty-bed, underground, bunker hospital ward was next door to the aid station, and next to that was the Dust Off radio bunker. The Dust Off crew had hooches next to ours, directly across the street from their helicopter. The dentist's office was between the underground ward and the Dust Off radio bunker. The usual wooden latrine houses were seen at either end of the company area. Hooches for the enlisted men and the NCOs were along the back street near the EM club. The motor pool buildings were on one corner of the back street. Four ambulances and several work trucks were spaced neatly in the adjacent parking area of the motor pool. Boardwalks and drainage ditches were everywhere, circling the hooches and the buildings, leading every which way. As Art and I walked around, we passed smiling soldiers who saluted casually, but with sincerity. Obviously Art had the admiration of his men, and they were comfortable in his presence.

All of Company D's above-ground structures were surrounded with dirt-filled fifty-five-gallon drums with sand bags on top of them, reaching almost to the overhanging eaves of their corrugated tin roofs. The drums had many irregular holes punched into their outer surfaces from a lot of incoming shrapnel. The fragment-damaged drums told a small part about the base's history; Art told the rest. In Tay Ninh during the infamous Post Tet Offensive in May, 1968, Art told of enemy soldiers walking the streets inside the base. At that time, in fact, armed NVA soldiers had walked down the very street we were now on! Art's face paled slightly as he remembered he saw those NVA soldiers erect only for a few brief seconds before they were cut down by GI rifle fire. The Post Tet Offensive was worse here in Tay Ninh than many other places, because the NVA had concentrated in the forest west of this province. During two weeks, enemy soldiers had reached the inside of the base on several bloody occasions. The fresh and well-supplied NVA regulars traveling down the Ho Chi Minh Trail couldn't resist attacking the Third Brigade base at Tay Ninh on their way to Saigon. That was why the American base was always on full Red Alert. Incoming rocket and mortar fire slammed into the base daily. So far, during Art's time here, no one in Company D had been killed or seriously wounded. There had been close calls on the perimeter, however. Company D had to supply soldiers to man a section of the perimeter of the base camp each night. Our soldiers were responsible for a one-hundred-yard section of the "berm," which contained one of the quad-fifties, an impressive piece of machine gunnery. As I saw from the air, there were several quad-fifties at intervals around the base perimeter. Company D's men used the standard .30-caliber machine guns, M-16s, and M-70 grenade launchers. Art told me that most of our medics were conscientious objectors (COs), leaving precious few Company D soldiers to man the perimeter guns each night. The cooks, the motor pool men, and some of the medics did double-duty on the berm, leaving the conscientious objectors to do double shifts elsewhere. Sometimes they had to fill in at the motor pool and mess hall while the nighttime defenders got some sleep the next day. Art assured me that even with the nighttime berm staffing problems brought about by the conscientious objectors, the esprit de corps of the company remained very high. The men got along very well together. The objectors were allowed to refrain from shooting, but the Army made them do other chores including being a frontline medic. Our conscientious objectors never balked at filling in with double shifts in other, non-combat jobs. They appreciated what the other guys were doing for them, and they tackled their extra work with resolve. Art told me he had learned a lot about COs, and he admired their bravery. In my short tour thus far, I could easily see the company's ability to work together caring for the fighting soldier; conscientious objectors with regular soldiers, medics with mechanics and cooks. This had to be a direct result of Art's leadership.

Art pointed out the latrine I would be using, a.k.a. the "crapper." The two crappers in the company's area were not segregated by rank. In this unholy place, a captain could sit next to a private without expecting the enlisted man to stand and salute. Art assured me this was very reasonable, as if I wouldn't agree. Neither Art nor I cared a great deal about Army protocol. Doctors in general, and especially drafted Army doctors, gave a fig about Army chicken shit, and our rank gave us that leeway most of the time. Out of curiosity, I looked inside the latrine. In bold letters was a sign that asked reverently, "Please, Dear Lord, Not on the crapper!" No one wanted to get shot in the latrine, and the sign was a constant prayer towards that end. Who said this was an unholy place?

Art pointed out that my bunk was next to his, and he suggested I take this time to settle in. Next to my bunk was a tall olive drab metal locker in which I was to stow my stuff and my clothes. A large wooden box under my bunk was mine also, and I put my stateside uniform in there along with the many other extraneous things I had carried with me that I wouldn't need for a long time. A lone table stood in the center of my hooch along with its four folding card table chairs. Directly over the table, a single naked light bulb hung in its socket from the rafters with a dog tag chain as its pull cord. Next to the front screen door, there was a "reefer," which was an Army issued blood refrigerator that Art had ordered for use in the aid station. The aid station had another one to use so this was ours now. It was brimming with soda, beer, and some perishables from the mess hall. I was advised the drinks in the reefer were obtained from the EM Club but officers were never to go inside the club. If an officer wanted a can of pop, he was to knock on the Club's back door to buy it. An officer or an NCO entering would disturb the men inside. I could live with that. Soda and beer were far less expensive at the EM Club than at the local PX, which was yet another manifestation of Sergeant Knoerr's expertise in procurement, and of course, no questions could ever be asked.

Art and I shared the hooch with the XO of the company, Captain Bill Myers, and Stuart Knodel, a first lieutenant. Bill and Stu were Medical Service Corps officers and did most of the administration work of the company. Two of Company D's doctors had DEROSed already, and Art was next to leave. Two new doctors were next door and a third was to come in a week or so. The number of doctors in the company would jump up to four, one more than usual. The company dentist next door dropped in to say hello. Captain Bob Friedinger, the dentist, was from Iowa, the same town Bill Myers was from. Imagine, two guys from Cedar Rapids, Iowa, in the same room in South Vietnam. This was a small world indeed. A tall lanky blond, Bob was deeply tanned. He would be leaving Vietnam next week too. Late for his afternoon clinic, he said he would sit and shoot the bull with me later and left. Bob was scheduled to leave with his good friend Art. They had worked together for over six months and had developed a close friendship. Art told me Bob was a very hard worker and had earned a very good reputation. Regarded by his patients as a very gentle dentist, his elective appointments were booked weeks in advance. A lot of high-ranking brass were his patients, coming from miles around to partake of his skills. He worked eight to ten hours each day, seven days a week. His nights were free, but he was available for emergencies anytime.

The doctors of Company D were to man sick call each and every day, seven days a week. Wounded soldiers and civilians could come in for treatment, any time, day or night, but with four of us working, I thought this would be manageable. Listening to us talk about work, Stu Knodel chuckled and assured us we would have plenty of time to look for bugs. All of us laughed at that crack, except Art. He sighed and said the insects in Tay Ninh were great and he would happily stick around to collect them, but he didn't like the other things that flew around here. Stu seemed puzzled at Art's comment, and inquired, "What things? Rockets?" "No, your bullshit!" Art said smirking. Stu deserved that response and shut up for a while.

Art then proudly showed us three large wooden boxes he was planning to ship back to the States. Each box had been filled with preserved insects of all shapes, sizes, and colors. There were beetles that looked like miniature rhinoceroses, majestic and beautiful butterflies, and stinging insects that looked like scorpions. All were impaled with pins, meticulously labeled and individually mounted on paper shelves. Art showed me an article he had recently had published in a very prestigious entomology journal. In it, he described a heretofore-unnamed type of beetle and gave a scholarly dissertation on its place in the classification of insects. He told me he had discovered several other not-yet described specimens, and he would publish information on them in journal form when he got home. There was no doubt Vietnam was a haven for insects. Most of us found them annoying, but not Art. I couldn't help wondering why Art left the insect field to practice medicine. He certainly talked more about insects than he did about medicine in the short time I knew him. I'll bet he went back to entomology. He would have made a very interesting Biology professor. He certainly had the passion for it. Stu piped up and told us that Art was no longer welcome in the Philippine Army compound. Evidently, he had gone to their area three nights in a row, turning on the special Philippine engineering lights for hours at a time to attract insects. Art spent many hours under those lights each night collecting insect specimens for his scrutiny. Unfortunately, on the third night, those lights also attracted VC mortar fire. The Philippine detachment's commander politely asked Art to "Stay the hell away!" This wasn't the first time Art's nighttime lights had attracted enemy fire, and Stu led me to believe Art would hazard enemy fire for insects any day! After Stu finished his story, several others unraveled tales of Art's shenanigans, drawing a small crowd. As the stories unwound, Art just listened and smiled. Those stories were funny, but they were also told with a certain reverence that I hoped to have assigned to me someday. Lunchtime broke up the stories that morning, and we ate a good meal, hamburgers specially made for "Doc Lewis" by Short Round.

Art had to get to sick call with the others that afternoon and I tagged along. I was given my own office in which to see patients, and I went right to work. After we finished up sick call, Art took me to meet his friend, Colonel Wair. Headquarters for the Third Brigade was several hundred yards up the main street across from the nice new Post Exchange. Entering the Headquarters's air-conditioned trailer, we ran into the command sergeant major. He was the highest-ranking NCO in the brigade. As a matter of fact, a command sergeant major is the highest-ranking NCO anywhere. The insignia for the rank had three stripes up and three down with a star in the middle of the opposing stripes. The star was in turn surrounded by laurel branches on each side. I had never seen this rank before, and I was pleased to find him a helpful and friendly veteran in every sense of the word. Men of high rank were usually great men. They had to be to get so far. The command sergeant major was no exception to my rule. He ran the Third Brigade Headquarters with all the spit and polish you could imagine. The personnel under him seemed to enjoy working there. The place buzzed with activity under a sign that read, "There is a war on you know!" Art and I took a seat while all kinds of brass went in and out of Colonel Wair's office. A loud, "ART," resounded from the inner office, and Art winked at me. We arose and he led me into the smoky office. If there ever was a sterner looking man than Colonel Wair, I have never laid eyes on him. The colonel stood and I stiffly saluted him. Bending over his paper-laden desk, he extended a strong hand and shook mine forcibly. "Have a seat!" he commanded and I did, stumbling a bit. He inquired about my quarters, asked where I had gone to school, and how I was finding the Army. Barely waiting for my answers, he would impatiently ask another question. I later learned that he had read my officer's evaluation forms and knew all the answers before he asked me any of those questions. With a great deal of pomposity, he assured me that if I ever needed anything, just ask him, and it would be mine. Parenthetically, he added, that if I did half as good a job as Art had done in running the medical company he would be very pleased and wouldn't have to "chew out my sorry ass!" Abruptly, he rose, shook my hand and called over me loudly, "Sergeant!" The meeting was over; I had been dismissed. A little befuddled, I followed Art's lead as we left the office. On the way out we passed a very serious looking command sergeant major rushing in. Thinking about how curt and brief the meeting had been, I

In front of the aid station in Tay Ninh

The mess hall at Tay Ninh, before sand bags

decided the colonel had a huge job to do, and I should admire the businesslike fashion in which he conducted his affairs. On our way back to the medical company area, Art strongly suggested I attend the colonel's Brigade advisory sessions every morning from 0700 to 0800 hours. First, the colonel liked the medical company CO to be there, and second, I would learn a lot about just how the war was run. As for drinking with the colonel, Art thought I should wait to be invited. The colonel got loud and overbearing when he drank his martinis and Art confided in me, although he loved drinking martinis, he didn't really enjoy those happy hours with "the colonel and his court." Art said he was really looking forward to having his martinis with his wife back home in the States. He became quiet after mentioning his wife and I kept quiet also, trying to allow him some space to dream.

Back at the company mess hall, dinner was being served. Tray in hand, I was proceeding through the chow line when I noticed several foil-wrapped packages on a steam table. The men in the line moved by without disturbing the wrapped packages. Interested in what this was all about, I watched a soldier take one of the foil packages back to his table. "That's kosher food!" Stu Knodel said. He was behind me, and had noticed the attention I was paying to the foil-wrapped packages. The specially prepared food was flown to Tay Ninh each day via a supply chopper from Cu Chi. Orthodox Jewish food, vegetarian meals for Seventh Day Adventists, and special meals for Muslims, should there be pork on the menu, were all shipped to accommodate the company's conscientious objectors. "The Army needs every mother's son and bends over backwards with special food and jobs for the COs. Out of seventy-eight men in the company tonight, twenty-four are COs." Going through the chow line, I was interested to see how little the non-CO company members cared about the special treatment. The special food, the special jobs and all, seemed a bit unfair to me, and I related my concerns about these inequities to Stu. He assured me that, although these conscientious objectors refused to fight, they were not in any way scared. Many infantry medics in the field were objectors, but they would brave all kinds of danger to care for a wounded buddy. The riflemen respected them for that and no one in this company complained about the special treatment given the objectors. In Company D, being a CO was simply a non-issue. They fit in the company admirably, and I was beginning to feel better about the special treatment some of "my men" were getting. I was to witness for myself the bravery the COs in our company would portray when things got rough in the not-too-distant future. I remember thinking Mohammed Ali should have been drafted into our company. After all, he was an avowed conscientious objector of those times, so why didn't he get the same treatment our guys got?

Art walked into the mess hall after the food line had closed for the night. Wearily, he sank into a chair at our table. Short Round brought him a plate of food and a cup of coffee. Art thanked him and dug into the food. Flushed with the colonel's martinis, Art told us what the old man had talked to him about this evening. The brigade was still on Red Alert, but the boys of the Wolfhound Battalions were "kicking VC butt" in a place called Trang Bang! There would be beau coup casualties tonight. The colonel said, if he had anything to do with it, the casualties would be all the "goddam enemy's." He was going to fly down there to see what's up for himself, after he ate his dinner. Art said the colonel could sober up as quickly as anyone he had ever seen. To me, Art seemed pretty sober himself, having imbibed two martinis a short while ago. I could never be expected to work after drinking like that, and there were no two ways about that. I planned to avoid the colonel's happy hour if at all possible. As I thought about how to excuse myself from the martinis in the future, Art said the colonel had asked that he bring me over for a drink tomorrow evening. Seeing no way out for tomorrow, I lied saying I would be honored to have a drink with the colonel that next night. Art added that the drinking sessions would only last twenty minutes or so. Like everything else he did, the colonel even drank fast.

This first day in Tay Ninh had been a long one for me, and I was bushed. I had expended a lot of energy in my move here, and I was looking forward to a shower followed by a good night's sleep. The other doctors would have to take care of the expected wounded. After all, I wasn't on call yet. Before I took my shower, there was the traditional officer and NCO versus EM volleyball game. This popular game was held every night possible. The officers and NCOs had very few players to field, so I was drafted for the game. The volleyball court doubled as the open-air movie theater, so we had to play before it got dark and the movie started. I played. Our side lost. They were great. Those nineteen-year-olds were in perfect shape, painfully pointing out the difference nine years made. Just as the sun set, the game was over.

Soaked with sweat, I asked which way to the showers. I was directed to an old rusty water tank propped up vertically on its long axis. A faucet was at the very bottom near the concrete slab the tank sat on. The tin roof overhead was held up by four corner two-by-fours, but there were no walls. I had to kneel near the faucet, naked, wet my body with a small amount of water from the tank, soap up, and then finally rinse off. Most used their steel helmets or canteens to hold the water to pour over themselves for the final dousing. Wow! What a major setback in my feelings about Tay Ninh. Just when I was beginning to like this place. Oh well, when in Rome. So I got undressed in my hooch, wrapped my olive drab towel around my waist and walked the short distance to the "shower" in my flip-flops. As I approached the tank a loud explosion and its concussion rocked me. I heard what sounded like a steam engine passing over my head. Startled by the loud, very close noise, I instinctively hit the dirt. When it seemed quiet for a few seconds, I got up and ran like hell for the safety of my hooch. Art and Stu were playing cards, seemingly unaware of the danger. As I burst through the door, Art smiled without looking up at me and remarked offhandedly "That's the eight-incher you heard. The artillery battery fired that huge sucker of a cannon from their compound on the next block." I remembered seeing those guns from the air earlier this morning. I was annoyed at Art because he was so calm. "When they fire across the base like that, it sounds like a train is coming right for you," he said. The guns had been quiet all day, but had just begun as I neared the shower tank. Really embarrassed now, I returned to start my shower. Dirty all over from hitting the ground, I also stank from sweat. A soldier, wrapped in a towel, was leaving the tank as I walked up. He said, "Goddam engineers!" as he passed by me. Kneeling down, I turned on the water spigot at the bottom of the tank. Nothing! No water at all, not a drop! That last guy was cursing because there was no water in the tank tonight. The engineers were supposed to fill these tanks but the tank was empty. The engineers probably had more important matters to tend to, no doubt, but what was I going to do? Going back to my hooch in a quandary, I noted the card game was still going great guns. Now there were four playing, and they all turned and smiled at me as I reentered the room. I supposed to others there was great sport in watching a rookie discover the ups and downs of Tay Ninh life, but I was really ticked. Calming myself, I asked if anyone had any suggestions. Everyone just shrugged their shoulders and went back to their card game. I wet a face cloth with water from my canteen, and wiped my body clean. My "sink bath" felt good, and I had to be a whole lot cleaner. The cool night air chilled me slightly, so I made my bed and jumped in. I could smell the iodine on my body left over from the canteen water. I tried to go to sleep, but didn't for a while. The noisy card game and the eight-incher's shells made sleeping difficult. Finally, I dozed off into the deep sleep of a very tired man.

Later that same night, I awoke with a start. The staccato of a lone machine gun sounding very close, woke me. I could see that Bill Myers was awake, lying in his bunk, smoking a cigarette. Bill thought one of the perimeter guards was most likely firing at some shadow he saw, and the perimeter was only about one hundred yards away from us. All of a sudden, the base camp seemed too small to suit me. Bill said he had been in Tay Ninh a long time, but gunfire still awakened him. The surrounding snores attested to the others' veteran status. They were able to sleep, despite the noise. The firing eventually ceased. The next thing I knew, I awoke to a beautiful morning. Birds were singing in the backyard grass and a cool breeze was blowing. A small wooden stand outside the back door of our hooch had a metal bowl on it for shaving, and brushing teeth. Supplying my own canteen water, I did both. Feeling pretty good after a fairly good night's sleep, I was relieved the night was over. Last night, I was afraid I'd never be able to sleep with all that noise, but now I had learned sleep was possible. One of the other doctors I had not as yet met came out to use the washstand. I introduced myself. His name was Charlie Guess, and he had been drafted after his internship year. He had graduated from the University of Mississippi's Medical School the year before and spent his internship year at Georgia Baptist Hospital in Atlanta, Georgia. With a soft southern accent, he told me he had to leave a wife and daughter back home in Mississippi, and he already missed them very much. The other doctor, Tom Zinn, and Charlie had been in Vietnam for two weeks, and they both hated it.

After a breakfast of chipped beef on toast, which will always be known as "shit on a shingle" in the Army, I went to the aid station to take sick call. Early mornings were very comfortable in sunny Vietnam and this morning the air was cool, and the sky was a deep blue. As I walked to the aid station that morning, I realized I always felt glad to be alive at times like these. The aid station building's design was a left over from World War Two and the famous "pre-former," Henry J. Kaiser. Consisting of pre-formed, half-circle corrugated tin pieces, the pieces were fit together to form a long Quonset hut about fifty feet long. The building had been bolted to a concrete slab, and two sliding doors were found at the front and back of the aid station. Small windows were situated about chest high along the rounded sides. Inside, the immediate front area held a receiving desk to one side, and the rest of the space was filled with folding chairs. Along each curved wall were stacked the all-too-familiar sawhorses and stretchers. When wounded came in from the heliport across the street, the chairs were removed, placing them out of the way along the walls. Then the stretchers were placed on the sawhorses, ready to receive the wounded patients.

The midsection of the building sported a narrow hall on one side with four tiny offices off to the other side. The offices were used for sick call, housing a desk for the doctor and a chair for the patient. When a patient needed to recline for an examination, he and the doctor would have walk to the rear of the building. In the rear of the building were two operating tables in a small operating room. Here the patients could lie down for a complete examination. There were also sterilizers, cabinets filled with surgical instruments, a small pharmacy, and a small laboratory that housed our only lab technician. Although very primitive, the room worked well. An average day in the aid station saw over one hundred patients with minimal wait and maximum efficiency.

Medics kept the patients moving from the doctor, to the pharmacy, to the lab, and to the X-ray machine. The X-ray was the biggest hang up. The X-ray machine itself was ancient and was kept in a small closet of a room in the back. We had to clear the area each time an X-ray was exposed, which took a lot of time. Even having to wait for X-rays, patients got good and quick care.

The windows were covered with screens to keep out the omnipresent, aggressive insects. Helicopters landing nearby stirred up so much dust the screens had to be covered with clear plastic. The dust had to be kept out to protect the wounds we were working on from becoming contaminated. With no air-conditioning and no provisions to get any, the plastic kept out the dust, but made the place beastly hot. The aid station was neat and clean, but nothing like the show place of Cu Chi. Cu Chi was air-conditioned and newer because that's where all the Army brass lived. That was good and bad. I felt the Army ran just as well without all the spit and polish. To me growing and cutting grass as was done in Cu Chi was a colossal waste of time in a war zone, and there was none of that in Tay Ninh. Life in Tay Ninh's boondocks was very different, and, so far, I liked what I had seen. Many of the medics in Tay Ninh had worked in Cu Chi, but they all seemed to like their life in Tay Ninh better. Even though the buildings were not as big, not as new, and certainly not air-conditioned, there was much less Army crap to put up with here, and no one wanted to go back. Considering the danger Tay Ninh harbored, compared to Cu Chi, the fact the men didn't want to leave spoke volumes about their morale.

Later that morning, I met the company's first sergeant. Sergeant Rossnagel was a stickler when he needed to be, I was told, but otherwise he let the medics do their job and supported them in their work. Army-trained as a licensed practical nurse himself, he understood the workings of military medicine, but his job with Company D was all on the military side. He was responsible for every enlisted man, NCO, and officer in the company and their welfare. He made sure we had replacements, supplies, gas, electricity and much more. Six feet tall, slim, muscular, and bespectacled, he had a short military crewcut and a friendly smile. Surprisingly, he was much more soft-spoken than I had imagined a first sergeant would be. Right away, I was impressed with his superior intelligence and the smooth way he had about him. About thirty-five years old, he was much older than I was, but he always treated me with the military respect owed an officer. There was never any doubt in my mind that he ran the Company D show. Comfortable in his position as the first sergeant, he made me feel at ease whenever our paths crossed. After I first met him, I knew here was another example of a good man in a high military position. Right from the get-go, I realized this sergeant was one fine man.

Sergeant Rossnagel had instructions to bring me to report to my military superior in Tay Ninh. I thought I had already met my boss when I met Colonel Wair, but evidently I hadn't. Sensing the confusion I had about Colonel Wair not really being my boss, Sergeant Rossnagel explained the medical battalion's chain of command to me. In short, Colonel Wair was the commander of the Third Brigade, but a Colonel Jenkins, head of Supply for the 25th Infantry

Division, was to be my commanding officer while I was stationed in Tay Ninh. To this day, despite the sergeant's careful explanation, I have no idea how Colonel Jenkins fit in the medical battalion. Sergeant Rossnagel did produce the orders that sent me to Tay Ninh, and they were signed by Colonel Jenkins! Not wanting any more explanations about the Army chain of command, off I went to report to my new commander.

Driving a jeep to the other side of the airstrip, Sergeant Rossnagel took me to a building marked "Supply Headquarters." All the while I was riding in that jeep I kept ready to jump out on a second's notice, but the jeep didn't overturn this time. The sergeant and I entered the building where a sergeant major instructed us to have a seat. After just a minute, I was called into Colonel Jenkins's office. Saluting as Sergeant Rossnagel advised me to, in a false deep voice I said, "Captain Snider, reporting as ordered, Sir!" "At ease, doctor," replied the colonel. Gesturing me to take a seat, I handed him my typed orders and sat down. Colonel Jenkins was tall and rigid, every inch the complete soldier. His uniform was perfectly starched and his posture was ramrod straight. His smile was warm, however, and immediately I felt at ease. Preoccupied with shuffling through the papers I had handed him, the colonel said, "Sooo, does Rossnagel have you in line yet?" "Yes sir," I replied, feeling myself smiling. I told the colonel that I was very impressed with First Sergeant Rossnagel and was looking forward to working with him. "Good, I never have any trouble when Rossnagel is on the scene. Listen to him about most things. Ask his advice often; he'll never steer you wrong, you can bet the ranch on that. Do you have any questions of me?" Not having any, we talked about little things, like where I was from, was I married, did I have any children, et cetera. When our conversation was finished, he followed me out of his office, talked with Sergeant Rossnagel for a few minutes, and then dismissed us. I only saw Colonel Jenkins one more time during my six-month stay in Tay Ninh. The scuttlebutt was that Colonel Jenkins was very nervous when in Tay Ninh, and he avoided the place, staying mostly in safer Cu Chi.

On the way back to the company in our jeep, Sergeant Rossnagel suggested we have a transfer of command ceremony that very afternoon, so I could settle into my duties sooner than later. I sort of got the feeling that the top sergeant didn't get along well with Captain Lewis, and he wanted to deal only with me from then on. That afternoon, in front of the whole company, the Change of Command was held for Company D. The responsibility I now had began to grate on me. I was now the commander of D Company 25th Infantry Medical Battalion. Seventy-nine men were under my immediate command as of this moment. As the commander of a "clearing company" I had to ensure our mission was carried out. The mission of Company D was to make sick call available to all those who needed it, 24 hours a day, 365 days a year, to provide an assembly area for war casualties and transportation for those casualties in and out, and, in general, to medically support the mission of the 25th Infantry Division. The design for a clearing company was created during the Second World War to disperse wounded soldiers into the proper paths for treatment and recovery. Clearing companies formerly functioned as field hospitals, and there was a huge tent full of the material used back then, including a lot of very outdated medical equipment. One of my tasks was to periodically account for all that obsolete unused equipment twice yearly to the Inspector General of the 25th Infantry Division. Why that tent with its old anesthesia machines, saws and dull knives, existed in Company D in 1968, I'll never understand. Clearing companies had been created to follow the fighting infantry and to set up a hospital tent on a moment's notice. The Army had a much different plan in mind for us now, but the old equipment had never been discarded. So, twice a year, I had to account for all this excess baggage and present the data to the inspector general.

In real life, the company had a huge triage operation. Company D housed the Dust Off crew that picked up the wounded where they fell in the field. Those wounded were then brought to us for inspection and treatment. Triage meant Company D would evaluate the wounded and decide where each man would receive the treatment he needed. Those who needed general anesthesia were transported across the street to the 45th Evacuation hospital. The 45th was an inflatable unit that was made to be highly mobile. This one had been across the street from us for a long time, and there were no known plans to move it. Shaped like a Quonset hut, the 45th Evac was constructed of connected black plastic tubes inflated with air. Inside, a beige-colored lining extended 360 degrees around, forming the walls, ceilings and floors of the buildings. Three fully trained general surgeons and an orthopedic surgeon operated in two fully equipped surgical suites, stabilized the post-operative patients for a day or so, and then evacuated them towards the States. Neurological injuries had to be flown to the Long Binh Evacuation Hospital on the outskirts of Saigon. This was the closest hospital with a neurosurgeon on the staff. The system seemed complicated and cumbersome, but the Medical Corps made it work beautifully.

Battalion surgeons were stationed in the field with infantry units. Usually General Medical Officers, they were often the first doctors to examine sick and wounded GIs. Battalion surgeons started life-saving resuscitation of wounded soldiers with plasma, saline, and morphine. A typical scene went something like this. When a GI was wounded on the battlefield, a call would go out for a "Medic!" The squad's medic on patrol with the men would ignore the grave danger, going to the side of the stricken man. Many times, the wounded soldier was cared for right where he fell. The medic would apply antibiotic powder to the wounds and bind them with dressings. Tourniquets were utilized to stop bleeding when necessary. An IV, possibly, would be started, and, finally, the wounded soldier was moved out of harm's way. At this point, the battalion surgeon took over supervising the care. Out in the field, or at the unit's base, the Dust Off was called in to pick up the wounded man! That radio message from the field would be received in the bunker right behind my hooch where the Tay Ninh Dust Off radio dispatcher was located. A messenger would run to the Dust Off crew's hooch next to mine, and the crew would scramble to their chopper in a matter of seconds. The Dust Off crews moved rapidly and efficiently! Pulling on their clothes as they ran to their helipad across the street, about fifty yards away, they would begin their life-saving mission. Getting airborne took only a few minutes, and they would roar down the street just inches over the traffic. Bystanders would wave good luck to the crew as they flew off. Those calls and scrambles were exciting to watch! Meanwhile, my medics would go into the ready mode at the aid station. The sawhorses and litters would be placed in orderly lines, far enough apart to ensure adequate working spaces. IVs were hung from poles in readiness. IV needles, fluids and basins full of Betadine were strategically placed about the stretchers. All the while the radio messages were broadcast overhead to monitor the progress of the Dust Off crew.

If the firefight were still raging and landing were too dangerous for the Dust Off helicopter, the infantrymen would wave off the helicopter by popping a red smoke grenade. When the infantrymen popped green smoke, the Dust Off knew it was safe to land. The wounded from the battle would be placed onto the helicopter through the side doors quickly, often in under sixty seconds. Inside, the patients would be secured in place with belts and off they would go. Specially trained medics would assess the wounded en route, communicating with the awaiting doctors, if necessary. Bleeding points would be pressurized, IVs maintained, and morphine administered, if needed. A paper tag was attached to the wounded soldier somewhere on his person. This tag was the beginning of the medical record for the patient. On the tag data were recorded such as, what time IVs were started, whether morphine had been given and similar other pertinent treatment data. As they flew, the crewmen on the Dust Off chopper would radio ahead with the number and types of wounds. Where possible, triage was completed in the air on the helicopter, and the wounded were taken directly to the Evac hospital or to our clearing company's aid station. The accuracy of the in-flight triage was very accurate. Usually covered with mud, the soldiers' wounds were hard to find, let alone evaluate. Coupling the obscuring mud with the cramped positions onboard ship, the accuracy achieved by the Dust Off crew was a tribute to their training and efficiency.

After the fight was over, the dead that had been left on the battlefield were picked up for transport to us. Company D had its own dead shed next to the helipad, complete with the sobering grenade pit. Usually very tired from taking sick call all day, and having tended to the wounded most of the night, the examination and carding of the dead was a tedious task. Graves Registration was always busy in Tay Ninh. In fact, we carded 29 to 30 KIAs weekly for long stretches at a time. During those weeks, the GI body count for the whole war was about one hundred dead souls a week. That percentage speaks a lot about the amount of action seen by the Third Brigade soldiers of the 25th Infantry Division in 1968-9. Usually the last thing I did after a long night was to record the names and diagnoses of those who didn't survive that day. The faces of those freshly dead boys haunted my dreams each night. Only after realizing those poor souls were now at peace could I finally get some sleep myself those nights. For the dead, there were no more patrols, no more K rations, and no more bullets. Their war was over! They were finally home.

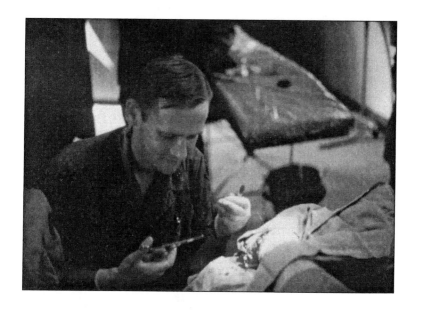

Operation on "frag wounds" in Tay Ninh

Two patients in front of a fragment-pocked Quonset hut in Tay Ninh

From left to right; Hal Shields, Stu Knodel,
Marty Bruggerman, and Charlie Guess

Art Lewis and Bob Friedinger left for Cu Chi, and home, the next day. Their send-off offered hope of leaving for the rest of us some day, and we were glad for them. I hoped to see our new physician and dentist soon, but so far I had no official word as to when they would arrive. I settled into my new life full of resolve to do a good job and to fix up the place. The first order of business to me was the shower situation. That needed immediate attention and was first on the list. The next thing I felt I needed was a bunker to sleep in. I definitely wanted to stay alive, and all the grunts I spoke to warned me about sleeping above ground. If an infantryman couldn't sleep in a bunker, he'd dig a foxhole to protect himself from unexpected mortar and rocket attacks. Protecting myself whenever and wherever possible just made sense. I knew I couldn't do these projects by myself, so I went to work convincing my fellow officers about the benefits of my two-phase plan. I didn't have to work too hard convincing others about the shower, because the heat, sweat and dirt made everyone's lives miserable. Necessity is the mother of invention, so we set about to invent that mother.

Within a day, our new doctor, Marty Bruggerman, and dentist, Hal Shields, arrived from Cu Chi. Marty was a partially trained internist from Minnesota and Hal was a practicing dentist from Washington, D.C. Like the rest of us, they both had been drafted, so later that night, we all drank a toast to Lyndon Baines Johnson for bringing us together. He sure drafted a lot of us! Marty and Hal settled into the hooch next to ours, and they became great additions to our group. Both had pleasant personalities and positive outlooks. Gloom and depression made time drag in Vietnam, and we certainly didn't want, or need, that. There was no doubt that we all hated this lousy war in Vietnam, but we were all here for 365 days, and we had to make the best of it. Each night we sat around the table in my hooch to tell each other what we had found out during the day concerning the shower and bunker missions. Like a medical conference, we would assemble, discuss, and plan possibilities. The shower would be the first project and, if we did well on that, the bunker would be next. Also, we had been in Tay Ninh for several weeks now, and thus far, we had no incoming rounds to accentuate the need for a bunker. That accent would soon change.

Sick call was energetically attacked by all four of the doctors. That meant most of the one hundred patients would have been seen by lunch time, most days. One doctor was to cover the afternoon's duties, freeing up three of us. The one that been on call the previous night was free to nap if he needed, while the other two carried out what we had planned the night before. Of course, when the wounded came in, we all went to the aid station and pitched in. There were wounded just about each day, but the projects went forward nicely and within two weeks we had a shower, and the bunker was finished a month later.

THE SHOWER

Here's how each went. First, came the shower. We could see a large elevated water tower about one block from us in the engineer's compound. From this tank, the engineers filled a tank truck to deliver water to the awaiting receptacles around the base. The engineers had yet unused pipe and they could lay it, but we needed a work order before they would lift a hair. Many of the soldiers in the engineering company came to our sick call and we got to be friendly with quite a few of them. In Cu Chi, the aid station had running water, as did the hospital ward. Tay Ninh, of course, had none. Carefully wording a request, I asked for running water to be made available for our aid station and below-ground bunker hospital here in Tay Ninh as was the case in Cu Chi. I also asked for an outdoor shower be built behind our aid station. Besides making showers available to our patients, the medics would be able to wash the mud off wounded soldiers. After all, this was the healthy thing to do. One night, early on in this process, I had a drink with Colonel Wair and suggested I'd like to get running water in our treatment area to better help our injured soldiers. "Goddam good idea, Snider," he said "I like the way you want to move things along here in the boonies. I can help. I love to jump-start those engineers every once in a while." The colonel continued, "Send your work order to my command sergeant major, he can push it through." I had a copy of the work order in my pocket at the time, but I waited until the next morning to give it to the brigade sergeant rather than chancing giving it to the colonel that night. The very next morning, a lieutenant from the engineers was at our aid station asking me to show him just what we wanted. Within a week we had a sink in the aid station, one in the bunker hospital, and a nice outdoor shower out back of the hospital. The patients loved it, lingering under the water as long as they could each day. An infantryman often had to go weeks without being able to shower. To him, it was a real treat to be sick and get a shower every day. We rigged a hose attachment from the sink in the aid station to be able to wash the mud from the wounded soldiers more quickly and efficiently, and it worked well!

Physicians in the Army were responsible for inspecting mess halls, latrines, and bathrooms. Back in Texas, we had been shown how to construct water drains in a land below sea level. The drains had to filter through something before seeping into the soil beneath. We used the ubiquitous and plentiful crushed soda cans as the filter for our drain. Borrowing the company's deuce-and-a-half truck, which I had learned to drive, I went into Tay Ninh village to obtain sand and cement to make the bathroom's concrete floor. Pacific Architects and Engineers had a sand producing operation there. PA&E was a civilian engineering and construction company hired by the Department of Defense to build a lot of the buildings, bridges, and other structures needed in South Vietnam. The employees of this huge construction company came from many different countries, and they were all cared for by the Army Medical system. Through sick call, we had become friendly with many of them, hence my opening to procure the small amounts of sand, cement and corrugated tin roofing I needed for my shower from their supplies in Tay Ninh village. The afternoon I picked to go into Tay Ninh city was extremely hot, and I was driving the deuce-and-a-half truck myself. Tom Zinn had come with me, as we were the two off duty that particular afternoon. We had taken off our shirts to enjoy the breeze on our drive. Leaving the Army base by the busy front gate, we were waved through by a preoccupied MP, who was arguing loudly with a Vietnamese man on a Honda scooter at the time. After picking up the supplies from the PA&E depot downtown, we returned to the front gate of the base. This time the MP was paying more attention to us and he glared when we passed his small elevated wooden platform. He blew his whistle so forcibly his face turned red. Startled by the whistle, I slammed on the brakes, stopping the big truck in the middle of the dirt road. "Put on those shirts," he ordered with a yell. He had stepped off his white platform and was walking over to our truck. He had the look of a state trooper walking to a car after someone went through his radar trap at eighty-five miles per hour. Confident in his position as an authority figure, he was going to give us a dressing down, no doubt. Tom and I were buttoning our shirts when he looked into the truck cab. Spying our black captain's bars, his haughty attitude suddenly vaporized. The now flabbergasted MP stopped dead in his tracks. He smiled, saluted and remarked, "I'll be goddammed, a couple of captains driving a deuce-and-a-half! Come on through."

We mixed and poured the concrete into the awaiting wooden frame we had crafted. Thanks to the tropical sun, the concrete hardened in a very short time, and we soon had a cement floor over our carefully constructed regulation drain. The sides and roof were furiously and quickly put up by a gaggle of sweating, swearing doctors, complete with hammers, nails, and battered thumbs.

Sergeant Rogers came over from the motor pool to fit the pipes for us. He had been a plumber by trade before being drafted, and he suggested we find a tank to store the shower water. The heat from the sun could then warm the water, instead of having the cold water coming directly from the engineer's tank. He could weld two fifty-five-gallon drums together for that tank but he didn't have any drums to give us. Tom Zinn and I paid another visit to the brigade dump to find two drums or an airplane wing tank for the shower water tank. The dump was located just outside the base camp's main gate. Once burned, Tom and I wore our shirts and took a salute from our new MP friend. To scrutinize the dump's treasures, Tom and I stood on the lowered tailgate of the quarter-ton truck we had taken from the motor pool. Without any warning, the chain holding the tailgate horizontal snapped, dropping the two of us onto the hard ground! As we hit, there was the unmistakable crack of a bone breaking. Tom rolled on his side in obvious and severe pain. He was holding his right ankle in his hands, moaning. The ankle's unnatural angle left no doubt that there was a bad fracture. Finding two sticks and using my belt, I fashioned a splint to support his ankle for the trip back.

The X-ray confirmed Tom's ankle had been broken in three places. Seeing his own X-rays caused Tom more pain, so I gave him a shot of morphine. Tom's fracture was badly displaced, and way beyond my orthopedic expertise. On a stretcher, the medics and I took Tom across the street to see the orthopedist at the Evac hospital. More comfortable now from the morphine, Tom began to realize the possibility of getting out of Vietnam with his injury. The thought of going home made him a little giddy, and he was smiling and mumbling to himself. The orthopedist confirmed Tom's hope announcing he would put Tom's leg in a cast, but surgery would be needed in a larger center, like out of the country! Consequently, he would ship Tom to Japan, the nearest place capable of doing the operation. He added that Tom would most likely be shipped all the way back to his home in Arizona. The fracture was going to take at least three months to heal properly. Tom smiled a drunken smile as the nurse got him ready for the casting. While Tom was getting his cast, I returned to our hooch to pack some of Tom things for his trip. I sent the rest of his stuff to his home address. Tom was the first casualty of Company D while I was the Delta Six! Unfortunately, he wouldn't be the last. The next morning we all cheered as the Dust Off left with Tom and others for the Tan Son Nhut airport and, ultimately, Camp Zama, Japan. Marty, Charlie, and I would run the medical operation without another doctor for the rest of my time there.

Two drums were later found and welded by Sergeant Rogers. He had the plumbing fitted and working in no time. The shower was finished! Hal Shields fashioned a V-shaped sink made from ammo crate wood and placed it beneath the faucet Sergeant Rogers had previously installed. We were all set. Each morning the tank was filled by one of us, by simply turning a faucet on the pipe that led from the engineer's tank into ours. Each day, the tropical sun would heat the water in the black tank in time for evening showers. Charley Guess was a pretty good artist. He painted a picture of Tom standing with crutches, a cast on his right ankle, and smoking his pipe. Below Tom's depiction, a caption read "The Tom Zinn Memorial Shower." The painting was placed over the new shower door for all to see. Sometimes, I imagine that picture and that shower room standing in the same place today outside of Tay Ninh. I imagine Vietnamese showering there and wondering who the heck is this Tom Zinn!

A month after Tom left Company D, we received a letter from him. The letter said the orthopedists in Japan had decided there was no hurry to operate, so Tom had been shipped to a hospital in Arizona where he finally had his surgery. At the time he was writing his letter, he was at his home, lying in his own bed with his wife at his side, and happily recovering. I wrote back to him enclosing a photograph of Charlie's painting hanging over our new shower room. I was sure he got a laugh out of that picture. After that, we often spoke of Tom, but I never heard from him again.

The "Tom Zinn Memorial Shower"

THE BUNKER

Being across the street from the Evac hospital, we sometimes worked in their emergency ward to help out, especially if ours was slow. I assisted their surgeons when time permitted, just to keep my hand in. The commanding officer of the 45th Evac was Lieutenant Colonel Jim Smith. He had come from the big Army hospital in Denver, and despite his being a lifer, he was a real nice guy who loved to drive heavy road equipment. Somehow, he had access to a great big bulldozer with a huge earth-moving blade on the front. I often saw him driving the earthmover doing chores for fun around the base. One day I asked him if he would consider digging a hole for our bunker. He came over to examine our proposed site and agreed to dig the hole for us that same afternoon. We had decided to place this bunker between our two hooches with entrances into the bunker from each hooch. During enemy shelling, going outside of our hooches in order to enter the bunker would unnecessarily expose us to danger, so the bunker entrances were logically kept inside the somewhat protected hooches. The one obstacle to digging the hole was a pipe that went between the hooches to the old shower area. Digging with our GI entrenching tools, we found the pipe hugged one side of one of the hooches. We marked it so that Jim would miss it.

The remarkable Lieutenant Colonel Jim Smith came riding up to Company D that day, mounted on his huge bulldozer. In several short passes the otherwise orthopedic surgeon had dug a huge, perfect hole just like a professional earthmover. Had we dug that six-feet-deep by ten-feet-long and six-feet-wide hole by hand, as we had originally planned, the four of us would have spent three or four weeks in back-breaking labor. The piled-up dirt at either end of our new hole was used to fill the sand bags that would cover the top of the bunker. For the ceiling of the bunker, using what I could remember about the command bunker in Cu Chi as my model, I suggested we first lay a sixteen-by-sixteen-inch, twelve-foot-long wooden beam over the hole lengthwise. Crosswise, over the central wooden support, perforated steel plates from the airstrip (no questions please) were placed as the first layer of the roof. Next, four layers of sand bags were placed atop the PSP, pounding each layer down for snugness as it was laid. Empty ammo crates came next, on top of the four layers of sand bags, to create an all important air space. More PSP over the ammo crates, in turn, held the final four layers of sand bags. The air space we created was necessary to allow a shell to "arm itself" on the empty layer. Armor piercing shells such as fired from a rocket-propelled grenade launcher, or a rocket itself, were engineered to first penetrate whatever it came in contact with, then it would arm itself at the first lack of resistance and explode at the next resistance it encountered. That way, these shells would "burn" their way into the protected cavity of a bunker, tank, or a pill box, and then explode, killing those inside, instead of exploding harmlessly on the outside, at first impact. Secure knowing we had done the necessary research, we felt confident that this bunker could withstand a direct hit from anything in the enemy's arsenal.

By the middle of November 1968, we had completed the outside of the bunker and I was extremely pleased. Seeing what we officers had done, others in the company began to build their own bunkers. Soon, many new bunkers were strategically located throughout the company area and people began to sleep more soundly at night. Security from the random enemy rockets that plagued the Vietnamese skies at night was very comforting. With pieces of left-over lumber we scrounged from the Brigade dump, bunks were fashioned inside the bunker and we brought our bedding down from above. A single Hitachi oscillating fan supplied air conditioning for the bunker when and if the company generator was working. More importantly, the fan kept the omnipresent mosquitoes away from us while we slept. I clearly remember watching the mosquitoes flying towards me, only to be blown back by the wind of the fan. When the fan turned away from me, the mosquitoes regrouped, flew back towards my exposed skin, and then, just as they were ready to land on me, the fan turned back my way and blew them away once again. This flying towards, and blowing away, went on all night long. If the electricity ever went off, and it often did, I'd wake up with a lot of bumps. Eventually we finished the walls in "ammo-crate knotty pine," which created a homey look.

175 mm. howitzer firing just behind my hooch

Time out in Tay Ninh

VENEREAL DISEASE

Marty, Charlie, and I decided to continue manning the aid station by the previous schedule. With one less doctor, things were certainly tighter, but we three worked well together and helped each other whenever possible. This way, by following the old schedule, one of us was still free each afternoon. As time passed, we became much more familiar with the types of diseases we were seeing and with treating the wounded. War wounds were almost second nature to us. After war wounds, sadly, the next most common group of illnesses we had to treat was venereal disease. PA&E workers, GIs and civilians alike were afflicted. The ironic thing about venereal disease was that it was so totally avoidable. Although we often did, telling young men, away from home for the first time, to consider abstinence from sex was next to fruitless. Gonorrhea was the most commonly isolated agent. Every day, young men showed up on sick call with the telltale sign of pus dripping from their urethras. In an effort to speed things up, these complaints were handled by our medics in an algorithmic fashion. If there was a complaint of dripping pus, a smear of the pus was made to look for the offending bacteria. If gram-negative intracellular diplococci (GNIDS) were seen on the smear, which took about ten minutes to do, shots were automatically administered and the patient was on his way in less than 30 minutes. At that time, most of these bacteria were not as yet resistant to penicillin and two huge shots of procaine penicillin, one in each buttock, would be curative. If an allergy to penicillin was elicited, then a week's course of oral tetracycline was prescribed.

The GIs would present with a whole host of imaginative complaints to keep their embarrassment over the disease they suspected they had down to a minimum. Cover-ups like "trouble urinating, a drip from the penis, groin pain," and, the best, "'a cold in the bladder" were used by reticent soldiers. Most soldiers knew that not to be treated, as if anyone could stand the discomfort urinating anyway, could possibly cause loss of their personal sexual function completely and forever. Stories of soldiers losing their penises, being sent to an island near Japan to live out the years in celibate isolation, or worse, circulated in the animated bull sessions of the American soldier in Vietnam. Scared by these rumors, most GIs reported to sick call at the first sign of any dripping, ulceration, or bumps in the groins.

Also of interest had to be the young men who had never been away from home, officers as well as privates, meeting a girl in a bar, and actually developing strong emotions for her. As they were injected in each buttock, many of these gullible men were chagrined to learn that these girls were actually prostitutes. Often, our well-intentioned medics would remark to a cringing patient receiving a painful penicillin injection, "That must have been some girl you had, you're still coming!" Although possibly cruel, that was said, not to be judgmental, but to embarrass, in order to possibly avoid this dilemma in the future. Whether it was the disease itself, with its very painful urination, the embarrassment of the treatment, or the painful injections, what we did worked fairly well. According to the medical records seen at some future point, the first time for this disease was very often the last. On the other hand, repeat offenders were discouraging to see. They immediately recognized their malady by the all-too-familiar signs, and faced the required painful injections with a resolve not to visit that particular girl again. I think the thing that bothered me the most was their idea that the girl was the culprit. Possibly, the man may have first inoculated a non-diseased woman who, in turn, passed the bacteria on to her next customer, and so on. Which came first, the chicken or the egg? Most GIs had no illusions about what they were getting for a few of their Yankee bucks. Boom-Boom girls were everywhere and often followed patrols onto the jungle trails as far as the sergeant would allow. I always had a hard time believing that a GI could have sex with a Boom-Boom girl on the side of a road in an old refrigerator box, the only privacy available. However, that refrigerator box encounter was a fairly common story, and must have been directly related to the soldier's lust at the moment. Both the sun and the passion made those boxes pretty hot.

At one time the Army wanted its doctors to inspect the women in the local houses of ill repute and, after a negative examination, issue a card to the girl signifying her freedom from venereal disease. Interestingly enough, the three physicians of Company D individually refused the request when approached. We had not conferred with each other about this beforehand, and we were proud to have come to the same conclusion independently. When a delegation of soldiers came to ask us why we all refused to perform this very simple task, I motioned their attention to our sick-call waiting room. Pointing out a big, gruff looking man, I hypothesized he had gonorrhea, and that he could be the next customer of the prostitute who had just been inspected. She would then harbor the offending bacteria in the pool of sperm he had left, and the next man then dipped himself into that pool. No amount of cleansing could remove all the bacteria. Only several days of antibiotics could do the job of eradicating the gonococcal bacteria, and the customers couldn't wait. Hard as it was to understand, the GIs probably got the Clap from each other, and the prostitutes were simply the partially innocent reservoirs. My explanation didn't go over very well with the soldiers. That certainly was not what they wanted to hear. They wanted us to make paid-for sex safe, and that was impossible for us, or anyone else, to do. Frustrated with our apparent unwillingness to help, we were asked if we then suggested the impossible, abstinence. I said that although abstinence seemed implausible, that was the logical first thing to consider, followed by a careful, and not a hasty selection of a partner. Next came taking antibiotics before and after an unknown exposure. I said if a soldier were waiting in the infamous line of horny GIs winding up the stairs in a brothel, he was very likely to get VD from one of the guys ahead of him, and there was nothing I could do about that. The delegation of soldiers left in disgust, and the local prostitutes were never inspected by the doctors from Company D. I was sorry they were disappointed in my (our) response to their plea, but, if the very next customer of the prostitute I had just examined inoculated her with VD, what good did I do? I realized this problem, but they could not, or, refused to, understand it. I did request the Army prophylactically treat all the local prostitutes with daily oral antibiotics, but my suggestion never got very far. The VD problem was more moral than it was infectious, and, moreover, not all sexually transmitted diseases can be eradicated by antibiotics. Even back in 1968, we were aware that some forms of hepatitis and other viruses could also be transmitted by sex, and this was even a stronger argument for abstinence. This all seemed so very logical to me as a physician, and moreover, the Company D doctors never flagged in our duty to do all we could with the male side of the VD problem.

SOME OF THE CHARACTERS
OF COMPANY D

Our company laboratory could do the appropriate tests for malaria, VD, and most other blood tests needed in Vietnam in 1968. The medic responsible for the lab work was Bill Adler, an extremely intelligent young man and a conscientious worker. Drafted after completing his first year of graduate school where he was pursuing a doctorate in biology, Bill contracted meningitis during basic training at Camp Leonard Wood in Missouri and almost died. He told me that experience sensitized him to the value of a laboratory in the practice of medicine, because the early accurate identification of the offending bacteria was primarily responsible for his eventual recovery. He was always keenly interested in the accuracy of his reports. Often, he would report his results to me in person, such as a positive malarial smear, and then he wanted me to look at the test to further verify and discuss his findings. He probably knew much more than I about laboratory medicine. His services were invaluable to the clinic, and to me. Tall and severely thin, he looked like he was still very ill. During his meningitis illness, he was so ill he had to have a tracheotomy cut in his windpipe so that he could continue breathing. That tracheotomy tube left him with a tracheal irritation causing severe paroxysms of coughing which lent credence to his still being ill. I suggested he get out of the military on a medical disability that I could arrange, but Bill wanted to remain in the Army until his term was up so he could be eligible for the GI Bill. Only the money he would receive from the GI Bill would enable him to finish his schooling, otherwise he would never be able to pay for his continuing education. I was very thankful to have this superb lab technician to depend on during my stay with Company D. Looking at his cachectic frame, one would think he would be on sick call often, but Bill never missed a day of work, and he had more stamina than I did. I never asked, but, according to the other medics, he was a conscientious objector who vehemently abhorred the war and killing. I thought it was odd that he never discussed his feelings with me, but he was one of those guys who could completely separate his religious convictions from his daily activities, and to me, that always is a commendable attribute. I wish I could have been that way, but I always shot my mouth off at the most inopportune times.

Hank Phillips was a tall, thin, blonde kid off a farm in Illinois. Very mild-mannered and quiet, I hardly ever knew he was around. His non-complaining demeanor was providential, because Hank was our X-ray technician. The X-ray machine he had to use, the only one there was, was the most cantankerous piece of machinery ever devised by man. This ill-natured electrical monster needed all the coaxing imaginable to work. To make matters even worse, the power supply of the company was run from a single generator. The entire company used this one generator, which was woefully inadequate for the periodic demands of the X-ray machine. If the cooks in the mess hall were using their various electrical food preparation appliances, Hank had to wait for them to finish before he had enough electricity to use the X-ray machine. I can still remember Hank many times gracefully loping over to Short Round to ask him to turn off his appliances for a moment or two so he could take an X-ray. Hank's requests never went over well with Short Round, always the temperamental cook. The whole company would get a big kick out of watching mild-mannered Hank come up against Short Round when Hank needed a picture, and Short Round was in the middle of preparing dinner. Short Round would rant and rave while Hank listened politely. Hank had that humble aggression that finally won out in the end. If the potatoes were ever lumpy, however, Short Round would blame Hank and his damned machine. I was finally able to procure an additional small generator that Hank was able to hook up with the company's existing generator. With this additional generator, Hank could finally get a good X-ray without giving Short Round a temper tantrum. The fact that we got any X-rays at all was directly related to the efforts of Hank Phillips.

Two of our medics, Phil Brandenberg and Paul Washington, had been trained by the Army as surgical assistants back in the States. Phil was a short, slightly stocky young man from rural California. A very devout Christian, he was a staunch objector to war and capital punishment. Phil had been drafted, and, despite his religious position as a pacificist, was eager to help his fellow man in the capacity of an Army medic. After basic training, he took extra training in surgical technique. Phil used to drive one of our company's ambulances, and more than once I saw him risk his own life to pick up wounded soldiers during barrages of incoming on the base. I remember him returning from a very risky ambulance run one day. I was amazed how he had exposed himself that afternoon. After he off-loaded his patients, he said smiling, "I hate this war. I just want to help." I believe he was a Seventh Day Adventist, a vegetarian, and a strong opponent of alcohol and tobacco. Despite all his personal religious hates, he had an upbeat personality and, never negative, he was always ready to pitch in and help. Rounding out an almost perfect picture was Phil's tolerance for the "sins" of others. Although he never openly objected to his fellow medics drinking beer or smoking cigarettes, we occasionally would hear "tsk-tsks" from him as he walked by behavior he didn't care for. Consequently, Phil was well-liked, if not admired by the men.

Paul Washington was a handsome young man with a trim moustache and a beautiful wide smile revealing a perfect set of white teeth. Gregarious, and always happy, he loved to talk with, and was very reassuring to, his GI patients. Like Phil, Paul was quick to comprehend, very good with his hands, and always eager to learn. Both Phil and Paul wanted to be physician's assistants when their Army days were over. They both ached to attend the new physician's assistant's school at Duke University. The three of us would talk for hours as we worked over wounded GIs. I wanted them to go to medical school. They had the intelligence, desire, and passion for what they did and would have made great surgeons. Both would listen politely to me, but neither would agree to it. Something deep inside both of them foiled my attempts at convincing them. I thought Paul felt being a poor black kid from the South, he didn't have a chance, and Phil felt it would take too long, and he didn't have the time to spend. I never could convince them, but I liked them so much, I never stopped trying.

When wounded came into our treatment area, they would be triaged as to whether a doctor should take care of them or if Phil or Paul could do it. Marty Bruggerman, being an internist, liked to relinquish his surgical duties to them whenever he could. He knew they carried out his instructions completely, and that they both could cut and sew better than he could, or wanted to. When finished with their appointed tasks, Phil and Paul always sought the approval of the doctors. I never found any job they did lacking in any way, and their GI patients would also be happy with their work. When suturing a wound, Paul would ask me if he could "tighten up this dude" evoking a quizzical look on his patient's face, and a smile on mine. Paul would then talk to his patient in such a way to put him at complete ease, a gift I always wished I could emulate.

One night, after midnight, three wounded ARVN soldiers had been brought into the aid station for care. Paul Washington called Marty Bruggerman on the phone explaining in detail what the injuries were. Marty asked Paul to proceed without him being there in person. Marty had just gotten to bed and the care needed was straightforward, well within the ability of Paul's expertise. While Paul was finishing up working on the last wounded soldier, Colonel Wair, of all people, walked in and inquired abruptly, "How are things going, Doctor?" Paul said "Fine, Sir!" but timidly added he was not a doctor, just a surgical tech. His face turning red at Paul's response, the colonel swore, and demanded, "Get the doctor right away!" Paul rang Marty. Marty ran down to the aid station and got quite an unjust earful from the "Old Man!" The colonel ranted and raved at Marty, and, as he was walking out, added, he wanted to see Captain Snider in his office at 0700 the next morning! Paul had done an excellent job! The ARVN soldiers looked great. When Marty came back to the hooch that night, he advised me what had just happened in "my" aid station! He was right, as the commander, I was ultimately responsible, but I didn't understand what was wrong. Certainly the colonel's own Army had trained Paul to do just he had done. What was the beef? I knew the colonel would soon enlighten me as to what the beef was, but I resolved to stand my ground.

The command sergeant major spied me as I entered the headquarters building the next morning and motioned me over. He warned me the old man really had "a bug up his ass" that morning. He had seen him this way before, and, if I knew what was good for me, I should "just listen and not say a word!" Just then, the colonel's door flew open, and I heard, "Snider, get in here!" Inside, he raged on in a loud steady voice something to the tune that he never wanted to find that the doctor had not seen the patient before treatment was started. Art Lewis would never do anything like that, and, if I knew what was good for me, I'd never let anything like he saw last night ever happen again. Wow, I felt like I was hemorrhaging. I had been chewed out like that once before from "Old Frosty," Gus Lindskog, the surgery professor at Yale. He didn't let me say a word in my defense either. As with both Dr. Lindskog and Colonel Fair, the time didn't seem right for me to speak, so I just looked down at my shoes. I rigidly awaited what was to come next. Colonel Fair stormed past me and walked into the waiting brigade briefing room. Timidly, I followed him in, red-faced. He began speaking to the others around the briefing table as if nothing had happened. He was calm, cool, and collected. Looking around, I saw several of the officer attendees smiling knowingly at me. I could feel my face turning even redder. Later, after that morning's eternal briefing was over, an infantry major took me aside. In hushed tones he told me he had lived through many such tongue-lashings. Like the command sergeant major, he emphasized that I not say anything in my defense. Doing so would only make the colonel angrier, which would do nothing for my cause. Sort of an Army tradition, standing there and taking the verbal assault was better than to react. History bore this out countless times, the major continued, no matter how mindless the superior officer's tirade, endure rather than react. Strange business was this Army, but the major seemed like someone to listen to. Patting me on the shoulder, the major moved away just as the colonel came by. Colonel Fair smiled briefly and passed, his smile quickly dissolving into his usual frown. The command sergeant major winked and gave me a pat on the butt as he passed me by, almost running to keep up with the rapid stepping colonel. As the colonel left, the meeting broke up, and I began to calm down. I was still smarting at the unfairness of the process, and I was especially ashamed at my silence. The long morning briefing meeting I had endured had done much to dampen my welling emotions, and now that I was alone, there was no one to hear me if I were to speak up. Shrugging my shoulders, and walking away, I guessed I sort came of age in the Third Brigade that day. Bobby Fair was "The Man," above reproach, and always infallible. I was late for breakfast, so off I went.

Our pharmacist, Brian Kelly was a magician. Although the American Army had to have been the best-supplied army that ever was, a shortage of medicines plagued us in Tay Ninh in 1968. We never had enough antibiotics, antifungals, and antimalarial medicines in stock to keep up with the demand. No matter how many forms I filled out, medicines were hard to get. Brian had a way of begging, borrowing, and stealing what was needed. He was a fun-loving guy who loved a good bull session. Many a night after the last patient had left, and after the last wounded soldier had been tucked safely into his bunker ward bed, we all gathered around in the front of the aid station to just talk. These sessions were about as egalitarian as possible. The medical corps in Vietnam had a comfortable relaxation of Army protocol, and the men of Company D became a close-knit band of brothers. Those end-of-day bull sessions were a lot of fun, and we were all topped in the funny story category by Brian. Steven Segura, Brian's pharmacy assistant, was much more quiet than Brian, but he loved to listen to Brian's stories, as we all did. Brian was able make Steven feel at ease and I'm sure Steven learned a great deal about life from Brian's tales.

Probably the most notable character in the company had to have been Lurch! He was blonde, six-feet-four-inches tall, and the proud owner of a remarkable basso profundo voice. The depth of his voice was so striking that, at times, he even impressed himself, eliciting a cocky smile on his face as a baby might, amused by its own, sudden sneeze. He really looked and sounded like "Lurch" from "The Addams Family" TV show of the time. Every one knew and appreciated our Lurch. He was the focal point of the company, and he relished the attention in an unobtrusive way. Although Lurch stands out clearly in my memory, I'm embarrassed to confess I don't remember his real name. My excuse is his real name was rarely used at the time. His nickname was ceremoniously given to him by the medics and of all the monikers bestowed by the men, his was by far the best. Lurch loved his adopted name and he loved his life in the company. Whenever I needed him for something, and called his name, he would come to my side, saying in his deepest voice, "You rang, Sir?" No matter how engrossed I was, and no matter whomever I was near, I would look up at this big amusing guy and laugh out loud when he spoke. He had the innocent face and the ruddy complexion of the farm boy from Iowa that he was. Patients coming to Company D's aid station had to register with Lurch at his front desk. His elevated large registration desk was off to the right side as one entered the treatment station and was hard to miss. A loud deep voice would notify you of your mistake, if you happened to pass without signing in.

In this war zone, for everyone's protection, there was a hard and fast rule. No weapons were to be brought inside the aid station by anyone, ever. There could be no exceptions! A carefully devised storage place for weapons was positioned outside the aid station for all to use. A rifle rack, an ammo table, and a sandbag pit for grenades were provided. It was like old Dodge City inasmuch as all guns were checked outside the saloon. When a soldier forgot, didn't see the sign, or decided not to care about stashing his weapons, and walked inside armed, Lurch's deep voice would rise above the loud conversation in the waiting room. In sarcastic manner meant to embarrass, as well as advise, Lurch would demand, "What's the matter with you soldier? Can't you read simple English? Take that M-16 (or whatever) outside and stack it where it belongs, or I'll make you eat it!" Any GI, so summarily admonished, would easily jump a foot into the air like everyone else in the waiting room. I think Lurch's commands got more attention and reaction than did the sound of incoming! After issuing such a command, without even so much as a sidewards glance, Lurch would look back at the papers on his desk and resume writing. You could hear a pin drop in that place for a while until someone got up enough courage to begin speaking again. The silence would often be broken by the sound of a truck passing by outside as the front door was opened by the guilty soldier to stow his weapon.

Lurch was the protector of the aid station, both by his position near the front door and his imposing presence. On two occasions Lurch saved me from certain harm. The first time was during an afternoon sick call. A frequent visitor to our sick call was a soldier the doctors nicknamed "Mr. Penis!" He was from the Bronx and liked to act the tough guy. He came to sick call at least once a week usually complaining about some dirty slut he had been with the other day, and he always wanted us to check him for possible VD brought on by his most recent sordid affair. A real hypochondriac, he had a very dangerous passive-aggressive personality. Deep down, he hated women and mistreated them out of sheer disrespect. He hated authority even more, and that is why, I believe, he would flop his penis on my desktop for me to scrutinize! When I wouldn't react, he would inspect every inch of his organ, pointing out any irregularity for me to comment on. Actually, in the half of a dozen times, or so, I saw his penis, I never found anything wrong. This was very unusual behavior for any young man. Most GIs were often too embarrassed to even mention they suspected venereal disease, let alone flaunt it. I guess, being naturally modest and a lot embarrassed, they would rather describe what they had, rather than let me see.

Marty and Charlie had both experienced the same encounters with Mr. Penis as I, and, like me, felt a little intimidated by his tough talk and gross actions. All his tests were always negative, but on many occasions, just to appease him, we gave him doses of penicillin, tetracycline, and Keflex. Nobody in the aid station liked him. When he left the front desk after registering, Lurch would curl his lip like a growling dog, signaling dislike. The last time I examined that aggressive hypochondriac, I decided that I had had enough of Mr. Penis. The time had come he be told I wasn't going to inspect him any more. I decided to let him tell me what he thought was wrong, and I would respond accordingly. Having said something to that effect to him, he glowered at me menacingly. Standing, knocking over the chair he was sitting in, he told me if he could get me back "on the street," he would kill me! Not knowing what to do, I walked swiftly from the small examining room out into the hall to place myself in clear view of Lurch and the crowd waiting. Sensing my alarm, Lurch moved around from behind his counter desk and stood by me. The fuming Mr. Penis came rushing out of my office zipping his trousers with a sinister look on his face. He abruptly stiffened when he saw Lurch standing alongside me. He brushed past me and went outside, obviously in a savage mood. Lurch sat back down behind his desk while I, shaken, returned to my office, sat down, and called for the next patient. Outside, my rebuffed patient shoved a loaded magazine into his M-16 and rushed back inside as he chambered a round! All the GIs inside instinctively recognized the unmistakable sound of a bullet slamming into the lock of the rifle barrel and tensed up. The patient in my room quickly ran out into the hall at the sound! Unwarned, as I was not at all familiar with rifle sounds, I arose and followed my patient into the hallway to see what the commotion was about. Blurred in front of me was the scene of Mr. Penis coming through the waiting room holding his now-loaded rifle in a threatening angle in front of him. He moved through the waiting room, into the very hall I was standing in, only about six feet away, and Lurch was upon him. Lurch pulled the rifle

Sitting at Lurch's desk, I hear a "noise."

from his hands with a downward jerk using his left hand. With his right arm, and the whole weight of his body, he shoved my assailant backwards causing him to land in the dirt outside the front door. The fallen startled soldier started to get up. Lurch's two strong hands grabbed his shirt. Lifting the soldier, he began to shake him like a dog would shake a rat. Growling, Lurch said, "Get out of here! If I ever see you back here again you'll be in the dead shed." Throwing him back onto the ground, the soldier landed in a heap. Lurch unloaded the offending M-16 and threw the rifle at the cowering soldier. Mr. Penis stumbled to his feet and ran sideways down the road, never to be seen by me again. Lurch went back to his duties as if nothing happened. He wasn't even breathing hard. I thanked Lurch so profusely that I embarrassed him. As things settled down, I went back to seeing sick call patients. My next patient was a Puerto Rican soldier who was eager to talk to me about that amazing incident. He said he knew that guy and he was a "real bad dude." He had given a lot of people a lot of grief. My patient laughed about how Lurch "tightened that guy's ass!" A lot more at ease now, I smiled and agreed. That all happened so fast that day, I felt as if I had been watching a movie.

The second time Lurch intervened for me was even more frightening. Once again, I would be beholden to Lurch's quick and decisive action. About 2000 hours one evening, MPs brought in an agitated soldier who had been found lying on the ground outside the Third Brigade headquarters with a loaded M-16, shouting threats at the then-vacant colonel's office. Colonel Wair was out in the field somewhere and missed the whole thing. A headquarter's sergeant heard the unintelligible shouts of the deranged soldier and called the MPs. Enter now my old MP buddy Sergeant Robinson, having been transferred from Cu Chi about the same time I had been, holding a much taller soldier tightly by the arm. The soldier had been disarmed and was held captive by the smaller MPs via a very efficient pair of twist handcuffs. Obviously agitated, the captive soldier was tall, African-American, and very muscular. He was sweating in the still night's heat, and he was very drunk. I could smell the alcohol and suspected drugs too, a very dangerous combination. Contained by those painful cuffs, he seemed docile enough now, and Lurch instructed the MPs to let him lie down on the stretcher so the doctor could talk with him. The MPs removed the handcuffs and told the soldier to lie down on the stretcher. The soldier told me he had been drinking and that he wanted to kill the "White mother f----- who was responsible for this war." Lurch chuckled and said, "I do too!" as he returned to his seat behind the reception counter. Sergeant Robinson asked if he and his MP partner could leave as they had received another call on their way over to the aid station and had to respond. I naively asked the now quiet patient if he would promise to behave. He said he would. With tight lips, he said was feeling better and would not cause anybody any trouble. I let the MPs leave, as I truly didn't expect any problems. I had seen many drunken men who took out their frustrations on authority figures. Usually, they took a punch at a sergeant and sobered up in the brig, penitent in the morning. The soldier and I talked quietly for some time while Lurch wrote at his desk. The three of us were alone in the aid station that night.

My interview showed the angry young soldier was more than just drunk and acting out. He was a very mixed-up kid whom I suspected was on mind-altering drugs, which added to his underlying mental condition. He kept saying over and over that he just wanted to go home and see his Mama. All GIs just wanted to go home. Unexpectedly, his next statement was, when he got home, he was going to join the Black Panthers and get in Whitey's face. If he couldn't get home, he was going to go AWOL and lose himself in Saigon's infamous "Soul Kitchen." The Soul Kitchen was rumored to be a place in Saigon where disgruntled black AWOL soldiers had an underground empire dealing in drugs and the black market. If such a place existed, this distraught soldier wanted to go there. With Martin Luther King Jr.'s assassination fresh in everybody's minds, young African-American soldiers couldn't hide their feelings of distrust for the Army with all its racism. This man's anguish seemed way out of line compared to most, however, and I suspected real mental disease. Anyway, his last statement concerned me. The only thing I could do with a sociopathic dangerous soldier was to have the MPs take him to the brig and make arrangements for a formal inquiry involving psychiatric evaluation.

He was becoming more agitated as we talked. I thought I could take the edge off his anger with a sedative. I chose paraldehyde, a potent sedative when combined with alcohol, forming what was commonly called a "Mickey Finn!" Putting a healthy dose of the drug in a can of Dr. Pepper soda, I suggested the soldier drink the soda to make him feel better on this very hot night. As he put it to his lips, he said, "This better not be any drugs! I don't want you to drug me, man!" The unfortunate thing about this situation was that paraldehyde has a very pungent odor. In fact, paraldehyde stinks to high heaven! Taking a big swig of the altered soda, my patient obviously caught a whiff of the paraldehyde. "Why you white mother f-----! I'll get you!" Off the stretcher he jumped and, in an instant, had me locked in a breath-obstructing bear hug. Tumbling backwards, the two of us toppled over the front desk! Seeing us coming, Lurch leapt out of harm's way with all the grace of a ballet dancer. The much stronger soldier let go of me with his right arm, pulling back to hit me. Lurch grabbed his swinging arm on its forward path. I could feel a jerk as Lurch yanked backwards on that strong arm, just about pulling it out of its socket! The soldier was quickly up on his feet facing Lurch. Still with a steely grasp on that right arm, in a move a karate black belt would have been proud of, Lurch spun the soldier around, pinning the soldier's arm behind his back in a painful half-Nelson. Yelling and cursing, the soldier was begging Lurch to let him loose. Pushing the soldier into a chair, in an instant, Lurch had both his arms behind him locking him into the seat. Almost as if on cue, Sergeant Robinson walked back in on the scene. The cuffs were reapplied and the soldier and the MPs went out to the waiting jeep. Sergeant Robinson said with a backwards glance, "This guy needs the pokey, not medical care!" I couldn't have agreed more. Lurch was righting his desk, calm as a cucumber. "Want me to take the paraldehyde over to the pokey? I can make him drink it." No, I didn't. He would be OK. On the way back to my hooch, I kept thinking what a man Lurch was! Twice, he saved me from significant harm, and he thought nothing about it. I have not forgotten him. I often wonder what ever happened to him. Once, in a rare moment, he told me he was a Mormon, a man of peace. He, too, was a conscientious objector and hated the war. Like the others, he was a devoutly religious person, but he never could have been called a coward. I often think that he's a hard-working farmer now, with a slew of big blonde kids. I'll bet he never talks about the war, and specifically, what he did for me and Company D.

I saw that patient again the next morning, at the request of the colonel, who had heard about the fracas after returning from his trip to the field. I couldn't believe I was seeing the same guy. He was fine! Polite and cooperative now, he was sober and facing a court martial. Speaking with him again, I still wasn't sure that he was actually mentally fit, and I ordered he be sent for psychiatric evaluation. Declared sane by the psychiatrist, he was court-martialed and sent back to the States to serve a short jail sentence.

The Army wanted all of its soldiers to try "to win the hearts and minds of the Vietnamese people." D Company's interface with the people was through the sick call we held for civilians. We could not have done that without Mae Lin, our interpreter. More than that, she was our Vietnamese soul. About twenty-five years old, and dressed in tight-fitting camouflaged fatigues, she was a striking example of Vietnamese beauty. She was working at the aid station in Tay Ninh when I arrived and was there when I left. She had been there for many years, and how she had come to be there is forever lost in time. An excellent interpreter, as far as I could tell, she told me she had been hired by the 25th Division when they selected Tay Ninh as a base camp. Initially she was to be a liaison between the 25th brass and the local people, but later fell into being Company D's interpreter.

Mae Lin demonstrated an impatience with her own people, as many Vietnamese interpreters seemed to harbor. Perhaps she fancied herself an American, and by her new identity, she felt aloof from common Vietnamese people problems. I did check with the local Army intelligence people concerning her authenticity once and was assured that she had been completely scrutinized. No one in Army Intelligence had any doubt she was legitimate, as well as a South Vietnamese patriot. No traces to the enemy, or with communism, were ever uncovered. I felt badly that I had any suspicions, as she always did her job well and was certainly appreciated by the wounded and sick GIs. Working so closely with Company D, 25th Med, she was privy to knowledge of American troop whereabouts, and other bits of sensitive information that could have been very valuable to the enemy. As the Delta Six, I just needed to know more about how she fit in with my unit. I did not want to leave any loose strings hanging around that might jeopardize our mission. I never did know who paid her, or if she was paid at all. She said she received money from the United States Army as a Tay Ninh provincial interpreter, and I felt uneasy about that explanation. There were a lot of things happening in Vietnam that seemed fishy to me, but the assurance I got from the Army Intelligence people was good enough for me to be comfortable with the fact that whatever she was doing, she was sanctioned by the United States. Indeed, she was a help to Company D!

Mae Lin had, at times, an almost disdainful approach to her wounded fellow countrymen. The same abrupt manner was also used on wounded or sick enemy soldiers and civilians. Her demeanor was much different when she was helping the American wounded. Her voice was light, and she joked incessantly when attending GIs. I thought she hoped to marry an American soldier, but she never seemed to follow up on her contacts. Marty thought that she blamed the Vietnamese people for the turmoil her country was in. She acted curt and aloof with her own people, no matter how bad their state of human plight was. Keening Vietnamese women seemed to bother her the most. The emotional outpouring of Vietnamese women towards death was certainly much different than occidental practices. Vietnamese men, on the other hand, were not demonstrative at all and would stare off into space when confronted with personal tragedy. A mourning Vietnamese woman would literally scream, emitting huge tears, followed by drooling from the mouth. These outbursts were mandated by their culture. This type of response wasn't local. I had seen it many places in South Vietnam. The wailing, drooling women made us uncomfortable, and nothing we could do would lessen their grief process.

How my memory relates this mourning process to Mae Lin is seen in the following story. Once, a young Vietnamese mother brought in her baby who had died several days earlier. I carefully examined the dead baby's body to assure the mother that there was nothing I could do. I asked Mae Lin to explain this to the mother in Vietnamese. She did and the young woman burst into screams and tears. Saliva drooled from her mouth, almost reaching the floor! Her sudden screams scared me, and I tried to comfort the crying mother, but to no avail. A little confused, I asked Mae Lin why the mother was screaming now? Surely she realized that her baby was dead. Hadn't she cried before this? I felt I knew the answer. The mother probably had heard that the Dai Wi Bac Si might be able to save her child, and she still held out hope of a miracle from the modern medicine of the Army doctor. Upset with the mother and the other crying women, Mae Lin began to shout at them to be quiet. She bruskly wrapped the baby's body in a blanket and sent the whole entourage back to their village. Why our female Vietnamese interpreter acted this way to her own people always irked me.

Despite the harsh treatment she gave her own people, I liked Mae Lin for the most part and got along well with her. I found it amusing to watch GIs lock onto her with their eyes as she strolled by. There was little doubt our soldiers all thought she was the prettiest thing they had ever seen in jungle boots! More than once, Lurch had to warn a GI signing in for the clinic to pay attention to him and not to Mae Lin. She never became involved romantically with anyone as far as I could tell. She insisted she wasn't married and was looking for a good man. As I said, Mae Lin was there when I arrived and was there when I left, and for all I know, she may still be there. The latter possibility would be highly unlikely, for when the NVA eventually won the war, Mae Lin would have been high on their hit list. I hope the United States government knew this, and made arrangements to ferret people like Mae Lin out of the country to a safe place.

Recounting the key players in company would not be complete without describing Sergeant Jackson Thomas. He was the NCOIC of the bunker hospital ward. He had four medics working under him who cared for the sick and wounded in the bunker ward. Thomas had entered the Army as a nineteen-year-old many years ago. He had been trained as a medical corpsman and had served in many huge Army hospitals all over the world. Rising in rank over the years, he functioned as a ward nurse. Although not a registered nurse, he was equivalent to a licensed practical nurse in training, and the Army relied heavily on men like him to supply a lot of the in-patient care. Caregivers, like Sergeant Thomas, were the hands-on workers in military medical care.

They were indispensable. When wounded or ill soldiers were admitted to our underground hospital, they entered into the world of Sergeant Thomas. His was a very comfortable and caring world. The ward was run like an efficient infantry unit. Everyone under Thomas's command knew his duties, how to do them, and where to turn for advice and help. Even his patients were expected to do their part, and it wasn't unusual for me to see a ward patient making his own bed. Slackers were treated swiftly and severely. Always the consummate medical teacher, Sergeant Thomas taught his medics tirelessly. Both the medics and I learned a lot from him.

Doctors made rounds in the bunker ward each day, and Thomas was always right with us. He rarely took any time off. If he were away from the ward during doctor rounds, the medic he left in charge was to fetch him so he himself could hear what the doctors said about "his kids." He would often say quasi-medical things on rounds that would astound me. An example that comes to my mind was, when on rounds with me, unsolicited, Sergeant Thomas told a patient of mine, not to drink any beer at all for the next two weeks while taking the tetracycline I had just prescribed. The soldier had a bad case of non-specific urethritis secondary to gonorrhea and had been receiving IV antibiotics. He had responded nicely to the IV drugs on the ward, and I was certain he would do well with an oral antibiotic. Dressed now, and ready to go back to his unit, the soldier looked puzzled by the no beer order, and so was I. "Why no beer?" I asked. "Tetracycline is compatible with alcohol, isn't it?" Ignoring my inquiry with a wink, Sergeant Thomas advised the departing soldier to listen to what he had said, or he'd end right back here with a worsening gonorrheal infection. Knowing something was afoot by the furtive wink, I waited until the soldier left, then asked Thomas about the "No beer!" His answer made so much sense, I was ashamed I hadn't thought of it on my own. Sergeant Thomas explained his purpose in advising against beer was certainly not that alcohol had anything to do with making tetracycline less effective. He just wanted that soldier to stay sober for the next two weeks. Sobriety might just keep him out of the brothel. A time-honored tradition, the Army told its men being treated for VD to stay away from all alcohol for at least two weeks. The best lesson I learned from Sergeant Thomas was not all medical wisdom necessarily comes from doctors.

Company D had its share of bad actors, also. One of them was a big stocky blond, named Montefiore. This character went about causing trouble for me and the company just about every day. He had been drummed out of the infantry because he didn't fit in. Infantrymen depended on each other to do their job. If the man next to you always broke and ran, your life would be in continuous peril. Although hard to imagine, if a soldier wouldn't fight, there was no way in the world you could make him. Infantrymen would talk to their own, keeping would-be shirkers in line with peer pressure. Constant prodding of men on the front lines just wasn't worth the effort, and untrustworthy soldiers were quickly transferred out of front line outfits. Thus, Montefiore was booted out of the infantry as unreliable, and indirectly came to roost with us. He had been with a supply company for a time because he really wanted to drive a truck. The problem with being in the supply outfit was his refusal to do any hard work. He gave the truckers such a hard time, he was transferred, and finally ended up in our motor pool as a mechanic's helper. My personal assessment of the man was that he was a coward. Despite his bully-like nature, deep down, he was much more afraid of getting killed in the war than was the average soldier. Obviously, he hated the infantry the most, because he was the most likely to get killed there. Convoy truck drivers were always getting shot at in ambushes or were setting off mines on back roads. That didn't appeal to our boy either, so he acted out until he was transferred once again. To his ongoing chagrin, Montefiore found Company D was no safe haven. The almost daily rocket and mortar fire caused him to act out frequently.

Sergeant Rossnagel made Montefiore his personal project. The first sergeant laid it on the line to this guy. Rossnagel said he'd freeze in hell before he'd let Montefiore get out of the Army with a dishonorable discharge without first serving time in Leavenworth. I don't recall a day going by without hearing Sergeant Rossnagel yelling at Montefiore. I felt Monte, as we came to call him, was incorrigible and would never change as long as he remained in Vietnam.

Things went along fairly well for a while thanks to daily threats from Sergeant Rossnagel, but an encounter between Montefiore and me finally brought everything to a head. One fine afternoon, I happened to be standing behind the EM club, waiting to buy some more Royal Crown Cola for the officers' fridge, when I was spied by Montefiore, who happened to be sitting at a table inside. Just that day, I had given Sergeant Knoerr the order that Monte was not to have any beer or any other EM club privileges. Montefiore was just finding out about my orders from the bartender when I showed up at the back door. Montefiore burst through the flimsy back screen door towards me, almost tearing the door from its hinges as he went. Seeing that big soldier bursting through that door startled me, and I began stumbling backwards. He was yelling curses at me and shoved me off the wooden back stoop of the club. I was no physical match for him, and, being the bully he was, he enjoyed his size advantage. Things were not looking good for me. I tried to reason with him, but he was too upset about my recent orders. Miraculously, Sergeant

Rossnagel showed up, shirtless, and slightly out of breath. He had been jogging by and saw what was going on. He wasn't the only one watching, as many of the club patrons came outside to check out the commotion. Most of these soldiers were from other outfits and didn't know I was an officer. Soldiers always enjoyed a good fight and one was about to start! Pushing through the gathering crowd, the first sergeant stood tall like a knight in shining armor. Sergeant Rossnagel was in perfect shape, while Montefiore was fat and sloppy. Rossnagel ordered Montefiore to stand at attention! When he wouldn't, the sergeant warned him he would have to use force. Montefiore could be seriously maimed or even killed if he didn't yield! Wow! I was impressed by Rossnagel's warning, even if Montefiore wasn't. Not phased at all by the sergeant's warning, Monte lunged clumsily at Rossnagel who promptly hit him one good punch right on the nose. The sound of crunching nasal bones and the resultant blood flow was impressive. Montefiore just slumped down and then fell backwards, crying. Sergeant Rossnagel sent someone for the MPs, and eventually good old Sergeant Robinson showed up, all by himself this time.

Monte spent that night in the pokey only to be returned to his hooch at Company D the next day. He seemed to behave for a while, but eventually began his disruptive behavior again. Sergeant Rossnagel had to call Sergeant Robinson and the MPs about him several times, but each time Montefiore came back to our company. One day, I witnessed quite a scene when Montefiore resisted Sergeant Robinson's efforts to take him to the MP station. Monte called Sergeant Robinson a racially explicit name, so the sergeant calmly took off his MP armband and laid his pistol on the ground. I was flabbergasted. Was the much smaller sergeant going to fight this man? I think the racial slur was too much for my MP friend to take, and he was going to unofficially put out Montefiore's lights. Sergeant Robinson put up his fists to fight. Realizing his size advantage and seeing his unarmed nemesis wanting to fight, Monte just laughed smugly. A few of us had gathered around, and we wanted to help Sergeant Robinson. The sergeant told us to stand back, he would handle this. He must have been really smarting from Montefiore's name-calling. Montefiore suddenly lunged to strike, and in an instant the MP hit his bigger opponent in an already sore and still swollen nose. Most of us bystanders instinctively said "Ouch!" as the punch landed and the nose bled again. Even though Montefiore had few real friends in our company, there was some genuine empathy for his nose at least. Tears welled up in Montefiore's eyes, and he began to bawl like a baby. He truly must have been in a world of hurt, but that's what he deserved. Sergeant Robinson calmly put back on his MP armband and re-holstered his pistol. He looked dignified and satisfied. His revenge was well-deserved and sweet. Now, Montefiore went along docilely like a puppy dog with his master.

Later that night Montefiore was in my hooch! I was very relieved the first sergeant was with him. Because of the Red Alert, the MPs couldn't keep anyone locked up in their non-bunkered jail, so Sergeant Rossnagel agreed to guard the prisoner tonight and then would have him flown to Headquarters Company at Cu Chi in the morning. In Cu Chi, a division-level court martial would convene to decide the fate of this pitiful misfit. The soldier guarding Montefiore that night looked like a little boy, a chicken guarding a fox. Since the brigade was still on Red Alert, Monte had to be kept in a bunker for safety in case of an enemy attack. He was to be housed in the company bunker near my hooch. Just as I was about to go to sleep that night, there was Montefiore standing next to my bunk while the little boy-guard was futilely trying to make his prisoner return to the bunker. Montefiore promised to behave if only I would allow him and his guard go to Montefiore's own hooch where they would be much more comfortable. As the company commander, I felt this seemed reasonable, so I agreed and off they went. All went well that night, although the base camp was raked with mortar fire off and on the whole night through. No one was hurt from our company, and early the next morning the first sergeant and Montefiore boarded the Dust Off helicopter that was returning to Cu Chi. I heard later that Montefiore was tried, found guilty, and returned to the transport company in Cu Chi as a loader. He was sentenced to remain in Vietnam for an additional six months as part of his punishment. As far as I know, he behaved and actually did a good job back in the safer Cu Chi environment. I was very glad to be rid of him and the problems he caused. I felt that Company D, like the infantry, didn't want anyone who wouldn't do his job.

During my time as the Delta Six, Montefiore had to be my biggest discipline problem. Occasionally, I did have to verbally reprimand several soldiers for things like drunkenness, disobeying orders, and other minor infractions. I was never threatened physically again.

Sergeant Robinson still kept popping up in my life. If I thought I had experiences with bad apples, I was in the minor leagues compared to him. One noontime, I was walking towards the mess hall, having finished with the morning's sick call. My reverie was interrupted by the sounds of shouts and men running behind me. Turning, I saw Sergeant Robinson leave his feet in a flying tackle, stopping a fleeing soldier. Dust rose as they wrestled on the ground. From the dust rose a triumphant Sergeant Robinson, holding the bad guy by the collar. The sergeant was alone and obviously had become exhausted by the chase. Hank Phillips, the X-ray tech, had been walking with me and was standing alongside me as we watched this scene unfold. Sergeant Robinson pulled out his Colt .45 pistol, cocked the hammer back, and handed the gun to a surprised Hank. "If he moves, shoot him!" the sergeant ordered Hank as he pulled on a boot he had lost in the scuffle. I couldn't tell who was more pale and shocked, Hank or the tackled soldier. The fleeing soldier was still lying where he had been tackled and his face was drained of blood as he panted. Hank and the pistol were visibly shaking. Robinson quickly retrieved his weapon, which afforded Hank the opportunity to regain some of his lost composure. By now, an MP Jeep pulled up and reinforcements were at hand. In a few seconds, the whole incident was over and the participants were gone. Hank and I laughed nervously as we continued on to lunch, both wondering if the whole thing had actually happened. Sic Semper Sergeant Robinson, quick, furious and just.

THE RAGING WAR

As the weeks rolled by, the wounding of American soldiers increased. The treatment station became a place of never-ending labor. Just as sick call ended, the Dust Off helicopters began to land with full loads of ripped and bleeding bodies. Sometimes, huge Chinook helicopters came down and spewed out as many as twenty wounded at a time. Marines, Navy Riverine men, and ARVN troops were dropped on our doorstep by means of all sorts of vehicles to have their wounds cleansed of metal shards and the debris of combat. Special Forces men would walk in from places they weren't supposed to talk about. These members of the vaunted Green Berets had war wounds as well as tropical diseases that came from camping for months at a time in hostile jungles. They offhand-edly mentioned places like Laos and Cambodia, only to clam up when I inquired further.

Sometimes we three doctors had to work twenty-four hours to-gether, leaving one doctor to handle the next morning's sick call all by himself. The other two got a few hours of fitful sleep listening to the continuous hammering of outgoing artillery barrages. As I would fall asleep, I tried to imagine the poor grunts being shot at for days and weeks on end. If they could do it, I could too. Short Round and his crew thoughtfully brought food and coffee to the aid station when they saw we hadn't shown up for chow. They knew what we were going through, and they wanted to help as much as they could. This was a medical company destined to treat the sick and wounded GIs. The whole company went about their business with a tireless esprit I will always be proud of. I used to imagine relatives back home watching us take care of their loved ones. That gave me a per-spective that urged me on when I was exhausted. All the men of Company D knew what had to be done, and they responded admira-bly, day in and day out. This sense of satisfaction for Company D, working beyond reasonable limits for unreasonable amounts of time, made me smile. I would think about the day's work, satisfied with what the company had done, and fall off to sleep in the wee hours of those noisy nights. I wanted all my men to get medals for what they did, but the colonel often reminded me that, "They were just doing their jobs." Yes, they were, but there should have been some consideration for the care they gave their fellow man. They had unflagging devotion, binding up wounds, getting wounded soldiers off to recovery, or back to duty, healed, and ready to fight some more. I've never really seen devotion like that in the medical profession since. To this day, I remain proud to have been a part of that dedicated team. Not only the conscientious objectors of Company D hated the war, we all did. We were all victims of the worst fate to befall mankind, war! Providence however, afforded a unique opportunity to do some good in those worst of times, and the men of Company D performed admirably.

The tropical climate was terrible for fighting. The heat could be so bad that the whole treatment area and bunker hospital would be filled with GIs, and even K-9 patrol dogs, getting IV fluids to combat dehydration. We gathered all the ice we could find to bathe the men and dogs. A lot of beer and soda had to be imbibed warm those days, thanks to the medical company's need for ice. Most of the ice we confiscated came from the many clubs on the base. Never did we take ice used to refrigerate food. Sergeant Knoerr even got ice from the colonel's own officers' club! Imagine, enduring a martini that wasn't chilled! Joking about the brass is an age-old tradition, but the colonel and the other leaders wanted our guys to have the best. There was no questioning that. I always had a hard time understanding how military leaders could care so profoundly about the welfare of their men one day, and the next day send so many to battle, and ultimately death. I was glad I never had that job.

Our sick dog problem got so critical that Division sent us a veterinarian to help! What a great addition to our company was Dr. Bill Veck. The night he first joined us, he told us that the Army drafted vets to be inspectors of meat, kitchens, and food processing, as well as to take care of the Army's K-9 forces. The Army used dogs as point men, sniffers of booby traps such as land mines, and in attacks. These dogs were magnificent. We all took childlike glee in petting and loving them whenever we could. Their soldier handlers were special folks, like parents, very concerned about their child's health and welfare. Having a vet to help in their care, the dogs thrived. Bill was much more qualified to treat dog diseases than we were. The great difference in outcome was soon appreciated by the dog's handlers.

One day Bill came into the hooch lugging a long, heavy, olive-drab metal container. He had been inspecting meat for the brigade, when he spotted a case of nice steaks! He confiscated them because, he said, they were contaminated with pseudomonas bacteria. He pointed out a streak of green slime on the meat to the mess sergeant who nodded in agreement. Actually, there was no green slime, but Bill had the knack of making people agree with him, even to the extent of seeing things that weren't there! That night our patients and the men of Company D were treated to a huge steak fry. The motor pool guys made a great barbecue grill from the ever-useful fifty-five-gallon drums. The smell of steaks cooking on an outdoor barbecue was irresistible. That was one of many barbecues we enjoyed using Dr. Veck's condemned meat. Word got out that if you got wounded, try to go Company D. You might be eating barbecued steak for dinner. Those steaks lent a touch of home that warmed the hearts of our soldiers so far from the USA.

Dr. Veck would often come back from the field with all sorts of snakes, monkeys, and rats. He especially liked snakes, and, like Art Lewis with his bugs, Bill Veck was in snake heaven in Vietnam. Of the twenty-six varieties of Vietnamese snakes, twenty-four were poisonous! Any snake spotted was killed on the spot. The worst of all the snakes was the king cobra. Cobras in Vietnam got to be huge, and their bites were excruciatingly painful and deadly. I treated a single cobra bite during my tour in Vietnam. Jumping out of a hovering helicopter, a Kit Carson scout landed on the back of an eight-foot-long cobra. Kit Carson scouts were NVA soldiers who had come over to our side and had been trained to find their old comrades for the US Army. These scouts often led our forces on attacks. Naturally, the cobra promptly bit the scout, sinking its long fangs deep into the flesh of the scout's calf. Immediately the scout began to scream in overwhelming pain! The cobra was quickly dispatched on the spot with a bayonet, and the screaming scout was transported right back to us in the same helicopter from which he had jumped.

On arrival, I gave him a healthy dose of morphine for his pain. I also gave him intravenous steroids and anti-serum (anti-venom made from horse serum) in hopes of arresting the damage of the snake's venom. Unfortunately, he still screamed constantly. His leg began to turn blue and harden spreading from the fang marks on his calf upwards towards his thigh. I needed help. Since the scout was Vietnamese, I had to go through their medical system. True to the past, I was advised to give him plenty of morphine, and I wasn't to bother to send him to their hospital. He was going to die and they couldn't help. Since death was a foregone conclusion, the Vietnamese ritual was to place the stricken victim of a cobra bite in the shade and then walk away. There, the victim would scream, awaiting his fate of a painful death in three or four hours. Not being Vietnamese, I had a different plan. After all, this man had been given the anti-venom and steroids. Surely he had a chance. Dr. Veck was on the scene and didn't have anything to add to what had been done already. We contemplated a hurried amputation of the bitten leg, but I wanted to give the anti-serum a chance to work. The anti-venom came from the World Red Cross and was made in India. Our batch was over five years old but should still have been effective. Housed in an old glass plasma bottle, the serum itself was a desiccated mass of brownish conglomerated powder inside the container. I reconstituted the powder with saline, creating a solution that looked just like a chocolate milk shake! Bill reassured us although he had never handled anti-venom before, "that's the way it should look!" I administered the anti-serum intravenously over a thirty-minute time period following the instructions that came in the package with the bottle. I felt sorry for the scout being surrounded by all these Americans, so I transferred him to the Vietnamese hospital in Saigon. The Dust Off crew flew him to Saigon promptly. That poor man never stopped crying from pain on the thirty-minute trip The Vietnamese doctors in Saigon told the Dust Off crew they would keep the man very comfortable. They hoped the anti-serum would kick in, and he would live. I never heard another thing about that unlucky man. Although, there were many horrible ways to die in Vietnam in 1968, this had to have been one of the worst.

Bamboo vipers and banded kraits were abundant in the fields and jungles. I was surprised more soldiers didn't get killed by them. Bill invited a herpetologist friend to stay with us for a week. The herpetologist taught us a lot about snakes, and, most importantly, how to treat their bites. During the week he was with us, a soldier was bitten by a bamboo viper and lived! The snake was identified as a bamboo viper, "Old Two-Step," by our resident snake specialist. After having been bitten, the victim would usually walk two steps and then fall over dead. That didn't happen to this patient, and, despite losing a fingertip, he did well. He also got some funky-looking anti-venom intravenously, as well as massive doses of steroids. He was discharged "fit for duty" after two weeks with us.

The Army was worried about rabies. Cases of rats infected with rabies were being found in the mid-section of Vietnam, and Bill Veck was given the task of looking for rabid rats in Tay Ninh. Soldiers would nibble on snacks while on guard duty at the perimeter. The remnants of the food would attract rats, and the cobras would follow the rats. Bill had set "have-a-heart traps" in strategic places around the berm. These traps would catch the animals live, which was important when searching for rabies. Bill killed the captured rats by a lethal injection, sending their heads to a lab in Saigon. The rabid rats would have black spots, known as "negri bodies," found deep in their brains. If rabies were found in local rats, a plan of eradication was to be implemented. The first step would be to trap rats, and Bill was hot on the trail.

One day one of Bill's rat traps held a very angry mongoose in it. The mongoose was a brown weasel-like animal, about the size of a big house cat. A mongoose liked to eat the snakes, that preyed upon the rats, that ate the food the GIs left behind. The trapped mongoose was very unhappy being caught in Bill's trap, and his growls sounded very threatening. Bill was deliberating how to free the mongoose when the medic Bill had borrowed from the aid station spoke up. "Stand back, I'll handle this!" he said as John Wayne might have in the same situation. The medic then fired a full clip from his M-16 rifle directly into the cage. With his mouth open down to his knees in disbelief, Bill saw only blood and fur left in the bullet-riddled cage! Needless to say, Bill was justifiably angry with the frightened medic, and his new assistant was never allowed to carry a rifle after that. Specifically, Bill was concerned the mongoose could have had rabies and now there was no mongoose head left to examine. Although no rabies were found in the rats Bill trapped, rabies was still all around in Asian rats. Bill felt obligated to order no more eating while on guard duty. His edict caused more grumbling than he ever imagined, and pretty soon hunger won out. Bill stopped his rat trapping, soldiers ate on guard duty, and the rats thrived. No rabies was ever reported in Tay Ninh.

One afternoon, a very tall and skinny soldier came to our hooch with a frenetic monkey on a leash riding on one of his master's broad shoulders. Knowing this couldn't be for me, I yelled for Bill. The soldier wanted to bring the monkey home with him next week. The monkey had been getting handouts from the soldier's outfit, and he became great friends with this guy. The soldier wanted Bill to give his monkey shots so the monkey could return to the States with him. Bill knew just what shots were needed, and he soon had them ready. Thinking the monkey would never hold still for the shots, I stuck around to watch the show. Bill assured me and the monkey's owner there would be no sweat. He had given monkeys shots before, and he thought the task was a piece of cake. I settled in to observe the whole thing from my vantage point at the central table. The soldier held the jumpy monkey for Bill to inject. The instant the needle penetrated his dermis, that monkey went into orbit. In a heartbeat, he was screaming and jumping from rafter to rafter up in the hooch's roof with the leash dangling and giving away his hiding place. Each time he screamed, ferocious-looking teeth were bared, making the animal look more like a big baboon than a small monkey. More determined than ever, Bill yanked the monkey down from the rafters by pulling on the leash. Then he and the soldier took off chasing that monkey all over the hooch. The screams of the now-crazed monkey and the shouts of the chasing men attracted a crowd. Instinctively, many of the men came armed. Afraid this melee was going to turn into a shooting match, I quickly gave up my vantage point and exited the back door. That observant, smart monkey saw me leave, and realized the door was his only way out. He bounded outside through the back door right behind me. Bill, the soldier, and the spectators followed in hot pursuit, rushing by me down the street towards the aid station. Later, when Bill returned, he was covered with scratches and his shirt was torn in several places. He looked emotionally spent and physically drained. He told me they had not been able to catch the monkey, who had climbed the company flagpole in front of our aid station. His soldier/master was still trying to coax him down with a banana. Bill lost interest and left. At times like those, I was very glad I didn't become a veterinarian! I had the pleasure of Dr. Bill Veck's company for several months, but when, for some unknown reason, the K-9 outfits were moved out of our area, Bill went with them. While he was with us, however, things were never boring, and he sure earned his keep.

SNIPPETS FROM TAY NINH

I had many memorable encounters with wounded and sick GIs that year in Vietnam. Although I hoped to remember most of those events, I know I didn't. Those that I am able to recall may still shed some frail light on the truth of what actually happened over there. From watching movies and reading books, I see the public's image of the American soldier in Vietnam as one of an intoxicated, marijuana-smoking, bloodthirsty, ignorant, and over-sexed murderer. When I was with the 25th Med in Tay Ninh, I did not encounter the soldier described above. Through my work as a physician, I saw thousands of soldiers of all ranks, privates to generals, and from most branches of the military, as well as Department of Defense workers, American civilians, foreign civilians, and soldiers from many other countries, including the enemy's soldiers. I would be wrong, and very misleading, to leave the impression that most of my contacts were the likes of Mr. Penis, Montefiore, and others I have recounted in a negative light thus far. Quite the contrary, ninety-nine percent of the men I encountered, including the enemy, were principled, moral, and very caring people, placed in harm's way by their well-intentioned governments. Not to follow my country's call was not a viable or prudent option for me or the men with whom I came in contact. We were accepting, fatalistic men who would rather have had that terrible cup pass. Of course, the cup didn't pass, and most of us did what had to be done.

Following are a few stories I remember about some of the people I encountered personally while a doctor in the aid station of Company D, 25th Medical Battalion in Tay Ninh Province from mid-October 1968 to mid April 1969. These snippets are not in any particular order.

A twenty-year-old combat soldier had experienced an annoying canker sore in his mouth for over a month. At first, his sergeant was understandably reluctant to allow him to fly to Tay Ninh from their position way out in the field for such a trivial complaint. The battalion surgeon had examined the patient in the field and had prescribed penicillin in the hopes that the drug would do the trick. When it didn't, the battalion surgeon sent the soldier to be seen at Company D. The day the soldier arrived in Tay Ninh, the aid station was very busy with wounded soldiers interrupting the morning's sick call flow on two occasions. I didn't get to see the soldier until after lunch. When I examined him, I saw a very small, half-centimeter ulceration between his gum and cheek which looked just like an irritated canker sore. The soldier told me he had noticed the sore over thirty days ago, and that he had already been treated with penicillin. My interest was piqued. Since there had not been any response to the antibiotics in the recent past, I decided to remove the sore surgically. Using local anesthesia, I cut out the area in question, and repaired the defect with dissolving sutures. What I removed, I sent to the pathologist in Saigon. Having removed what was bothering him, I sent my young patient back to his field unit with instructions to check back with me about the test results in two weeks. Saying he would with slurred speech from the anesthetic, the soldier went off in the direction of the PX. In a few days, I received a telephone call from the pathologist in Saigon. Amid the static and operator interruptions I heard the word "cancer!" There was malignancy in the lining of the cheek! A type of cancer called an adenocarcinoma, the tumor was formed by the tiny mucous glands lining the cheek of the mouth. Never having seen a similar case, my instincts warned me this was a very bad thing. I tried to contact him in the field. I was frustrated at every step and gave up trying to contact him by phone. His company was out on patrol so I had Brigade Headquarters call him right away. If they couldn't reach him by radiophone, the command sergeant major assured me he would send a messenger out that very day. At dinner that night, I discussed his case with Charlie and Marty, and we all agreed this was a very rare tumor in such a young patient. The Dust Off pilot at the dinner table heard the story. He wanted to fly out that night to retrieve the soldier. I thanked him, and suggested I would take him up on his offer if I didn't hear anything by the morning. I couldn't help thinking of the tragic possibility that the Dust Off helicopter might crash in the jungle at night trying to pick up this soldier for something that could have waited until the next day.

The next morning, the soldier's outfit notified me the patient was on his way into Tay Ninh! I saw him later that same morning. Telling this now suspecting and very anxious soldier he had cancer of the mouth was very difficult for me, but I was able to stammer through. He took the bad news fairly well. Smiling, he said, "The ulcer was gone, cured!" I saw nothing but a tiny scar where the offending ulcer had been. No doubt the excisional site had healed, but the cancer could still be in the surrounding tissues. I felt obligated to send him back stateside for further consideration. "Fine with me!" he said, and I made arrangements to send him to the tumor clinic at Walter Reed Hospital in Washington, D.C. Of course, I never heard of him again. The decision to do the biopsy was fortunate and the fact that the specimen wasn't lost was providential. Hopefully, he did well.

GIs were always cutting and nicking themselves, creating small openings through which any one of thousands of bacteria could enter their bodies. The inflammation caused by the invading bacteria in the subcutaneous tissues around the cut is termed "cellulitis." Most cases of cellulitis are caused by the streptococcus bacteria which was, and still is, extremely sensitive to plain old penicillin. One day, I saw a young soldier who had an area of tender redness around his right elbow. Because of a fever of 101 degrees Fahrenheit, I admitted him to our hospital for intravenous penicillin. I ordered the penicillin be given intravenously rather than by mouth, a standard treatment of cellulitis with a high fever. The next morning, I visited him in the bunker ward on rounds. Standing, he was intent on making his bed. I couldn't help noticing the IV fluid was white, not colorless, as it should have been. The pure white fluid running into his vein suggested an error. He was getting procaine penicillin used for intramuscular injections, rather than the plain penicillin manufactured for intravenous use. Procaine penicillin obviously had procaine in it, which was novocaine, an anesthetic used to dull the pain pure penicillin causes when injected into a muscle. Procaine was dangerous when administered intravenously, causing cardiac irregularities.

I corrected the problem and began to administer the proper form of penicillin intravenously. The cellulitis seemed slightly better, and he was now without any fever. His heart action was normal despite the procaine he had received. Taking his blood pressure, I noted it was now 80/60, having been 120/80 all night. I thought the low blood pressure was an indication of a worsening infection, which was causing septic shock. There was an internist at the 45th Evac across the street and I asked him to see my patient. The internist agreed the patient was critically infected, and he suggested we transfer him to the Third Field Hospital in Saigon where an infectious disease specialist could take care of him.

That same morning, he was flown to the hospital in Saigon by our Dust Off helicopter. When he left us, his blood pressure was back to normal, and the patient himself said he felt "fine!" The next day, to my amazement, I heard that the patient had died! A rare and deadly infection was suspected to be the culprit, but confirmation was pending. The ID specialist was sure this was a rare form of a pseudomonas cellulitis and would advise me of the culture results when he got them back from the lab. I never heard the final outcome of those tests, and I never saw another similar case. All my subsequent cases of cellulitis got better quickly on IV penicillin. Vietnam held mysterious diseases unknown to modern medicine, and this had certainly been one.

Calling someone a coward who ran during an enemy attack was difficult for me to understand. The strongest instinct of man has to be self-preservation. Running from certain death seems only natural, and at times must be a very wise thing to do. At the time of the American involvement in Vietnam, the term "cowardice" had been replaced with the more medically correct terminology, "battle fatigue." At Fort Sam Houston, we were taught most soldiers who became too frightened to fight were to be given every consideration. They invariably recovered and eventually could be returned to their units. The fighting was intense in the areas surrounding Tay Ninh when I was there. The large numbers of dead and wounded attested to that fact. Grunts were being pushed to the limits of human tolerance, day in and day out. One night, I witnessed a case of "battle fatigue," and I quickly became pleased with the Army's handling of this condition.

Company D had been working on wounded GIs most of the night. A battalion of NVA attacked a small American infantry firebase near Trang Bang. The fighting had been fierce. Starting just before sunset, rocket-propelled grenades pounded the small defensive bunkers created earlier that day. Mortars thudded in, and the enemy riflefire was deadly that evening. Eleven KIAs were waiting for me to tag that night, but I would do that grisly task only after the living had been tended to. At two in the morning, I was very relieved to see all the wounded had finally been treated. Although the aid station was still crowded with wounded GIs and medics, the worst of the night's work was over, for now at least.

Lurch saw that I was not actively treating anyone at this point, and he advised me a soldier who had been "lightly" wounded was still sitting outside, waiting his turn. Lurch brought him in for me to see. The new patient took a seat on a stretcher next to a severely wounded GI who was being readied to go to the bunker ward. Sitting on the stretcher, I noticed Lurch's new patient seemed nervous and very ill at ease. He was fully dressed, so I asked him where he had been wounded. He pulled at his unbloodied shirtsleeve and began to sob. Tears came as he told me he had climbed aboard the Dust Off chopper just to get away from the fight. He told the medic on the helicopter he had a frag wound of his arm, which he deftly covered with his other hand to hide his phony wound. The Dust Off crew had seriously wounded soldiers to care for. He was taken at his word, and no one examined him. He was dropped off on our doorstep with the other wounded soldiers. Triaged by our medics, he was asked to wait for his turn outside on the benches placed there for the "walking wounded."

With no wound to show me, he was now busted. Remembering another case I had once, I did examine his head to make sure he didn't have a small dink there. In the recent past, I had seen a soldier who had been near an incoming rocket explosion and helped bring in his comrades who were wounded by that same rocket. That soldier didn't sign in to be seen himself, never realizing he had been wounded. After his buddies were taken care of, he began to cry, not knowing why. I examined his head and took an X-ray. Inside his skull was a tiny metal fragment, probably from that nearby exploding rocket. I finally did find the entrance wound made by the fragment, and subsequently sent him to a neurosurgeon. The point is, a soldier could have a tiny fragment wound and not even know he had been hit. I wanted to be sure my current sobbing soldier didn't have a hidden wound. He did not.

Now the poor guy was sobbing so hard that he was shaking. He had deserted his friends while under fire. Absolutely the worst thing that could happen to an infantryman had happened to him, and he was mortified. Running away from the fight by boarding the Dust Off flight was a reactive, impulsive action. Now he wished he had never fled. I tried to reassure him that he reacted the way many other guys do in the same situation, but he wouldn't buy into my consolation. He sobbed less violently after he told me his story and heard what I had to say. I thought he was terribly embarrassed now, both to be found out by us in the presence of his brave wounded buddies and to have to face going back to the buddies he left at the front. The latter seemed worse. He needed absolution from someone, somewhere, and a pardon came from the severely wounded soldier next to him. Hearing all that was said by the battle-fatigued soldier, the bloodied soldier lit a cigarette, as if on some supernatural cue, and offered a smoke to his sobbing buddy. The lighting of a cigarette for the frightened soldier was a conciliatory offer, and then the wounded grunt said, "Rough out there, wasn't it?" The crying lessened when the battle-fatigued soldier saw the proffered cigarette and realized the forgiving implications. Nervously wiping his tearing eyes with his dirty hands, causing a black smudge, the fatigued soldier responded nodding, "It was hell!" Beginning to loosen up now, he took a big drag on his Marlboro, and went on. "I was in a forward foxhole about fifty yards out from our perimeter listening for the enemy when the attack came. I had to 'dee dee mau' hot and low back to our lines! I emptied my M-16 as I ran." He was getting more excited now, as he remembered and as he went on. Listening intently, I got goose bumps hearing what had just happened to these guys. "I had to dive over the goddammed concertina wire as Sergeant Lee was about to fire the claymores! He saw me coming and waited until I got in, and then all hell broke loose. An RPG must have followed me in, because as I went to thank Lee, he was dead! I fired those claymores, and then ran back towards the center of the base. I heard the helicopter, saw the green smoke, and—and," he faltered and stopped talking. Tears welled again, clearing white lines in the dry smudge on his cheek.

"Shit, you were lucky to make it back from that foxhole, nice going," the wounded soldier said, breaking the silence. The wounded soldier went on, "God, I hate those f------ RPGs." The crying soldier nodded in agreement, and the two looked down at the floor. "What a story!" I thought to myself. Truly, it must have been pure hell out there. I was sure I would have boarded the helicopter myself! Nothing else was being said, and being afraid guilt feelings were going to reappear, I told those two in a paternal way to "pipe down!" The medics took the two soldiers to see Sergeant Thomas in the bunker ward where they would stay the night. I said I would be by to see them in a little while. The battle-fatigued soldier took one end of the stretcher that held his wounded friend, and with a medic on the other end, off they went down the stairs into the ward. About an hour later, after all the KIAs had been examined and carded, I made "goodnight" rounds on the soldiers I had admitted that night. Carding those KIAs had been grisly. That must have been one hell of a fight out there, judging by those mangled bodies. The RPGs and AK-47 rifles of the enemy did effective jobs on our boys that night.

The two soldiers were still talking when I came by their bunks. The unwounded guy was fully dressed and jumped up when he saw me. "I'm ready to go back, Sir," he snapped. He was smiling. His new friend suggested he stay the night, but he said he would be needed back at the firebase more than ever, so, if it was all the same to Captain Snider, he wanted to try to get back tonight. Turning, he shook the hand of his friend and uttered a "Thanks, man!" with a now cracking voice. That had to have been the most sincere thank you I had ever witnessed. "Keep your head down," came the reply from his wounded buddy as the resolute soldier climbed out of the bunker ward to meet his fate that night. I followed him outside. There was a helicopter belonging to his company parked just outside the aid station. They had dropped off more KIAs for me to tag. That helicopter took him back to the base with them when they returned. I watched the chopper lift off and burn its way into the dark jungle night. The battle-fatigued soldier had been rendered whole again with a cigarette and the caring support of a comrade who had the experience to realize the magnitude of the fear of battle and the kind wisdom to help his buddy who had been temporarily overcome by that fear.

Soldiers at the front fight for their buddies, and not for any political reasons. Being part of a team allows men to face the dangers of war and gives them the strength to persist. A man alone is more likely to surrender than if just one other buddy is left alive. Most GIs don't realize a bond of love develops between men in battle. Even if a GI realized this bond existed, male pride wouldn't allow him to admit to it. This bond was a very powerful force. One night after a battle out in the field, our treatment area was once again filled with wounded men. One soldier had died on the way in, before anyone had seen him, and his body was placed along a side wall of the aid station, out of the way of rushing medics and doctors. As I was debriding a wound on a wounded soldier, I was positioned beside that corpse that night. A fully clothed and armed GI burst through the open front door. Lurch was up and right behind him in an instant. Lurch hesitated a second, then backed away a few steps. The sweating and out-of-breath soldier stood behind me along the flank of the dead man. Looking up, I could see tears streaming down his face. Kneeling alongside the body of his slain comrade, the soldier buried his forehead in his grimy hand and sobbed. After a minute, not having uttered a word, he grasped the arm of his dead friend and said in a low, composed voice, "See you on the other side." Standing up, he wiped his face, and looking dejectedly down at the floor, walked out of the aid station with heavy steps. I'm not sure, but I think I saw a tear in Lurch's eye. The soldier I was working on began to cry. "We lost a lot of good men out there tonight, why?" he asked. I tried to say something, but not finding my voice, I just kept on working. I had no right to speak anyway. Only these men had earned the right to question fate with "why them?" There was no answer to that question. Later that night, Lurch and I had a discussion about the profound faith that soldier expressed with his words, "See you on the other side." We agreed he must have ardently believed in a heaven for fallen soldiers, and by what he did and what he said, he had expressed his faith better than any gifted preacher ever could have. After the last of the wounded had been cared for, we examined that dead body with new-found reverence. I found myself saying a prayer for him and for his buddy who had lived. The encounter I witnessed that night touched me deeply, and helped me to shore up the little war-shocked faith I had left.

I was always amazed at how polite the wounded soldiers were back then in Vietnam. Hosing down a naked nineteen-year-old soldier was a very cold thing to do to him, but necessary, so his wounds could be clearly seen and examined by us. The thick jungle mud and crusted blood could obscure large wounds, and we didn't want to miss any of them. After dousing the soldiers, they would shiver from the cold water, and the cold night air, not to mention the loss of blood. Always polite, they would smile despite their grave wounds as I approached, and, above all else, they would answer with a "Sir" on their trembling blue lips. I found it impossible not to admire and become very fond of men like that. Most of the wounded GIs hadn't a single entry in their medical records when I saw them. They never complained. They demonstrated profound courage by genuine smiles and politeness despite incredible pain and shock. They always impressed me as truly being a great group of men. Before they were wounded, they only wanted to do their duty and just go home. When wounded, they accepted their fate with a dignity I didn't believe was even possible. Life afforded me quite an honor when I was allowed to care for those wounded men. Such unexpected courage was not only seen in our guys but in the enemy also. I will never forget tending a wounded NVA captain. He was a Di Wi also and was probably my age. His eyes politely told me he would kill me if he had a chance. Despite the hot day, he was shivering. He was clad only in short black pants. He was thin and muscular, and he had one small frag wound on his calf. I debrided it, removing a small piece of metal from his subcutaneous tissue. This wound was not deep enough to make him as ill as he appeared. The Army Intelligence people wanted to take him, but I needed more tests. After a heated discussion with the Combat Intelligence Division (CID for short), I prevailed. Fortunately, not even the CID could go against medical orders. I ordered a malaria smear and waited the thirty minutes for Bill Adler to complete the test.

Using Mae Lin to interpret for me, I spent the half-hour it took for the test to talk with this man. I found he had walked all the way from Haiphong to Tay Ninh, a distance of approximately 1,500 miles! Unlike me, no commercial airliner had brought him to his war; he had to walk! His only remaining possession was a small wallet. Producing a picture from it, he showed Mae Lin and me his wife and children. He told us he missed them a lot. Tears welled up in his keen, dark eyes as he talked about his family. Someday, he said, he would get to see them again. Our conversation had begun to draw a crowd, and those gathered around were very quiet after Mae Lin told us what he had said about seeing his family again. All of us wanted him to get his wish. He smiled a brave smile and lay back, still shivering. Washington gave him a blanket. The CID soldier said, "No! No blankets," and pulled the cover off the prisoner. I piped up and said, "Yes, he needs that blanket!" Washington gave it back to the prisoner and leveled a menacing glance at the CID man. CID personnel wore no rank insignia and we didn't know whether we were dealing with a private or an officer. Washington was very indignant at the CID's lack of concern for this man's obvious illness and probably would have punched him if only he could be sure the CID man was of a lesser rank. Mumbling to himself, Washington eased off, more content now that the prisoner had the blanket.

Adler walked over and advised me that the prisoner had two types of malaria, falciparum and ovale. Washington had taken the prisoner's temperature, which registered 105 degrees Fahrenheit! I ordered an intravenous infusion of two drugs and gave him pills to take with him. Mae Lin told me in a whisper that the CID guards would probably take his pills away. I continued the IV meds, knowing they couldn't take those away from him. The prisoner Di Wi stayed with us for another eight hours until his fever broke, and we were sure the quinine had a chance to work. Reluctantly, I turned him back over to the CID people, and he was whisked away for more interrogation. There was no doubt, brave men existed on both sides of this war. I prayed my prisoner patient eventually got back to see his family.

Our bunker ward could hold as many as forty wounded and sick patients, and did much of the time. The more seriously wounded were sent on to special hospitals in country, or evacuated out of country to places like Japan, the Philippines, or the United States. The bulk of Company D's patients just needed a few days to heal and would recover in the bunker ward hospital. The patients on the ward increased the number of men in the company to be fed. The large cooking team we had struggled at times to keep up with the 5,000 calories the Army said each man required per day. Our patients were easily spotted walking about the company area in the distinctive sky-blue pajamas they had been issued as patients. They could wander around as much as they liked, and they often ate in the mess hall to get away from the damp and smelly bunker. They would buy beer or soda pop in the EM club. If they didn't have any money, Sergeant Knoerr saw to it that they got what they wanted. They would easily devour one of the sergeant's BLTs, or linger over pizza and beer, talking about the girls they left back home. Our nightly volleyball games attracted many of the hospital patients as spectators, and they always cheered for the enlisted men rather than the officers and NCOs. The officers always lost. No one ever felt the least bit sorry for the officer underdogs, but we didn't mind. After the volleyball game each night, a movie was shown by our company in the volleyball court. There were many titles available in the cinema library, but the movie most requested was "The Green Berets," starring John Wayne. These battle-hardened veterans were something to watch as they hooted and hollered at the scenes in that movie. I'll never understand how they could tolerate watching a Vietnam War movie, let alone love it. Although our patients took a lot of Company D's time and energy, there were never any complaints from the men.

Soldiers in Vietnam had to get used to the fact that there were no defined front lines. The enemy was everywhere, hiding in tunnels, in jungle bunkers, and even masked as citizens walking down the main streets. GIs learned the best opportunity to encounter and destroy the enemy was with nighttime ambushes. Ambushes at night were also the major plan of the NVA and the VC. Two events stand out in my memory as being particularly sad. The first story was that of an eighteen-year-old rookie infantryman who had told his buddies many times that the enemy was simply misunderstood. All an American soldier had to do was to explain to them their faulty reasoning. Hearing the logic of the explanation, they would lay down their arms. None of his platoon members took him seriously. They thought he was just kidding, or crazy. One night, on patrol, an American ambush was set up, and, for his first time, he saw actual enemy soldiers walking down the trail his platoon had been watching. Accounts of that night came from surviving platoon buddies who were very angry. These soldiers said that the soldier with all the answers stood up, abruptly calling out, "Hey, you guys! Let's talk!" The patrol's ambush position given away, the enemy he had hoped to "talk to," stitched him across his middle with machine gun fire, killing him instantly. The resultant firefight wounded several of his platoon-mates, who were the ones telling me the sad story.

Equally as sad was the problem of "friendly fire." I took care of several groups of wounded soldiers in Tay Ninh who were accidentally ambushed by their own soldiers. Friendly fire was an unfortunate reality of the stealthy ambush fighting seen in Vietnam. This story was even more ironic because the friendly fire that killed one soldier was his own. His friends told me the nineteen-year-old was very gung-ho. He thought of himself as John Wayne. One bright day his patrol received small-arms fire from a village hut, pinning the American patrol down. Rather than endure the bullets spitting all around, our man wanted to charge the hut. With infantry hand signals his sergeant gave him the OK, and the eager soldier ran up to the straw hooch, flattening his back to the wall. Pulling out the grenade pin with his teeth, he lobbed the smoking oval through the open front door of that hut. The explosion followed, and he fell mortally wounded from his own grenade shrapnel. The one fact he failed to consider was that the straw wall of the village hut couldn't stop the exploding grenade fragments from killing him. The grenade toss seen in multiple war movies proved lethal to this thrower. The shaken platoon sergeant who related the story to me shook his head and said, "That's sure one tough way to learn."

The Third Brigade Headquarters base camp at Tay Ninh was in the thick of the war in 1968-9, receiving incoming rocket and mortar fire almost daily. The nightly bombardment exacted quite a toll of men's lives and made the survivors very jumpy. Recognizing the sound of incoming shells from the many outgoing salvos was never an easy task. No real veteran of incoming barrages considered reacting defensively to mistaken sounds of danger in any way cowardly. My hooch had a dog we had inherited from our ancestors, and her name was "Short Round," the same as the mess hall sergeant. We called her "Round," dropping the "Short." She was very friendly, loved to play, and always gave us her undying love and devotion. She loved Marty the most, probably because he spent the most time with her. Marty first recognized "Round" would whimper when a mortar or rocket had been fired and was headed in. She had the unique ability to hear a shell headed towards us long before our human ears could pick up those sounds. First she would nervously whine and then quickly scamper under my bunk to hide. Becoming aware of Round's early warning capabilities, we reacted to her whines and whimpers ourselves by violently scrambling into our bunker at the first hint of Round's unrest. Round was always correct when it came to identifying incoming, and many times we were safely under cover when the incoming rounds exploded. Round herself, however, refused to venture into our bunker, and no one could

Short Round had her own "dog tags"

This dog saved our lives

ever guess why. Once, fearing for the dog's life, Marty dragged her into the bunker with him. In her struggle to get away, she growled and tried to bite him. When Marty released her, she bounded up the stairs to hide under my bunk, her favorite spot for waiting out the enemy barrages.

A sound that most mimicked the whine of an incoming rocket was that of a deuce-and-a-half truck's transmission in low gear, slowing down. There was a crossroad in front of our aid station, complete with an olive-drab octagonal "Stop" sign. When big trucks geared down to stop at that sign, the noise was so convincing that GIs would hit the dirt. If one GI decided the truck whine was the sound of incoming and he hit the ground, others joined him by diving for the shallow trenches alongside the dirt road. When the truck rolled away from the stop sign, the soldiers would arise in disgust, swatting the dust and mud from their clothes, realizing their mistake. No words were spoken, and no one dared to make fun of the reaction to the false alarm. Deciding what was the sound of incoming was serious business, and only the foolish wouldn't react.

Hal Shields, our dentist, almost took off his head one time. In a scramble to get into our bunker during an enemy incoming attack, Hal didn't duck fast enough, hitting his chin and neck on the pipe between the hooches. Afterwards, he developed a moderate sized bruise beneath his chin on the front of his neck causing a hoarse voice for a while. At the recognition of that terrible sound of incoming rounds, all caution was abandoned by those seeking shelter. Besides Hal, I saw serious injuries from those frantic searches for shelter during incoming. The worst were broken bones and lacerations, but they were nothing to the wounds and deaths caused by those "zingers" from the sky.

One beautiful morning, I was shaving in the Tom Zinn Memorial Shower Room. As I rinsed the lather from my face, I thought I heard a round exploding inside the base camp's perimeter. There were a lot of other noises from outgoing artillery, trucks, and helicopters that morning, so I didn't think more about it. I sauntered over to the aid station just as Brandenberg and Washington were putting a soldier on a stretcher onto sawhorses. They had just made an ambulance run to pick up a soldier from another base camp company who had been hit by an incoming rocket this beautiful morning. As they lifted their patient onto the sawhorses, they said they feared he was probably dead. They were right! Looking at that unlucky GI, I saw he was shirtless and that he had shaving cream on his face. Only a single rocket had been fired into our base that gorgeous morning, but enough to snuff out his life as he shaved. I reflected on the possibility of my body lying there! The sound I heard that morning must have been the rocket that killed this soldier. We had both been shaving at the same time. I had been lucky and spared, but he wasn't. Was that all that sustained life: luck? If true, when was my turn to be unlucky? Those kinds of thoughts unnerved me, so I tried to put them out of my mind. I'd go crazy dwelling on them. The crazy reality was that luck was indeed the determining factor of survival. So far, no one in Company D had been "unlucky," but that was about to change.

The evenings in Vietnam were pleasant because a cool breeze would arise and start to blow away the oppressive heat of the day. After dinner, we would stretch out, shirtless, on our hooch's corrugated tin roof and bask in those cool evening breezes. From this elevated vantage point, there was an unobstructed view of the Black Virgin Mountain, which loomed dark into the starry sky. Flares, shot from our mortars on the berm, floated lazily back down to earth illuminating the base camp's perimeter, hoping to expose any creeping enemy to the scrutiny of our machine guns. The flares created a beautiful halo of light in the dark night air as they floated down to earth. Every once in a while, a light would click on, halfway up the mountainside. Any light on the mountainside had to belong to the enemy. We owned the top of that huge mountain, the ARVNS occupied its base, and the enemy owned the sides. As we watched, a helicopter gunship would soon appear spewing mini-gun fire onto the previously lighted spot. When the light would go out, the helicopter would eventually fly off. All would be quiet for a little while. Then, rudely, the light would click back on! The whole process would then be repeated. This cat and mouse game with the mountain light happened often and was actually fun to watch. The scary thing to realize was just how close the enemy was, and we couldn't eradicate him. Charley was just thumbing his nose at the American giant, and the giant couldn't stop him.

From the vantage point of the hooch roof, I could easily see the "Snoopy" plane as it rained its deadly fire onto the hapless enemy below hiding around our perimeter. Flying at one thousand feet, or even lower, this converted propeller cargo plane would bank to one side, and through opened side doors stick out several mini-guns. A machine gun sounded like a "rat-a-tat-tat," while a mini-gun had a constant roar. The plane's mini-gun, developed during the Civil War by R. J. Gatling, was a circle of eight or more barrels that rotated, filling their barrels with cartridges at the top of the circle and firing them at the bottom. The mini-guns could also fire twenty-millimeter rockets at the same speed. Snoopy was very impressive to watch, but sobering when considering the death it dealt. When all those bullets and rockets hit the jungle floor, fire and smoke welled up from below with a fury straight from hell.

One night, while on the roof, I saw an enemy 37.5-millimeter anti-aircraft gun fire back at a departing Snoopy gunship. That was a mistake! The whole area where the anti-aircraft gun had been, exploded in the return fire from the Snoopy ship. The next morning at the daily brigade briefing, I saw pictures of the captured weapon. The enemy had pulled that big gun through the jungle down the Ho Chi Minh Trail and probably only got to shoot it once! The anti-aircraft gun was only one of many weapons positioned to strike at Tay Ninh. The enemy had hidden all kinds of large weapons throughout the hamlets and in camouflaged jungle bunkers. This was very remarkable since the enemy was harassed day and night by our determined and experienced troops. Yet enemy attacks were coming more often and with greater force. I always thought the enemy meant business and was bound and determined to win this war.

The Black Virgin Mountain, Nui Ba Den, was honeycombed with tunnels and was used by both the Japanese and the Vietnamese during World War II. NVA troops lived in those tunnels, coming out at night to harass the ARVN bases at the bottom and the very important 25th Infantry Signal Corps' relay station on the top. Company D, 25 Med, often supplied medics to spend time with the units on the top of the mountain. I flew up to the top of that mountain on several occasions and can attest to the breathtaking beauty found there. This mountain was the only elevated land around as far as the eye could see. Jungle vegetation lined the sides of the mountain, and a large Buddhist Monastery was precariously perched on a rock outcropping halfway up one side. Practicing monks still inhabited the brightly glistening and serene monastery, which was mercifully untouched by the war. The 25th Infantry position on the mountaintop consisted of a series of bunkers in a circle around the summit. The once lush top vegetation had been burned back by infantry soldiers wanting clearer fields of fire, and by the almost daily fire-fights that took place there. Almost every night, the enemy would emerge from their tunnel sanctuaries to attack. Those particular tunnels were too close to our guys on the mountaintop. Artillery fire from our guns below would hit our men also, and couldn't be used. Consequently, the fights on the mountain top could have gone either way, except American helicopter gunships would fly up there to render precise, up-close fire on the enemy. On several occasions the American position would be overrun for a while until the helicopters would come and rout the enemy. This was yet another example of the cat-and-mouse game the enemy kept up to discourage the American troops. Morale was low for the men who had to fight and die to protect this advantageous signal position.

Our medics on the mountain switched regularly, always leaving fresh men to take over the daily duties. Once a nervous Dr. Marty Bruggerman volunteered on a whim to stay overnight at the top, and, as chance would have it, not a shot was fired. The guys on the top wanted Marty to come back more often, but he never did. Spending even one night in the combat zone up there would qualify a medic for the Combat Medic's Badge. The CMB was a coveted piece of metal signifying the wearer as a veteran of combat who served in a medical mode. This medal is usually reserved for front-line medics and is equivalent to the infantryman's Combat Infantry Badge. Most men who wore the CMB or the CIB had gone through hell to earn them, and, in my opinion, I didn't think a "one night stand" should qualify a soldier for the honor to wear the badge. Major Rogers, from Headquarters Company, the one the men called Buck Rogers, desperately wanted to get a CMB. Earning the Combat Medic's Badge would look very good on the major's military resume, and he decided to risk one night on the top of Nui Ba Den to accomplish his goal of securing the medal. Major Rogers came to Tay Ninh one day to overnight on the mountaintop. A little jumpy about leaving Cu Chi for the Tay Ninh boondocks, he settled into my hooch to spend the first night with us. As far as I knew, this was the first and only time Buck ever left Cu Chi to stay overnight at Tay Ninh or Dau Tieng, even though he was the executive officer of the Medical Battalion. That night we got blasted with incoming all night long! Rockets at first, then a long mortar barrage. Buck, who had downed a few beers earlier, was a nervous wreck. Acting the brave Tay Ninh veterans, we let Buck sleep in our bunker and consoled him from time to time. Actually, we were all scared. This was the beginning of a stepped-up enemy effort to wipe out the base at Tay Ninh. The next night Buck went up on the mountain and stayed overnight. Little happened up there that night, nothing like we had the night before down in Tay Ninh. When Buck returned the next morning, he had a cup of coffee and then "dee-dee maued" right back to Cu Chi on the first available helicopter. He got his CMB, which I thought he really didn't deserve. I never saw Major Rogers again.

Time was passing rapidly now. Thanksgiving came, and we ate turkey with all the trimmings. Sergeant Knoerr outdid himself. He arranged for a huge piece of ice to be sent from Saigon, and he carved a huge turkey from it. The sculpture was very well done and lasted quite a while, even in the tropical heat. He had been an ice carver at Fort Meade in Maryland, and he wanted to show off his skills to his Philippine friends. The Philippine government sent a group of dentists to our Tay Ninh base where they were to treat the Vietnamese civilians. The Filipino group became very friendly with our sergeant, and he had invited them to share in our Thanksgiving dinner. Sergeant Knoerr had obtained good French wine from the Michelin rubber plantation near Dau Tieng, which he set out for that sumptuous Thanksgiving dinner. When I sat down to eat that day, I could hardly believe what I saw. Let alone the slowly melting ice carving, there was good Chateau Neuf de Pape red wine served in fine wine glasses to go with the food. When I inquired how he got the wine, the good sergeant said, "No questions." In the middle of the meal, Lurch came and stole me away from my turkey dinner. There had been a helicopter crash killing several men. I was summoned to examine and card the bodies. Over in the dead shed, the fantasy I was living in the mess hall quickly evaporated. There were six "crispy critters" to tag. The six men had been burned beyond all recognition in a helicopter crash, and the sight was ghastly even to me, a seasoned veteran of viewing war dead. In order to reduce weight enough to fly, helicopters were made from an alloy of magnesium and aluminum. Magnesium was the same metal I burned in high school chemistry class. When lit with a match, magnesium burns white hot for a second then goes out. Helicopter crashes were the same. They flashed white-hot and cooked anyone unfortunate enough to be even near the flames. Unable to identify any of the men from the crash, I filled out the forms for each body, leaving out the names. The remains were forwarded to Graves Registration where they hopefully would be identified by their teeth. I remembered how carefully my teeth had been examined back at Fort Sam Houston. At the time, I innocently remarked to the dentist how nice it was for the Army to take such good care of our teeth. In a curt answer to my naive statement, the dentist told me he was only checking my teeth now to record information about my fillings, missing teeth, and position of my teeth so that I could be identified by my teeth if my body was too decomposed otherwise! After seeing those horribly burned bodies, I was thoroughly disgusted with the war, my job, and that dinner. All I wanted to do was to go home to my wife and child, but short of that, I settled for returning to my hooch. I had a headache from the wine and felt sick to my stomach. I vomited twice before I took a nap to revive myself.

Christmas in Vietnam was very different than anything I had ever experienced. Realizing getting in the holiday spirit would be next to impossible in tropical Tay Ninh, the men of Company D and I wrote lots of letters and dreamed of home. There was a new sign over Sergeant Rossnagel's desk that read, "Think Snow!" Even though the big mosquito standing on the snow sign brought the tropics back into focus, I couldn't stop thinking about snow for weeks. The most popular Christmas song in Vietnam was sung to the melody of Jingle Bells, and went something like this:

"Jingle bells, mortar shells, VC in the grass,
Take your Merry Christmas and shove it up your a--."

Bob Hope came to Cu Chi that season, and a lot of our guys went to see his show. They came back flushed with stories about the beautiful round-eyed women they had seen. Bob must have put on a great show; our guys really loved it. Christmas and the New Year came and went. Every GI who had one, fired his gun at midnight on New Year's Eve. I fell out of my bed at all the noise. I was sure all those gunshots meant the base camp was being overrun. The noise sounded like Armageddon for about thirty minutes. When the firing finally stopped, my jangled nerves wouldn't let sleep come, so I went for a walk in the dark. I finally got to sleep about four in the morning, the first day of 1969.

After the Christmas holidays, the enemy stepped up his activity in our area, and things were hopping down at the aid station. Colonel Wair's daily morning briefings were replete with details of enemy sightings. There seemed to be a lot more activity on the Ho Chi Minh Trail these days. Old Charley and the NVA weren't going to let up at all, despite being pounded by us all the time. Our scouting units felt a new NVA regiment was headed our way. I used to come away from those briefings with the hair standing up on the back of my neck. We were in for it. As more enemy soldiers were sighted, more battles were fought, and more wounded streamed into our little aid station. Each night we received more and more incoming rounds. With the increased shelling we took, I began to get a taste of what an infantry medic undergoes out in the field. Every time we got hit with mortars and rockets, the wounded would holler "Medic!" The poor medic would have to get up and move around under fire while all the rest of the soldiers would be seeking more cover. That just didn't seem fair. For me, that meant as I was hugging the floor of my bunker, the phone would ring. Phil Brandenberg would say, "You're needed here at the aid station, come on in." Just about the time I was to leave the safety of my bunker, the incoming would increase, of course. Donning my flak jacket and helmet, I'd start along the boardwalk towards the aid station, about one hundred very long yards away. The exploding shells sounded like the word "crap!" as they hit nearby. The metal fragments would strike the tin roofs making a ringing sound while they hit the sand bags with a thud. Each time I heard a round coming in, I'd hit the dirt. I would even seek a drainage ditch for cover, if one were handy. I got so I didn't mind the ditch water with its smell and taste of toothpaste. Any old port in a storm. Everyone else was able to seek cover and stay there, but not the Medical Corps people. By the time I reached the aid station I was usually angry to have risked my life on the trip over, but my anger would evaporate when I saw the writhing wounded, and the fearless Brandenberg and Washington walking about quickly and efficiently, setting up the things they knew I would need to treat the casualties. When I saw these guys doing what had to be done, I would think to myself ashamedly, "They don't show any concern for their exposure, why should I?" Hank Phillips would be out in the open, trying to start the finicky auxiliary generator, kicking it, stopping only to hit the dirt when a zinger came in. You were not supposed to hear the "one that gets you," which is probably true. That adage kept some soldiers from seeking cover. Their logic was that if you could hear the incoming round, you wouldn't get hit. Unfortunately my all-too-human nature made me hit the dirt and tremble when those frightening sounds passed overhead. Once, I actually saw two rockets passing over me about ten feet up in the air. One of the two rockets hit a fuel dump tank by the airstrip, and I was sure we were all going to die. That fuel tank was over one-half a mile away, but I could feel the heat from the burning where I was lying!

Once, Hank Phillips came to my hooch to get me in the middle of the night. The phone wasn't working, and there were several wounded to be seen. We crawled and ran in the direction of the aid station. Mortars were "walking" along all around us in the usual enemy linear fashion. As we passed behind the mess hall, the shells were beginning to fall closer, and we sought refuge in the new drain the cooks had been digging behind the now deserted mess hall. Pitch black, Hank and I made out the edge of the drain hole by the flashes of the explosion. Hank leapt head first into that hole, and I followed feet first. We both imagined the hole would only be a few feet deep, but the cooking crew had been busy digging, and that hole was eight feet deep! When Hank hit the bottom of the hole, he let out a scream I could hear above the noise of the explosions. Hank told me with a groan, he broke his arm jumping into the hole. I couldn't see anything at all inside that dark pit. Catching my breath, I tried to think what to do next. Hank was holding his broken wrist in his good hand for support. A few moments went by, and then there seemed to be a lull in the explosions. Getting out of the hole first, I gave Hank a hand and somehow was able to pull his long body out. We ran to the aid station where I could examine Hank's injured forearm. There was little doubt about the fracture. An X-ray confirmed a wrist fracture, with significant deformity. Despite the fracture, Hank took the other X-rays we needed that night. To Hank, the wounded came first, and he continued working. When the wounded were all tucked in, and after the KIAs had been carded, I set Hank's fracture and put him in a forearm cast.

The next day I expectantly filled out the forms needed to get Hank the Purple Heart. The regulations stated, in order to be eligible for the Purple Heart, "You have to be injured as a direct result of enemy fire." My request for Hank's Purple Heart was turned down at Division Headquarters. My personally calling the Decorations

Office at Cu Chi didn't help either. Breaking a bone escaping enemy fire was not good enough to merit the Purple Heart. I thought this was wrong, as did the company. They gave Hank a present. Short Round, the cook, not the dog, baked Hank a chocolate cake. Despite the taste of powdered milk and eggs, the cake tasted good. Hank was very appreciative, and he just beamed that day. The grease pit was kept covered until it was finished, lest someone else fall in.

The Black Virgin Mountain (Nui Ba Den) in the background

THE PALE HORSE CAME

First Sergeant Rossnagel kept the tired medics busy with work details when they finished their shifts at the aid station. The leaking sand bags had been hit many times with rocket fragments from the frequent shelling we had experienced over the past several weeks. Those bags needed to be replaced often, and the first sergeant kept the men busy filling new sandbags to replace the torn ones. One day, a Wednesday, I joked with several of the medics working on sandbag duty as I was making my way back to my hooch after a long day of working in the aid station. The pleasant day promised a beautiful evening. The mid-day heat was dissipating early that evening, and the cool breezes had already started. The guys were in a good mood as they filled the bags with dirt and pounded them into place. They were joking and laughing with each other as I left to continue walking the boardwalk towards my hooch. As I passed the mess hall, the smell of Short Round's dinner was very appetizing. My stomach began to growl. Brian Kelly's loud voice was clearly audible in the quiet evening air as he began another one of his famous stories. I could hear his buddy, Steven Segura interjecting his comments. There was a peaceful hum of activity about the area that evening, I felt glad to be alive.

Entering my hooch, there were two of Margy's letters lying on the center table, waiting to be read. Stu Knodel was crunching some homemade peanut brittle his wife had sent that day. That brittle smelled great! Goodies from home were always a real treat, and we all enjoyed those gifts from our wives and moms. I sat down to open one of Margy's letters when the dog, Short Round, began to whine, and then she ducked under my bunk. Stu looked at me, and in a heartbeat, we were into the bunker. Within a second, Charlie Guess and Hal Shields followed us inside from their hooch. Hal missed the pipe this time. The explosions seemed closer than usual. As I recall, only four or five hit. Just to be sure no more incoming was on the way, I decided to wait for a minute or two before leaving the bunker. Marty was not with us. He had stayed behind at the aid station to finish up with some sick call stragglers. Footsteps fell heavily on the wooden floor of the hooch above us. Just then, a bare-chested, sweating, and very pale Sergeant Rossnagel came down the steps into our bunker. Right away, I suspected the gravity of what he was about to say. Catching his breath, and gasping at times he said, "Captain Snider, Captain Snider! Segura and Grimmenstein are dead! Brian Kelly is severely wounded! Several others got hit, but they're not too bad. It's just awful!" Sergeant Rossnagel sobbed a slight manly sob, and he said "Holy Shit!" as he ran back outside.

All four of us ran full-tilt towards the aid station. My legs felt wooden as I passed in front of the mess hall. A few moments ago this was a happy peaceful scene! Running by the front of the mess hall, I could see two large holes the rockets had left in the dirt where they had impacted. There were several bloodstains on the pale, dry dirt by those still-smoking holes. Unfilled sand bags were strewn about, and pieces of torn fatigues and part of a boot were alongside one of the rocket holes. The smell of spent gunpowder was irritating my nose, and I felt like I was going to vomit. This spot was quiet once again, but, oh, what mayhem must have been there just a few seconds ago!

The aid station had its customary orderly chaos, but the looks on the faces of the medics told all. We had been hit. The war wasn't just happening to the other guys, the combatants. Now the war was happening to us. We had a Geneva red cross on our military ID cards, but the rockets didn't notice. We were in up to our necks, and we were vulnerable. All the mental safeguards of being medics, allowing us to feel safe from the war, evaporated in the horrible scene before me. Blood was everywhere. Marty was desperately trying to resuscitate Grimmenstein. He seemed agitated, very unlike his usual cool self. Marty's face was pale, and he was sweating profusely as he continued closed chest massage on Grimmenstein's ashen, lifeless body. All alone in the aid station when the injured men were brought in, Marty had been working furiously, and he was in panicked disbelief, as we all were, at the new and unwanted sight of our men being the victims this time. Marty looked up at me, his voice cracking, and said, "It's no good, he's bled out. What do you think?" I agreed there was nothing more to be done. Marty had been correctly administering blood and saline. "No heartbeat, no pulse. It's over!" I could hear myself saying. Marty turned his face from us, hiked up his loose fitting pants and blew his nose. The gloves he had not yet removed bloodied his handkerchief. Taking off his gloves, he threw his handkerchief on the floor with them. All of us converged on the stretcher holding Brian Kelly. He was sobbing, obviously scared to death. Washington and Brandenberg had been with Marty all the while in the aid station, and they had started large bore IVs in Brian's good arm. The other arm, his right one, had been injured at the convexity of the elbow. The injured elbow looked like it was separated from its attachments to the upper arm, but closer inspection showed that the flesh in the front of his elbow was still intact. All the vessels and nerves had been spared when the metal fragment from the rocket passed through. He would be able to keep his arm!

Segura and Kelly had remained sitting on the boardwalk facing the mess hall, right where I had left them, when the big 120 milli-meter Chinese-communist (Chi-com) rocket had exploded twenty inches to their rear. A large piece of shrapnel hit the top of Segura's head, killing him instantly! He never knew what hit him. We all took some consolation from that fact. Brian had been hit on the el-bow by a glancing piece of shrapnel, sparing complete severance of his arm by inches. Brian had a second wound, which was the worst by far! A piece of metal over 12 inches long, 5 inches wide and one inch thick entered his back just above the left kidney, and passing through his abdominal cavity, was now grotesquely pushing the skin on the front of his abdomen tenting out at least four inches into the air! His blood pressure and other vital signs were remarkably nor-mal. Although he looked nightmarish at this point, he was very sal-vageable. After assessing his condition, I told him that he would be "Just fine!" but he wasn't buying that right now. Grabbing my arm with his good arm he sobbed, "Don't let me die, Captain Snider! Don't let me die!" I told him he wasn't going die and he would be telling stories again tomorrow. He began to sob some more and whimpered the name of his friend, Segura. Whether he knew Segura had been killed, I didn't know. As far as I recall, no one ever told him his friend had died. With the help of the medics, we whisked Brian across the street where, within five minutes, he was in the op-erating room. Knowing he was taken care of for now, I hurried back to help care for the rest. Fortunately, the remaining wounded had only minor injuries. Grimmenstein, Segura, and Kelly were the only three left working when the rocket hit. The rest of the ill-fated work detail had already left to clean up for dinner. I'll bet Brian was in the middle of a story and the other two remained behind to hear the end of his saga, the last words they were ever to hear.

When the last of the wounded were gone either to their hooches or to the bunker hospital, Marty, Charlie, and I sat on stretchers while the men mopped the floor clean. In low voices we discussed what we thought had happened. Sergeant Rossnagel joined our group and advised me I needed to report this to Division Headquarters. Our numbers would be included in the Army's report to the press that day and the number of those reported killed in Vietnam on the six o'clock news that evening would include two from our Company D, 25th Med Battalion. I had just talked with both of them! How could they be dead? May they enjoy eternal peace.

Chaplains Manning and Vernon walked in on our group that grisly evening. They had been advised about what happened in our company and came to console the men. The chaplains were tireless comforters of the sick and the wounded, and they frequented our aid station. They were greatly appreciated by the men of our company and all our patients. Lieutenant Colonel Manning was a Lutheran minister from the Midwest, where a wife and kids awaited his return. Pastor Manning was short, had balding blond hair, and had the soothing voice of a person good at rendering solace. Captain Vernon was a Catholic priest from New Jersey. He and I played cards together from time to time, and he, too, was a warm and friendly guy.

By now, several hours had passed since Brian had gone into the OR, so our group of doctors, chaplains and First Sergeant Rossnagel went across the street for an update on Brian's condition. Captain Keeley had been the surgeon, and we found him in the recovery room tent. Things had gone well. "Brian was one lucky so and so," he reported to our group. Sometimes a surgeon will paradoxically say someone is "lucky" who just got the stuffing kicked out of him. That huge piece of metal had just missed Brian's kidney and adrenal gland. Brian's stomach had been cut in half, but no other organs were injured. Keeley had simply sutured the stomach back together, and washed out the peritoneal cavity with an antibiotic solution. Brian had lost about a liter of blood, but none needed to be replaced during surgery. Captain Keeley advised us to come early the next morning if we wanted to see Brian before he was shipped out. The plane was coming in at 0700 to pick up the transfers. The next morning about forty of Company D's men visited a very happy Brian Kelly. He was his old self. The good news about his surgery and the fact he was headed home made him euphoric. We all wished him well, shook his good hand, and never saw or heard of him again. He never asked about the other guys, but I am sure he knew. If he didn't ask me, I had made up my mind not to tell him. I sure didn't want to tell him that morning and drag his high.

The bodies of our slain buddies disappeared into Graves Registration and were gone. Vernon and Manning arranged a service for Segura and Grimmenstein to be held at the brigade chapel. The service was interdenominational, the kind the Army offers so that all the men of various religions can attend. Many of our company's soldiers were deeply religious, but they did not seem to be intolerant of the other guy's religion. Reverend Manning gave one of the nicest services I had ever attended. The brigade chapel was just down the street from our aid station, next to Third Brigade Headquarters. Having a four-foot high brick base, the chapel was open to the roof. I liked that chapel. Tiny birds flew all about, sometimes landing on the altar or the priest's shoulder. The openness of the chapel made me think that was the way God wanted his houses of worship to be built, wide open and free for all to see.

As I entered the chapel that beautiful morning of the memorial service, I was handed a program. The full names of our dead were printed with Scripture passages and songs noted. I heavy-heartedly said a few words and sat down. Many had tears in their eyes and the voices of those singing soldiers were lifted on the morning breeze and surely were heard in heaven. I personally felt so sorry that they had to die, so far away from their family, in such a forsaken place, for such a foolish cause. I especially remember the short epitaph near the end of that program:

> Not for fame or reward,
> Not goaded by ambition or lured by necessity,
> But in simple obedience to discipline as
> They understood it,
> These men. . .
> Dared all - Suffered all - And Died!
>
> Anonymous

I still have that memorial service program, and I will always cherish it. A very quiet line of young mourners filed out of the chapel that sunny morning into the tropical heat and back to the company area.

Their dying seemed unfair, a real downer for all of our company. Word got out of our loss, and wounded GIs would tell us they had heard what happened and how sorry they were for us. Imagine that! The condolences our company received from wounded and sick GIs were impressive to me. The soldiers of the 25th Division appreciated what we were doing for them, and we needed to know that.

As the Delta Six, I had to write letters to the Segura and Grimmenstein families. There was an Army guide to help a commander write those letters, and I read everything it said. I figured the Army had been writing these types of letters for almost two hundred years, and they had a lot of experience in it. Commanders were encouraged to personalize these letters as much as possible. The War Department had already sent a telegram to the unfortunate families, making my letter anti-climactic. I wrote and rewrote the letter, but I didn't like any of what I had written. Bill Myers was our new Executive MSC officer. He jotted down a letter, when he saw that I was having trouble. His letter was perfect. I threw away my inadequate attempts and used his. I pray some comfort was afforded those unfortunate families by my letters. Several weeks later, I received a nice letter from Steven Segura's father. He thanked me for taking care of his son and trying to talk him into going to college. Steven had evidently written his dad about our bull sessions, and I was pleased Steven's dad knew how much we liked his son. His Dad had received Steven's personal effects, but he said a small refrigerator was missing. Sergeant Rossnagel and I looked all over, but never could find the missing refrigerator. I believe the men took up a collection and sent the money to his dad. I still have the letter Steven's dad sent and read it over again every so often.

THE FIRST AIR CAV

Our company couldn't escape the enemy pounding. The NVA had no reverence for our losses. In fact, they wanted to kill more of us. The increased enemy activity brought about the transfer of a brigade of the First Air Cavalry to Tay Ninh. They took up residence on the base next to our officer hooches. Although most of their men were out in the field, their headquarters and medical companies were to be located inside our base. One memorable day I noticed an Air Cav Dust Off helicopter off-loading at our helipad. Off that chopper jumped my old friend and fellow Yale surgical resident, Bob Dragon. I was surprised and glad to see him. I had last seen him in Long Binh where he had been assigned to the First Air Cav and was trucked away. He was the same old Bob. As he greeted me, he told me in his Boston accent just how much he hated the goddam Army. Notably he had lost a lot of weight. The anti-malarial pills had given him unrelenting diarrhea, which made him afraid to eat. On top of the diarrhea and weight loss, Bob complained of a fungal infection at his belt line, his feet hurt, and now, he had to move. "I tell you, Rick, I'll never say a bad word about New Haven again. I'd give a year's pay to be back there right now. Wouldn't you?" I agreed with him. New Haven seemed very far away. Lately, I imagined I had been in the Army all my life. Seeing Bob helped me remember that I hadn't. I fixed a place for Bob to stay at least a few days with me, until his unit got settled.

Bob had been assigned to a medical battalion as a partially trained surgeon, just as I had been. Phouc Binh was where the First Cav had been and where Bob had worked prior to coming to Tay Ninh. We shot the baloney for hours that first night, and drank a few beers for "old times sake." Marty and Charlie got a kick out of Bob's Boston accent with its flat "A." His animated stories were both amusing and comforting. Here was someone else like us, who had the same problems we did, and Bob could gripe with the best of us. After a while, we stopped talking so much about the Army, and began to swap medical school stories the rest of the night. Bob stayed with me two more days. Each morning he would disappear into the mass of First Cav people who were very busy setting up an aid station nearby similar to ours. True to Army irony, the First Air Cav stayed although Bob was transferred back to Phouc Binh. I never saw Bob again while I was in the Army.

Bob Dragon shows up in Tay Ninh. It's a small world.

HELICOPTERS AND GUN RUNS

The Dust Off pilots became great friends with the officers of D Company. They played on our volleyball team, spent long hours playing poker with us, and ate with us each night. Despite a lot of war activity, paradoxically, there were long days of unending boredom, also. When the Dust Off guys weren't flying, we doctors could take it easy, and, with a helicopter nearby, we were always "air-mobile!" Surrounded by guns, we all wanted to fire them. With Berrigan as the pilot, we often went on "gun runs." When war things were quiet, three or four of the company officers would go with Berrigan and his Dust Off crew to fly over the Mekong River towards a small pond in the middle of the jungle. Circling the pond we would take turns firing our M-16 rifles, my M-1 carbine, grenade launchers and our Colt .45 service pistols. These "gun runs" were always a lot of fun, allowed us to blow off steam, and learn to shoot our weapons in case we ever needed them. One fine day, however, a potential disaster rose up and bit me in the butt.

The Dust Off chopper's radio reported a thunderhead coming our way as we were returning from shooting at our favorite pond. Berrigan was headed for Tay Ninh, twenty miles away. Huge black clouds were blocking our way home. They extended up about five thousand feet into the air, and I knew Berrigan couldn't fly over them. We were headed right into the teeth of the storm! The wind picked up and the chopper began to pitch and yaw violently. Suddenly we began to fall straight down towards the dense dark jungle below. Plummeting down, I held onto my seat for dear life. The crew seemed not to worry, but I had no idea why they weren't. They should have been scared out of their skins, as we were falling to our deaths!

With a loud "whoosh," I could feel the two long rotor blades catch solid air, and we began to ride forward rather than straight down. The whole episode took only a few seconds, but those seconds felt like an eternity to me. Berrigan, wanting to talk with us, turned on the intercom with a loud click. He and the crew were familiar with what was happening to the helicopter, and this was a common experience for them. The helicopter had been caught in a down draft, and dropped over one thousand feet. Air pockets like this one were common around storms like the one we had just hit. "Nothing to worry about. We'll be on the ground in a few minutes," he said after he finished his explanation. Safely back on the ground, the driving rain brought me to my senses, and I re-examined my policy. I had clearly violated my philosophy of no unnecessary risks. Unless something drastic came along to make me change my mind, no more gun runs for me.

I remained good friends with the Dust Off pilots and crew throughout my stay in Tay Ninh. My guard relaxed on my policy, and I began to fly with them again. The commander of Dust Off for the Division was Major Ken Moore. About 30 years old, and with his crewcut, he still looked like a college kid. He called his men his "boys" because so many were young warrant officers, about twenty years old on the average. I rode with the major several times, transporting patients, getting blood, supplies, and such. Although I usually sent a medic on these routine missions, I loved the thrill of flying in Huey helicopters and would often opt to go myself. The engine noise in Hueys was tolerable and their maneuverability was invigorating. The Huey helicopter seemed to be the safest flying machine around, and there were huge numbers of them. One fine day I headed to Cu Chi with Major Moore in his Dust Off helicopter to pick up some much-needed bottles of blood.

Unknown to me, the NVA had just began an all-out attack on a fire support base somewhere near the Boi Loi woods, and our Dust Off was needed right away to pick up the wounded generated from that battle. The call for help always superseded any other mission for a Dust Off helicopter, so Major Moore aborted our original mission and, turning the Huey around, headed for the caller's location. At the proper coordinates, a green smoke signal was easily seen, and Major Moore's chopper, with me aboard, swooped down for a landing. I was ordered off the helicopter, and the wounded were loaded in my place. Teasing me, Major Moore suggested I find an M-16 and start shooting at the enemy. He chuckled as he took off with his load of wounded soldiers and was soon out of sight. Panicking a little standing there, I nervously looked around for some safe place to go. As the engine noises of the departing helicopter diminished, the roar of the pitched battle surrounding me filled my ears. An Infantry sergeant spied me standing there out in the open. Calling over to me, he suggested I get down and start crawling towards him. That was exactly what I did, and I was soon crouching next to the sergeant. I noticed he was talking on a field phone with his headquarters, wherever they were, and I didn't say a thing. Intermittently, when he wasn't talking with someone else, the sergeant would talk to me.

Looking around, I could tell to my relief, I was in the middle of a protected area. The earthworks around us would stop any direct fire, so I relaxed slightly. The sergeant spoke to me in interrupted sentences and broken paragraphs. His men had repulsed the attacking NVA, and our guys were chasing them back, towards the jungle and cover. He told me he had been on the phone with the 25th Division artillery, but they had refused to take the fire mission on the fleeing NVA. Why, I didn't know, but now the sergeant was talking with the Navy. The Navy? That blew my mind. There wasn't any water around, so why the Navy? Finally finishing talking on the radiophone, the sergeant sat on his haunches and began speaking with me in earnest. He advised me to stay where I was. He was going to confer with his captain and would be right back. The captain was the commanding officer and was directing his men's pursuit of the fleeing enemy. The very loud noises continued for a few more minutes, then the din began to abate. At this point, I could hear only an occasional machine gun firing or a muffled explosion. The sergeant and a group of men came running low over the rise and sat nearby. They were engaged in excited Army talk, but there wasn't any sign of panic. These were professionals doing their job, and who wouldn't be excited when a fight was going on! Seeing those men in action, up close as I was, was a rare privilege for a base camp medical type like me. Although I was scared, I felt safe where I was. I knew Major Moore would need twenty minutes to get back from Tay Ninh, so I might as well enjoy myself out here with the infantry.

I could see GIs running low. They swarmed over the outer berm returning to their original defensive positions they had left to chase the fleeing enemy. The infantry captain was on the radiophone next to me. He was telling someone about the fight. He felt the main body of NVA was still close by, and the enemy was trying to avoid a major engagement with him at this time. The elusive enemy was apparently moving away to find safe cover in the nearby jungle. The captain said he was expecting Naval support any time now.

The sergeant motioned to me to join him on the berm. He assured me that there was no more danger, and I would "get a kick out" of what was to happen. Pointing so I could see a small silver speck on the sunny horizon, the sergeant shouted, "Here he comes!" The small silver speck was a Navy fighter plane with another jet right behind the first one. Div Arty (Division Artillery) couldn't take the fire mission today for some reason, and Navy planes nearby would respond. These powerful fighting jets would deliver a knockout punch to the retreating NVA soldiers. The planes were off a carrier on the South China Sea somewhere to our east and were heading our way! The speck I had seen on the horizon an instant ago was now a silver giant screaming by at a mind-boggling speed. First he and then his buddy flew over our area to spot targets. Slowing to turn, the jets banked and swooped low over a section of jungle several miles from our elevated berm position. The jungle exploded with fire as the Gatling gun rockets spewed forth from the wings of the passing jets. The earth I was standing on shook from the exploding bombs the jets had dropped. The high-pitched screeching noise from the passing jets was deafening. The bomb concussions tugged at the hat on my head. Suddenly I felt I was too close! Then came the napalm. What an awesome sight! Balls of flames ran along the ground sounding a loud "whoosh!" I wondered how anything could be still alive in that hell! As quickly as they came, the jets left. Only the crackling flames could be heard in the eerie silence that followed. I had never seen anything like that in my life, and I had never imagined anything that destructive even existed. Seeing my mouth agape, my sergeant friend said, "Aren't you glad the NVA don't use MIGS?" I had never thought of that, but I was sure very thankful they didn't. I would never want to be on the receiving end of such punishment.

Major Moore landed nearby in whirling green smoke, and this time there was room on the helicopter. Looking out on those soldiers, the scorched jungle, and the still raging flames, I realized how little I had seen of the war that raged daily around my little world. Multiplying this relatively small battle many times a day, and 365 days a year I could see why so many wounded and dead were generated.

Safely back at my company, I went back to work with renewed devotion on those men who endured that kind of a scene everyday. I now had a much better understanding of the war, what grunts saw on a daily basis, and "battle fatigue!" At dinner that night, Marty asked me what I had done that afternoon. I launched into a detailed account of my brief encounter with the real war and continued for about an hour. After eating dinner with us, and hearing my story, Major Moore remarked, "You know, you guys really ought to get out more." Marty and I both said, "No thanks!" in unison.

MORE AND MORE INCOMING

The loss of our two men became less painful as the time passed, but their deaths were always just under the surface. Most of us in the company slept underground in bunkers, and we jumped at the slightest sound suggesting incoming. This was a good thing, because the incoming kept coming in. No longer was that sound most likely from a truck; the real thing was now more common. Most nights held the rude entry of incoming mortars, rockets, and recoil-less rifle shots. The latter were rare, but did occur from time to time. Company D's area on the base was becoming noticeably more crowded with the First Air Cav's contingent right next to us. The Cav outfit was the new kid on the block and they didn't seem to give bunker safety much consideration, not like our company did anyway. One rainy evening, incoming mortar rounds began hitting a block away, just down the dirt street. Then the rounds began "walking" right up to the front door of my hooch. I had been reading by the light hung over the center table, and, cocked back on the rear legs of my chair, I had been resting my bare feet on the table edge. Round wasn't in the hooch that night, and by the time I recognized the reports as incoming, three or four had hit, coming closer with each round. They were so close, I sort of fell backwards, in a clumsy position, onto my back on the wooden floor. The next round struck just outside my front screen door with an ear shattering crash, sending metal fragments through the screens, the door, and the roof of my hooch. Knowing the next one would be right in my lap, I rolled over onto my stomach, clasped my hands over my head, and waited. Trying to crawl the twenty feet to the bunker seemed a waste of time, as the next shell would be on me in the next millisecond, and I awaited my fate! I remember trembling and gritting my teeth. The next one never came! Pure and uncomplicated fate saved my life that evening. The enemy soldiers probably ran out of mortar shells, and I got to live.

My nose wrinkled at the smell of burnt gunpowder from that last round. The blast had knocked over my locker, which landed alongside me on the floor. The door of my locker had been blown open and I could see fragmentation holes in my uniforms inside! Quickly counting my appendages, I found all four. I had not been hit! I decided to stay put, just in case Charley might have one more shell left! Lucky for me, he did not!

After all the noise and confusion of an enemy incoming attack comes an eerie moment of almost complete quiet. The period of serenity that follows the mayhem of fire and noise may last several moments, but is more commonly over in a few heartbeats. During that moment the victims probably are assessing themselves, much as I had done, or are waking up. Finding no injuries there may be a subsequent short-lived period of glee, or, on the other hand awakening pain may tell you that you've been hit. This night, that silent moment with the patter of the falling rain on the tin roof above, was pierced with a pitiful, whimper-like cry, "Medic!"

Several of the new First Cav soldiers had been mangled by those shells, and they were now beginning to feel pain and realize their injured state. By this time in my Tay Ninh tenure, I had lived through several of those quiet moments after incoming, and had heard several of those weak calls for help that follow. Those pitiful calls for help are so moving, so unnerving, that resistance is impossible and a response is immediate. I found myself running with several others, looking for the men who called for help. I quickly found two severely wounded soldiers and rushed them to the newly created Air Cav aid station where I helped care for them. One was stable, but the other had signs of intestinal injuries. He was hurriedly carried down the street to the MUST hospital a block away. Although I was to hear that eerie moment of silence many more times in the near future, I never did hear the quiet punctuated with calls for help quite so dramatically as I did on that fateful night. When I got back to my hooch later, I saw how close those mortar rounds had hit. The front steps of my hooch were peppered with shrapnel, and the next one would have had my name on it.

The next week, the aid station of the First Cav had another disaster. Sitting out in the back of my hooch, I was basking in the tropical afternoon's sun reading a book, when a helicopter attempted to land in front of the First Cav's new aid station fifty yards away. In front of their aid station a small cinderblock yard had been positioned for Dust Off helicopters, but the landing zone was extremely small, making any approach difficult. The helicopter coming for a landing that afternoon wasn't a Dust Off ship and was badly listing to one side. The pilot aborted his first attempt to land and was having trouble regaining altitude to retry his approach. Askew, ten feet up, the listing chopper just descended onto the hard dirt of the road, missing the landing zone by a few feet. The rotor blades hit the ground before the skids, broke off, and the shattered pieces filled the air with whirling fragments. A small explosion erupted as the body of the helicopter hit the hard ground, and a small fire started up in the tail section. Standing now, I was unsure whether to rush over to help, or to take cover from the fire that would surely rage in a moment or two. My answer came when several medics rushed out from the First Cav's aid station brandishing fire extinguishers. They soon extinguished the flames, and a crowd began to gather. I ran over to watch. The helicopter pilot was dead, still strapped into his seat with his safety belts. The co-pilot had been shot through his thigh and the red puddle at his feet told me he had lost a lot of blood. In shock and only half-conscious, he had managed to land that chopper and get out alive! Flying that chopper was a tribute to the co-pilot's strong desire to live and spoke volumes about his ability to fly.

The Air Cav medics deftly unstrapped the co-pilot and whisked him inside their aid station, and I followed. He was given blood rapidly and his response was evidenced by more purposeful motions. I later found out that their helicopter had been attempting to land in a jungle clearing. The helicopter was to pick up some Cav soldiers who had been out on a patrol. The infantrymen had popped green smoke as the chopper was hovering overhead. In the swirling green smoke the chopper touched down. Almost immediately a .51 caliber machine gun opened up on the soldiers and the helicopter! Several soldiers on the ground were killed and more wounded. The pilot was instantly killed and as the co-pilot began to lift off, he was struck in his leg from a bullet coming through the floor of the cabin. The helicopter's crew jumped off at the landing zone and sought cover with the grunts. Wounded, bleeding, and in severe pain, the co-pilot managed to fly out of there and back to Tay Ninh, a few miles away.

Chagrined the landing zone hadn't been secured, the GIs on the ground made quick work of the hidden enemy machine gunners. Part of one of the helicopter's rotors had been shot away during the ambush, which explained why the co-pilot couldn't gain altitude after his first attempt at landing at the base. That co-pilot lived, and the next day the whole base watched a huge flying crane helicopter lift the remains of the bullet-riddled Huey from in front of the Cav's aid station. You could see the crane toting its smaller buddy for miles. The dust swirl that huge helicopter stirred up took two hours to settle that hot, still day.

As if our lives were not exciting enough, adding the First Air Cav to the Tay Ninh base kept the joint jumping. Each night we would dodge incoming, watch outdoor movies, and play volleyball with our neighbors. Every night our hospital was nearly full with recovering wounded. Sergeant Knoerr kept those famous BLTs and pizzas coming. His fabled EM Club delighted the many troops on stand down, the wounded from the hospital, and the base GIs. Morale on the base was high those days, while drug use, alcohol abuse, and rambunctious behavior were rare. By what we heard on AFVNTV and read in newspapers, marijuana use and hard drug takers had to have been all around us. We of Company D in Tay Ninh rarely saw any joint smokers, drug users or even harsh treatment of Vietnamese civilians by our soldiers.

In Vietnam, there was no law against killing yourself in one of the many opium dens that dotted the countryside. Oriental society turned its head away from drug addiction, so, if you wanted to do drugs, you could, out in the open, and very inexpensively. When a fighting soldier was taking drugs or alcohol routinely, he wasn't doing his job, and that couldn't be tolerated. The self-policing was real and very effective and kept bad actors from getting other people killed. To infantrymen, keeping drug use under control was a matter of simple self-preservation.

The Tay Ninh base camp saw GIs come in for a one or two day rest after several weeks of hard marching under the hot sun, looking for Charley. The soldiers on their "stand down" would drink a beer or two, and then eat as much junk food from the PX as they could hold. Most of the time, they would just sleep. Rarely would they drink too much or do drugs. Occasionally, an exception would pop up like a sore thumb. The worst drug problem I encountered in

Vietnam was from the plastic explosive, C-4. C-4 was carried by most combat GIs to blow up things. Not long after the World Trade Center buildings were attacked on September 11, 2001, someone tried to blow up a commercial airliner with C-4 packed in his shoes! That was the same C-4 used by our soldiers back in 1968. Like many potent explosives, a plastic explosive was inert without something to detonate it. So inert by itself, GIs would light it with a match. The plastic whitish material would burn slowly allowing the soldiers to use the flames to cook their field rations. The C-4 gave off more heat than the canned Sterno that was supplied to cook those rations. Rumors circulated that eating C-4 would result in a terrific high. Unfortunately, as I came to find out, there was no high associated with ingesting this very toxic and deadly compound, but only sure death.

A soldier was brought to me having had a seizure. Brought in from the field by his buddies, he was semi-comatose when I first saw him. He responded to my pinches by unpurposeful movements and slurred speech. I put a Foley urinary catheter into his bladder, and pure blood filled the reservoir bag. He experienced several more grand mal seizures and then quickly went into profound shock. Within two hours, he died! Not having a clue why he died, I sent his body to the pathologist in Saigon for an autopsy. Later that day, one of his buddies came in and told us the dead soldier had eaten C-4! I sent this information to the pathologist in Saigon, who promptly advised us that there had been several deaths reported from soldiers eating C-4. Soon, a bulletin circulated to all military units explaining that eating C-4 would result in seizures and sudden death. The description on the bulletin fit my patient to a "T." I saw one more case of C-4 ingestion while in Tay Ninh, and the same result followed very quickly. The soldiers learned a harsh lesson, and I believe the C-4 deaths discouraged drug use in general.

Lighter moments were appreciated by GIs, and one of the funniest gags around was the sign outside Hal Shields's dental office. The official motto of the 25th Medical Battalion was "To conserve the fighting strength." We displayed a large sign with the motto and the 25th Infantry emblem, on a large sign in front of our aid station. The emblem of the 25th Infantry Division was a bright red Hawaiian taro leaf with a serrated yellow edge and a yellow lightning flash down the center. We in the division proudly wore that patch on the left shoulder of our uniforms. Two doors down from our medical sign was Hal's dental counterpart. As a joke, Hal repainted his sign to read, "To conserve the biting strength." "After all," Hal said, "that's what I am doing." Soldiers would laugh themselves silly if they were sharp enough to pick up the subtle change in that commonplace slogan. Soon the altered motto was pointed out by all who passed by. Colonel Wair never noticed the sign on his visits to the dentist. When confronted with the gag, Hal would just smile and say he was trying to live up to the motto. All good things come to an end, and Hal's sign was no exception. An officer passing by noticed the altered motto and stormed into Hal's office. He insisted the sign be put back to its original form immediately. Hal stopped what he was doing and reluctantly fixed the sign. Wise to the change, Hal's sign was scrutinized daily by the local brass, and the "biting strength" was never the same.

THE THIRD MAN

My hooch gradually took on an air of home. Pictures of Margy and Beth Ann were strategically placed about my personal area. There were cookies to munch on, sodas to drink and beer for the card games. My duties had become fairly routine, especially in the aid station and hospital, and I was beginning to get the hang of being the Delta Six. When a new soldier was assigned to the company, I would interview him in the Army fashion. Sergeant Rossnagel taught me how to do my Army duties and how to do them well. The reporting soldier would salute me as he entered the office. I would return the salute and bid the new man to take a seat. Next, I would talk to him, welcoming him to the company. A warm welcome was always nice, and helped to start someone off on the right foot. Most of our soldiers were very pleased to serve in Company D. The company had a reputation for good duty in a fair outfit with a caring first sergeant. I was more comfortable doing my Army duties, thanks to Sergeant Rossnagel. He was invaluable to the company and me because he saw to it that the company practically ran itself. Just as things in the company were beginning to settle down after the deaths of our own two men, tragedy visited us once more. I had just interviewed a nice kid from down on the farm in Missouri. He was to be a cook's helper, and his innocence was refreshing. He told me he loved the Army, saying, "Why, I get to sleep in until six each morning and I get to eat all I want at the mess hall!" I couldn't help thinking he must have had quite a life back on the farm, i.e., getting out of bed before 6 A.M. and not getting enough to eat. Discussing this with Sergeant Rossnagel, he told me many Army recruits remark how good the food is in the Army, and how easy the work is. These guys had much harder lives as civilians than most of us could imagine. The hard lives they had lived made them good soldiers. Many a recruit had his first shower in the

Army! I found that hard to believe, but I had every reason to expect that the sergeant was telling the truth, without exaggeration. I saw Private Everette Briggs the next day and asked him how things were going so far. He flashed a broad toothy smile and said things were just great. He liked working with Short Round and was sure he would be happy here. That very afternoon, while he was taking a nap on his cot, a single 107-millimeter Chi-Com rocket landed right next to him, practically cutting him in half! Not another rocket fell that day.

We gave him a nice church service. The aid station was closed that morning and the whole company turned out for the service at the chapel. Although only a few in the company had met this new kid, there were few dry eyes in the chapel. The irony of being so new in country and being killed was hard for us all to understand. I can still see his pleasant smiling face and remember those innocent comments he made about his Army life. I thought he never got a chance to really enjoy life, but, then again, no nineteen-year-old who died over there did either.

Now there had been three members of Company D who had been killed under my command. I'll never be able to shake free from the memory of those three men who died so far away from home in a war that was so hard to understand. Somehow, I feel that by re-membering them, I can give them some more life, for, other than some family members, who else will remember? As the years pass, they still seem very real to me. I can see them alive, walking around, and talking with me. Sometimes, I think I can actually hear their voices! Perhaps I'm a little crazy, and just hearing things that aren't really there, but I don't think so. I strongly believe they are still there, and I'll get to see them one day.

Unpleasantly, I also still remember the sound the rockets made that hit and killed them. Those are nightmarish sounds, loud and very real. I hear these sounds on the highway, in crowds, and mostly at night as I awaken from a deep sleep. "No, No!" echoes and re-echoes in my mind, recalling my reaction to the tragic news. There's no escape, their deaths happened! Maybe hearing those sounds again and remembering is good. My heart rate slows and my shakes lessen when I realize remembering is OK. I will never forget! I won't!

VIETNAMESE PEOPLE

At times, isolated as we were in our base full of Americans, Vietnamese people seemed to not even exist. There was the enemy, of course, and he was Vietnamese, even local Vietnamese. Those Vietnamese people I did come in contact with were very likable. Most of my contact came from those local citizens who came each day to work on the base. Mostly they were women, but I got to know some men. The younger generation spoke English very well, much better than I spoke Vietnamese, that's for sure. They were cheerful, polite, and nice to be around.

A few of the locals who worked in our company area were actually displaced North Vietnamese who escaped the religious intolerance of the Communistic regime in the North. They came with their priest, Father Tzu, a Roman Catholic, who fled with a lot of his village's people. These escapees settled in a lush valley nearby Tay Ninh and built a church that looked like a picture from Vermont. I saw that church once on a MEDCAP (Medical Civilian Assistance Program) mission to a nearby village. Glistening white in the sun, the steeple took on a holy aura. Very unusual for me to see a church in Vietnam, I was especially surprised to see one with an occidental spire. Coming closer to the steeple in my jeep, I couldn't help noticing two machine gun barrels sticking out from each side. I remembering smiling to myself as I imagined those guns were where the church bells should have been. The sinister-looking guns were supported by sandbags, lending credence to the fact that these parishioners were not going to give up easily to the Viet Cong who surrounded them and who threatened them regularly. Father Tzu was certainly not a pacifist!

I had the privilege to meet Father Tzu once at our hospital. He had come bearing gifts for our wounded soldiers. His visit was unsolicited and certainly unexpected. He and his whole entourage showed up one weekday carrying Vietnamese dolls, flashing beautiful smiles, and demonstrating a great deal of good will. He thanked me and my patients for our efforts to rid South Vietnam of the North Vietnamese oppressors. He told us that Catholics and other organized religions had been persecuted by the communistic government of North Vietnam. Atheism was the order of the North Vietnamese government, and they rooted out religions wherever they found them. Many of his fellow priests had been killed by the communists. He said he migrated south so he could continue to preach God's Word. He longed for the day when he could return to his home and live in peace. His message was heartfelt and seemed real to us. His tale gave a little more substance to the reasons the United States decided to help fight this war, and we were all impressed with this charismatic character. Father Tzu asked me if I had any children. When I answered that I had a daughter, he gave me a beautiful doll representing a Vietnamese woman dressed in a light blue ao-di with white pants. She was wearing the conical rice straw hat that just about every Vietnamese wore to ward off the cruel sun. I mailed the doll to my daughter, Beth Ann, who still cherishes it today.

Vietnamese women wore a top made of fine lightweight cloth for comfort in the heat. The top had a long flowing skirt that extended below the knees. A long slit on each side of the top went from the waist towards the floor allowing the front and back sections to flow gracefully with the breeze. The top was called an ao-di, and white or black pants were worn completing the Sunday outfit. During the workweek, women wore black pants and pajama-like tops, mostly black also. They were never without their straw hats to keep the sun away. I never saw a tanned Vietnamese woman. They used a shuffling gait as they walked, and they usually walked with several other women, giggling and gossiping as they went. I always thought the people shuffled because they wore thongs on their feet, but this wasn't the case. That shuffling gait was present even in bare feet.

The Vietnamese language was pleasant to listen to. Intonations, up or down the scale, changed the meaning of the same word, making the language difficult for me to learn. Men often held hands as they walked together with their shuffling gait. This was a strange sight for Americans to see, but nothing was signified by this action. The men mostly wore black shorts with black pajama-like tops.

They too wore the conical straw hats. Young children wore shirts, but nothing else. Diapers did not exist, and the children naturally eliminated anytime and anywhere! Children eliminating was not perceived as a problem in this rural, laid-back land of serene rice paddies and steaming jungles.

As a whole, South Vietnamese people were thin and well muscled. I observed the average rural man was about five feet, five inches tall, and weighed less than one hundred pounds. The women were slightly shorter and weighed about eighty pounds. They were hard working and uncomplaining, and I often saw a family of eight or ten toiling in their rice paddy. Men and women of all ages worked in paddy water up to their knees, wearing their conical hats with sweat pouring off their bodies. Men doffed their shirts, while the modest women rolled up shirtsleeves and shirt waists to keep cool. No one could have been cool under that sun! Little children gave stern orders to the water buffalo they tended while their parents did the manual labor. These buffalo pulled plows and turned bamboo water wheels to keep the water level up in the paddies. I was always amazed to see the little kids leading a huge water buffalo down a road, talking to it, and occasionally striking the beast with a bamboo switch.

Once, I saw a soldier who had been badly gored in the buttocks by a water buffalo. Remembering those children, and looking at this unfortunate but fully armed soldier with belts of ammunition around his shoulders, I had to ask, "Why didn't you just shoot that buffalo, rather than letting him gore you?" He replied, "I did, Sir! I emptied a full rifle clip into him! Twenty rounds!" Maybe a bamboo stick would have worked better than his M-16. Water buffalo always got a wide berth from me.

North Vietnamese people were taller than the South Vietnamese. They had more of a Chinese look to them, i.e., paler skin, thicker beards, and generally heavier and taller. They had darker hair under their arms and more body hair than their South Vietnamese neighbors. Their facial features had a Mongolian configuration, but only very slightly. Cambodians and Laotians, whom I saw from time to time, were also small, lightweight and sparse in body hair like the South Vietnamese, but their skin color was darker like Thailanders and Indians. The variations of the Asian people were easy to recognize; as south gave way to the north, the dark hues gave away to the lighter, the short to the taller and the light to the heavier.

There had been a lot of Chinese, Cambodian, Laotian, and especially French influence in South Vietnam. Most Vietnamese people spoke decent French and some Chinese. The vernacular of the day, especially when speaking to Americans, was made up of all these languages. We were Bac-si's, which was Chinese for doctors; dee-dee-mau meant to high-tail it out of there, and that was Vietnamese. Beau coup was French for many, and so on. Truly "pidgin English," this ersatz language was remarkably effective.

Each Sunday, Rosie, a middle-aged woman who worked in our mess hall's kitchen, came to the Catholic mass at the base chapel with her whole family. She always looked pretty, decked out in a washed and well-ironed ao-di with white pants. When I walked past, she and her whole family bowed in the old oriental manner. She always smiled and made polite conversation when we met. The politeness and shy nature of the Far Eastern culture was refreshing to a city kid like me. The occidental pushy style paled in comparison to genteel eastern manners. Rosie had come to South Vietnam with Father Tzu, and, like the good Father, she often talked about one day returning to her hometown to live once again with the relatives she had to leave behind. To live in peace, free from government harassment, was her dream. I don't believe her dream ever came true. Surely Father Tzu and his band of Catholics had to have been hunted down and executed after the North Vietnamese took over. I can only hope that never happened, but I'll bet it did. I dream of someday returning to find out what happened to Rosie and Father Tzu, but perhaps not finding those answers would be better. The kind and silently struggling people I met on my tour in South Vietnam were very likable, and I found it was easy to admire their persistence during a time of national upheaval.

WINNING HEARTS AND MINDS

MEDCAP missions, which stood for Medical Civilian Assistance Programs, were events where groups of doctors and medics traveled into the local villages to treat the civilians in their own town square. This was part of the Army's attempts to "win the hearts and minds of the people." Company D, 25th Med organized many MEDCAP missions, but maintaining security was always a difficult proposition. I couldn't help imagining that free-roaming bands of VC would have liked nothing better than to ambush a MEDCAP mission and kill Army doctors. Being a non-combatant in fact and in heart, I wanted to avoid any and all hostile enemy contact.

Of the two incidents that made me avoid MEDCAP missions, the first occurred when we had just returned from a nearby village late one evening. Our group saw and treated more than thirty patients in the town square of the village that day, and I was bushed. I remember the evening meal tasted pretty good that night, and I retired to my hooch for some well-earned rest. As I sat at the center table in my hooch, reading Margy's letter for that day, several rockets hit in the company area. Luckily, no one was hurt. Sergeant Rossnagel's hooch had been severely damaged from one of the rounds. A huge 240-millimeter rocket had demolished one side of his hooch wall and peppered his furniture. I walked over to see the damage for myself. The rocket crater in the hard dirt next to the sergeant's wall was up to my waist when I walked into it.

A team of artillerymen came to inspect the impact crater from that large rocket. This team of ballistic technicians, using the crater configuration, could plot the flight path of the offending rocket and determine the coordinates of its origination. Having done the calculations, the team went to where they figured the rocket was fired. Two crossed bamboo sticks with the tell-tale scorch mark in the dirt behind were found right in the middle of the same town square we had just left earlier that evening! Typically, no villagers were around to interrogate at the time. When one lone old woman was found, she cried and said VC had done this and they had left. Had the VC deliberately fired on our company area, or was this attack just a chance happening? The brigade couldn't opine; there were too many variables. Personally, I thought they were trying to hit the medical company with a clear message to "Stay Away!" My enthusiasm for MEDCAP missions was waning rapidly, and I canceled the next day's adventure.

The second incident of MEDCAP mayhem was the crowning one. Returning from a peaceful MEDCAP mission one late afternoon, our unescorted group of two ambulances and one jeep was fired upon by machine guns. The clumsy ambulances with the big red cross on their sides were great targets, and a bullet passed right through one red cross in a perfect bulls-eye. No one was riding in the back of the ambulances at the time, and I didn't find out about the bullet hole until I had returned to the base camp. The only defense we had was a single Colt .45 sidearm, mine, because the conscientious objectors accompanying me that day were, of course, all unarmed. Quickly dismounting from our vehicles, we took cover in a convenient ditch by the side of the road. Fifty-caliber machine gun bullets were sent our way, and they looked as big as basketballs as they kicked up the dirt on the road behind us. Very nervous, I kept thinking, "This is not good!" but the attack ended as abruptly as it started. With no more bullets coming our way, I peeked out to look in the direction I suspected the bullets had come from. There I thought I saw olive-drab uniformed men with camouflaged helmets on their heads. My thoughts were that these were ARVN soldiers, but surely they wouldn't have fired at us. After waiting a while, all remained quiet, and I gave the order to mount up! Our small entourage returned to the base at Tay Ninh.

At the motor pool, the bullet hole was found on the side of that ambulance! The motor pool sergeant, who had been in the infantry, said he thought we had been shot at by an ARVN unit, because the caliber was that of an M-16 rifle which the ARVNs used. The VC usually used a .30-caliber AK-47 rifle, but were known to pick up and use M-16s when possible. The sergeant also said he knew ARVNs would occasionally take pot-shots at GIs! Allegiances were cloudy, and common knowledge was that "Marvin the ARVN" could not always be trusted. I had heard rumors that ARVN units sometimes ambushed GI patrols, and shot at the helicopters that had just dropped them off. They had been known to have stormed aboard Dust Off helicopters, sent to pick up only the wounded, so they could get out of the battle. The South Vietnamese soldier was not always a brave fighter, would not always follow orders, and would desert on a dime. Moreover, rumor was that many ARVN soldiers were, in fact, Viet Cong guerrillas in allied uniforms.

In any case, the fact remained, we had been shot at, and the command sergeant major told me at the brigade briefing the next morning, that ARVN soldiers had been in that area at the time we had been fired upon. That incident greatly dampened my efforts to "win the hearts and minds of the people" with MEDCAPs. After all, our aid station was always open to any civilian for treatment, any-time. I no longer wanted to risk my life, or that of my medics, on those unprotected and poorly thought-out MEDCAP missions. My negative position on MEDCAPs lost me any favored status I might have enjoyed with Colonel Wair, but I could tolerate his cold shoul-der. I insisted we needed better infantry support to venture into those villages, and he agreed with me. He just didn't always have the troops to spare. Consequently I didn't plan any more of those missions.

AN OLD FRIEND

By March of 1969, I was getting to be a seasoned veteran. The war continued to rage around us and sometimes on us. Sick call became routine, and caring for the never-ending flow of wounded GIs became second nature. In April, R&R in Hawaii loomed as the next major event in my life and I was eagerly looking forward to it. Every day, I got letters from home, mostly from Margy, and some from my mother. Beth Ann was growing up rapidly and was talking a blue streak. She had learned to say "Tay Ninh" and missed her daddy. I sent and received voice-recorded tapes every week. I so longed to see my family again. At least R&R would allow me to see my wife.

As I was taping a message to Margy one night, we got a soldier with a head injury in the aid station. He was semi-awake and X-rays showed a large fragment deep inside his skull. A little bit at a time, he slipped deeper into coma, and I felt he would need neurosurgery soon. If he bled into his brain anymore, he would surely die. I called the neurosurgeons in Long Binh, and they agreed that if there were to be any hope of survival, this soldier needed surgery soon! The evacuation hospital at Long Binh was about 30 minutes away by helicopter and our Dust Off ship was readied for the trip. Concerned the patient might get worse on the trip I made plans to go along. Before the helicopter was ready, the patient worsened, and I had to place an endotracheal tube for respiratory support. I would breathe for him on the way to Long Binh using a hand squeezed ambu bag hooked to oxygen as a respirator. I brought along tracheotomy instruments just in case the tube came out and I couldn't replace it in flight. The ride was mercifully uneventful. We arrived at the evacuation hospital about midnight, and the patient was whisked straight into surgery. While I was talking to the nurses, the helicopter went back to Tay Ninh without me! The sergeant in the Long

Binh ER said they got a call and had to leave ASAP. The pilot said he would get me in the morning. The ER sergeant suggested I go to the POW camp down the road where he thought I could find a place to sleep until I could get back to Tay Ninh in the morning. Alone, I walked down that dark dirt road towards a lighted area that I assumed was in the POW camp. As I neared the light, I could hear men shouting and laughing. "It must be a nice POW camp," I thought. "They seem to be having a great time!" Soon it was obvious that some American soldiers were playing a game of basketball, and I thought I heard a familiar voice. As I neared, sure enough, the familiar voice was Duncan Morton's! We had played a lot of sports together in Cu Chi, and I recognized his shouts of glee. He loved sports and always was an excited participant. I called his name. I could see him peering into the darkness, squinting to see who had called him. When he recognized me, he said, "Ain't that some shit! Rick Snider! What are you doing here?"

Over a cold soda, I told him why I was walking down his dark road that night. We stayed up several more hours, just talking. He told me he had been transferred to the POW camp to run its hospital a month or so after I left Cu Chi. He was busy taking care of the many POWs brought to him with all kinds of wounds. He loved his job! The work was demanding, but he was up to the pressure, and he got help from the docs at the Evac hospital when he needed advice. He looked great! Seeing an old friend like Duncan was a good thing and made me remember my old friends in Cu Chi. Duncan got me a place to bunk in for the night, and I slept like a baby despite the fact I was sleeping above ground for the first time in many months. The next morning, Duncan and I made rounds on his patients in the POW hospital. Duncan was very friendly to his prisoner-patients. They smiled broadly when he talked to them, but I doubted they could understand him. Duncan was truly a wonderful doctor. He had that gift of being a genuine friend to his charges. His patients sensed his true concern for them, and they felt better, even as prisoners, just by seeing him.

The helicopter came to bring me back to Tay Ninh and I waved good-by to Duncan. I have never seen him since. I am sure he became a very successful surgeon and physician. Remembering him has been easy and I have tried to emulate his demeanor. As I flew back on that beautiful morning, I couldn't help smiling having seen Duncan again. The crew chief asked me if that was Dr. Morton, remembering him from mutual encounters in Cu Chi. When I said that it was, he smiled and told me what a good doctor and fine man he thought Dr. Morton was. I couldn't have agreed more. Touching down on the familiar tarmac of Company D, I was glad to be "home!" I knew my days were limited in Tay Ninh. The Army liked to transfer docs from forward units to the rear after six months and I had already been forward for seven months. Heck, nothing could bother me now. I was heading for R&R!

Margy and R&R

R&R

R&R stands for Rest and Recovery and was arguably the most sought after event in the life of a GI in Vietnam short of his DEROS day. Leaving Vietnam was a good thing, even for just a short while. Once back in country from his R&R a soldier could focus on his Date Estimated to Return from Overseas, but an R&R first was extremely nice to think about and to long for. In early 1969 there were many exotic and wonderful places to choose for your R&R. Taipei, Singapore, Kuala Lumpur, Hong Kong, Sydney, Manila, Penang, Tokyo, and Honolulu were on the list. Margy and I quickly picked Honolulu because it was in America, closer to Margy, who hated to fly, and Hawaii was a paradise! Most married men chose to spend R&R in Hawaii, while the unmarried men chose the oriental destinations because of the pretty women found in those destinations. R&R was going to be a second honeymoon for Margy and me, and I couldn't remember anything I looked forward to with such excitement and passion. Five days in paradise with the person I'd like most to be with was more than any man could ask for! Margy made reservations for us on Waikiki for the first night, and then, we were to spend the next four on the island of Kaui. I had a hard time keeping my mind on business while I waited for those happy upcoming days.

Sergeant Rossnagel made the arrangements on the Army side of things so nothing would go wrong for me. He had orders cut for my R&R and made arrangements for me to travel to and stay overnight in the Army's huge Third Field Hospital in Saigon. Close to Tan Son Nhut Airport, I could easily catch my plane the next morning from there. My basic training friend, Dr. Ron VanderMolen, was working at the Third Field Hospital, and I made arrangements with him to stay that night in his room in the posh Massachusetts Bachelor Officers' Quarters.

Sergeant Rossnagel personally made sure I had the proper uniform with which to travel. As Delta Six and a representative of Company D, our "mother hen" first sergeant wanted to make sure I was dressed with all the proper adornments on my uniform befitting a combat commander. Totally ignorant of the Army way, I gladly accepted his help in outfitting me for the upcoming trip. To my mind, all I needed for the trip was a bathing suit, but I would never let the sergeant pick one for me. He would surely pick an olive-drab one, and that I didn't want. The sergeant ordered my khaki uniform to be washed, starched, and ironed with great care. The khaki uniform was not usually worn inside Vietnam but was mandatory for travel.

Light green felt strips were wrapped around each of the shoulder epaulets on my khaki blouse, and through each of these green felt strips were affixed the Vietnam Army Force shield. The ribbons, captain's bars, and other insignia were properly and expertly placed on that now stiffly starched shirt. After he determined everything to be perfect, Sergeant Rossnagel allowed my uniform, a symbol of the Army's pride in its dress, to be carefully placed on hangers and covered with a plastic protective carrying bag to ward off wrinkles and the ever present Tay Ninh dust. Only after he was sure I would correctly represent Company D, could Sergeant Rossnagel relax enough to wish me safe travel and a good time.

When that day finally came, I left my envious friends to board the Dust Off helicopter which would fly me to Cu Chi, where I would spend the first night of my sojourn with my old outfit. That night I was on familiar turf. I had a fine time catching up on all the news with some of my old buddies. After a good meal in the bigger, more modern Cu Chi mess hall, I enjoyed a few drinks at the officer's' club. Later that night, I watched a movie in the outdoor theater. "Guess Who's Coming To Dinner" was playing, and I laughed out loud several times at the situations Sidney Poitier got into with Spencer Tracy and Katherine Hepburn. Towards the end of the movie there was an unexpected loud explosion nearby, reminding me of incoming in Tay Ninh, and I was thoroughly confused. Nevertheless, I hit the dirt with all the instincts of the veteran I had become. Following the flow of rushing men, I scrambled into a nearby bunker to wait out the ongoing explosions. The bunker was packed with sweating and breathless GIs, and, since this bunker served the Officers' Club, the smell of alcohol was strong. No one seemed to know what was happening. From the protection of that large bunker, I could hear sounds of small-arms fire alternating with incoming-like explosions. Over the next five minutes, the sounds lessened and finally ceased. Leaving the bunker, I soon found out what had happened.

A Navy Riverine Force helicopter had just dropped off several wounded at the nearby 25th aid station. Having dropped off the wounded the Navy helicopter began to fly away. Striking an unseen wire strung across the road, the Navy chopper crashed. Cu Chi helicopter pilots were familiar with those wires and avoided them. Striking an unseen wire, the Navy helicopter crashed onto a road near the outdoor theater, immediately caught fire, and burned rapidly because of the magnesium in the chopper's hull. Jet fuel and ammunition exploded from the heat. The helicopter's rockets and bullets "cooked off," adding to the mayhem. By the time we movie-goers arrived on the scene, all the explosions had stopped and the flames had been put out. A grotesque scene remained for all to see. The blackened twisted frame was all that remained of the Navy helicopter and was barely recognizable in the center of the street. White ash left from the burning magnesium outlined the former extent of the helicopter. The helicopter's hull was made from an aluminum-magnesium alloy which, being very flammable, burns intensely and quickly. Two charred bodies were frozen in crawling positions! They had been caught by the rapidly expanding flames as they tried to make their escape. The explosion and cooking ammunition caused several pedestrian casualties and these victims had already been taken to my old aid station nearby. A large portion of one of the helicopter's rotor blades was sticking out from the roof of the NCO club nearby. The occupants of the club had quite a scare when the large piece of the rotor blade came hurtling through the roof! Luckily, no one inside was seriously injured. I couldn't go back and watch the end of the movie. Instead, I found an empty bunk and tried to concentrate my racing thoughts on R&R. The charred bodies of the crawling men who tried so desperately to get away from the flames was all I could see. Mercifully sleep finally came later that night. I awoke early the next morning surprisingly refreshed and eager to get on with my trip.

After a good breakfast, I hitched a ride on a helicopter heading for Tan Son Nhut. I was dropped off on a helicopter landing area at the airport, which, in April of 1969, was the busiest airport in the world. Screaming Air Force jets took off at frequent intervals to begin their harassment of the enemy. Large commercial passenger jets were landing and taking off in another direction, and the South Vietnam Air Force prop planes were taking off and landing every few minutes. On my way out of the airport's front gate, I passed one of the largest PXs I ever saw. As crowded as Macy's in New York City at Christmas time, the airport buzzed with all kinds of activity! Next door the South Vietnamese Air Force Officers' Club was going strong, even though the time was only eleven in the morning. Vietnamese airmen in gray flight suits were milling about ogling young Vietnamese girls in tight skirts and low-cut tops. This complex was too busy for me, and I felt better as I passed through the front gate. As if on cue, as I passed through, the ARVN guard on duty at the gate pulled his .45 and fired two shots into the air to stop another ARVN speeding away on a motor scooter. The frightened ARVN on the scooter almost fell off as he spun around trying to stop. The guard ran up to him excitedly shouting Vietnamese words in a high, shrill voice. I gave that fracas a wide berth as I briskly headed for the Third Field Hospital about a mile down the road.

Motor scooters whizzed past with as many as five Vietnamese people on one scooter. Vespas and Hondas were the common brands of scooters and their numbers were prodigious! Military and private automobiles were also in abundance, not to mention jeeps, armored personnel carriers, and an occasional tank. This commotion was a lot for a rural soldier like me to take, and I was relieved as I turned into the Third Field lobby. There was air-conditioning! What relief from the oppressive heat outside. I called Ron and he said he would be down to get me in a few minutes. I told him to take his time, I wanted to enjoy the cool lobby. I sat down on a small waiting room sofa to wait for Ron and to enjoy the air-conditioning. During my trip thus far, I had become covered with fine dust. I began to slap myself with my soft hat to remove the dust. Looking up, I saw an Army major standing over me with his arms akimbo, Army style. His smile was reassuring as he asked me where I was coming from. Standing to be polite, I could see the major was with another man. This second man also smiled and repeated the major's inquiry in a very friendly tone, "Where are you coming from, Captain, and where are you headed?" At ease by their friendly interest, I told them I was headed for R&R! Unable to suppress a smile, I embarrassed myself with my effervescent reply. "Captain," said the major,

"Meet General Goodpasture, second in command in Vietnam!" At that instant, I noticed the four black stars, all in a row, on the general's lapel and began to realize the possible gravity of this situation. The general was hatless and seemed way too young to be a general. I wasn't sure whether I was going to salute or run. To be safe, I gave him the smartest salute I could muster. The major then asked if I had anything I wanted to say to the general. All I could respond with was, "My God, Sir! I've never seen so many stars!"

Both the general and the major laughed, putting me back at ease and allowing me to smile at what I had just uttered. The general then shook my hand warmly, thanked me for all I was doing for our soldiers, and wished me a wonderful time in Hawaii. He asked me to give his regards to my wife and family. He said this was a hard time for America, and he was thankful for soldiers like me. With a final wish for my future good fortune, both men turned and left me standing there, desperately trying to digest all that just happened. What a great guy that general was! I was very impressed! I was to notice more and more that most generals were like that, really good men. That's how they got that far.

Just as the general was leaving, Ron walked up and we shook hands. "Who was that?" he asked, turning his in the direction of the departing officers. "General Goodpasture," I said with new-found authority. "He came to greet me." "Did I see four stars?" Ron asked, whistling. "Yup, four of those little suckers. Equal to Westmoreland," I said. Ron just smiled and shook his head in disbelief. With that we left the lobby and Ron took me on a tour of the huge Third Field Hospital. Most specialties were represented at the hospital, including a cardiologist and a complete catheterization laboratory. On the other hand, no neurosurgeons were on the staff, and cases needing neurosurgery were flown the short distance to Long Binh. I told Ron about my recent experience in Long Binh and about meeting Duncan there. Ron and Duncan had met in basic training at Fort Sam.

I threw my gear in Ron's room at the Massachusetts BOQ. Ron didn't have a roommate at the time, leaving Ron's room with an empty bed. His room was air-conditioned and had its own bathroom complete with a sink, commode, and shower. A flush toilet was strange to see again! There was hot, as well as cold, running water, and reliable electricity enabling the use of an electric razor. These little things meant a lot, since they had not been available to me for quite a while.

Ron had been in a similar situation as I, having been initially assigned to a clearing company with the "Big Red One," the First Infantry Division, in central South Vietnam for the first half of his tour. He had been transferred to the Third Field about a month ago, and he loved it. He worked in the emergency room at the hospital, doing the same type of surgery he had done with the Big Red One, but he had other duties too. Although there was no "sick call" in the ER at the hospital, many patients came there to see a doctor for non-emergent illnesses. Many walk-in clinics were scattered throughout Saigon for minor complaints, but the Third Field Hospital's ER was more convenient for many to use. Ron said he saw civilians, merchant marine sailors, all kinds of government workers as well as many Army wounded. I made up my mind to request a transfer to the Third Field when I got back from R&R. To work in such a well-fitted and modern hospital would be a welcome change, and I knew I would enjoy working with Ron.

Going one step further, Ron petitioned the hospital commander to formally request that I be transferred there in the near future. Getting the commander's promise to request my transfer lifted me even more, making my upcoming R&R even more enjoyable. Ron had gone to Hawaii a month earlier and he loved it there. I was getting excited. I found sitting still for any length of time difficult. Luckily, Ron and I kept busy, topping off the day with a great dinner of steak and beer in the restaurant on the roof of the Massachusetts BOQ. The view from the restaurant revealed some bustling streets of Saigon below and a large soccer stadium across the noisy main street. A pleasant evening breeze cooled me as I ate, and the realization a war was going all around was the farthest thing from my mind. After dinner, I had a couple of drinks at the Circle Thirty-Four, a local Officers' Club. The club had tablecloths, air-conditioning, and entertainment; it was different from the bamboo clubs I was used to. The entertainment group in the Circle Thirty-Four that night was Japanese. They sang most of the popular songs of the day, and I remember stirring renditions of, "I Reft My Heart in San Flancisco," and "We Got To Get Out Of This Prace!" Their voices and the pretty dancing girls more than made up for any pronunciation errors. Later that night, I got the best sleep I had in many months. Not having to sleep in a bunker with mosquitoes and heat made for comfort unknown to me for months.

The next morning, I was up early. Ron said goodbye as he was leaving for work at 0700 hours. I pulled my crisply pressed uniform from the protective bag and got dressed. The uniform was tight on my body and made me uncomfortable. Even though I had lost a great deal of weight since I last wore these clothes, jungle fatigues were looser fitting and much more comfortable than the khaki uniform. Wearing the shirt outside of the pants made a lot of difference because tucking the shirt inside the pants kept in a lot of heat. Wearing an undershirt made me even hotter. I hadn't even left the air-conditioning yet! The regulation black shoes though were a comfortable respite from the jungle boots I had worn for eight months. I could see my reflection in the spit shine Sergeant Rossnagel had put on my shoes. Those shoes would never look that good again.

Finally confident I was wearing my uniform correctly, I set out for the TWA counter at Tan Son Nhut Airport. I walked the mile to the airport under an overcast sky that mercifully made the day fairly cool. I didn't soak my neat uniform with sweat. Things moved right along at the airport, and the next thing I knew, I was flying to Guam in an air-conditioned jet and eating real food! An Air Force major sitting next to me was also headed for Hawaii to see his wife. He talked all the way to Guam. An interesting guy, I enjoyed his company, and his talking made the twelve-hour ride go by a little more quickly.

The stop on Guam was interesting. Guam was the home base for many of the B-52 bombers that were operating over Vietnam. They were so numerous, they took up most of the runway space at the airport. Their long heavy wings touched the ground at the tips. Painted an ominous black and brown camouflage, they looked every inch the killers they were. The B-52s rained down their five-hundred-pound bombs near Tay Ninh many times, and the earth would rumble so hard that my bunker light shook fitfully on its chain during those attacks. How the enemy ever tolerated that pounding, I'll never understand. I had seen many dazed and dumbfounded NVA soldiers after some of those B-52 bombing runs. They wanted to surrender just to get away from the bombs. Stunned by the concussive force of the huge bombs, many of those enemy soldiers had blood coming from perforated eardrums. The concussions exacted a huge toll on their own, without needing shrapnel to inflict wounds. The look of terror in the dark eyes of the B-52 victims was unforgettable and very understandable. I always thought the B-52 bombs alone should have ended the war, but, of course, they didn't. Most of those bombs probably missed the major concentrations of enemy troops, and that is how they were able to continue fighting. I used to pray that the NVA would never get these black giants on their side. I'm sure I would have surrendered if they did. The B-52s flew so high I never saw or heard them. I only heard and felt their bombs. I was glad when our plane left that island, and for some reason, the return flight didn't stop there.

Landing in Hawaii was exciting. The plane emptied quickly in five minutes, rather than the usual 30 minutes. No doubt everyone was eager to see their loved ones and start the long awaited R&R! A lot of men did a lot of waiting in Vietnam, and this was the first payoff. In single file, we were led up to a closed gate in a tall cyclone fence with barbed wire on the top. We had landed on the military airstrip at the Honolulu Airport, which was separated from the public airport by this MP-guarded fence. I soon found out why MPs were necessary.

About fifty long-haired people looking unkempt in sloppy clothes had gathered outside our exit gate. "Hippies" were not new to most of us. I had some knowledge of the counterculture movement before I had shipped out. The hippies began jeering at us and calling us names like warmongers, baby killers, and squares. That really hurt my pride and stirred up angry emotions inside. I had imagined people would have been pleased to see us and would have been proud of what we had been doing. Certainly in previous wars returning soldiers were treated like heroes, getting a warm welcome home with bands and parades, not jeers and cat-calls. This was far from the warm welcome I had imagined. The venom these people had for us was frightening, and the confrontation was getting scary to me.

I had been standing next to a young three-striped "buck" sergeant who, like me, was decked out in a nicely pressed khaki uniform that proudly displayed his Combat Infantryman's Badge above his left breast pocket. His badge declared he had been a combat soldier, a veteran of untold numbers of firefights, and he was lucky to be alive. R&R had to have been especially priceless to him. Infantrymen made up only about thirty percent of all the troops in Vietnam, and I always felt they deserved R&R more than the seventy percent of us who were just support troops. Seeing that the young sergeant had the green felt strip under his Vietnam shield too, I felt even more proud of mine. He was wearing his wedding ring and I suspected he was going to meet his wife in few moments also. I couldn't help thinking that his wife would probably fall in love with him all over again when she saw him in his spiffy uniform, not to mention his having been gone for the past six or seven months.

One of the demonstrators lit a string of Chinese firecrackers that made sounds just like a VC machine gun. The sergeant's strong combat instincts compelled him to hit the dirt, and, unfortunately, he dove into a small mud puddle, which soiled his neat uniform. Getting up from the puddle, he saw the water and mud all down the front of his once immaculate uniform. He let out a string of oaths that would have embarrassed a Marine as he vainly tried to wipe away those muddy water stains. Snickers and more jeers were hurled from the other side of the fence when the hippies saw his misfortune. The longhaired antagonists taunted him by saying, "Afraid of a little firecracker? What a wimp!" Feeling very emotional, the sergeant, a survivor of life-threatening combat, began to wrinkle up his face as if he were about to cry. The taunts kept coming, "Oh, too bad, mamma's boy is all dirty! Dirt spots wash out easier than blood spots."

His fellow soldiers recognized the absolute unfairness of all this and quickly became inflamed. The sergeant regained his composure after hearing the savage threats his buddies shouted back to the demonstrators. Deleting the many foul expletives, the soldiers said that when they got hold of the hippies, they were going to tear them to pieces! That gate had been locked by some quirk of providence, or lives of the hippie antagonists would have been jeopardized for certain. The soldiers were hopping mad and would have easily killed a few of the protesters for revenge. The muddied sergeant was now smiling. His mind clearing from the disappointment of meeting his wife with a soiled uniform, he knew this was only a small problem in the big picture. Tempers cooled as the MPs cleared away the demonstrators. We passed through that gate to climb on a bus that would take us to nearby Fort Derussey on the Waikiki Beach and to our wives! I kept straining to see that sergeant. I wanted to see him greet his wife, but I couldn't find him in the crowd. In fact, I never saw him again. That whole encounter took only a few moments, but I'll never forget that sergeant. I can still see his face clouding up, that strong man, near tears. The injustice of it all! Jeered and mocked by the people he had been fighting and risking his life for. Vietnam was a crazy war. I really couldn't blame anybody for being caught up in the struggle as I had been, or for protesting against the United States' involvement. What happened to that infantry sergeant was an indignant experience for all of us to endure that day.

Seeing my wife waiting there made me forget everything else instantly. I thought I was going to have a cardiac arrest on the spot! She was more beautiful than I could ever have remembered. When she spied me and smiled my legs grew so weak I could hardly walk. Greeting her that day had to have been the best moment in my life. To me, Margy embodied all that was good and wholesome in life, in the whole world, all that ever was and all that would ever be. Her innocence and devotion washed free all the inequities my soul had accumulated in the Army and in Vietnam. What the war had hardened in me in the previous eight months, she melted with her beautiful smile right then and there. Seeing Margy made the anguish and hardship I had endured all worthwhile. When my heart finally settled down, we began to look at the new pictures of Beth Ann she had brought along to show me. My daughter was almost two years old now, and seeing her pictures made my soul sing. I was overwhelmed and exhausted with joy at that moment.

The Army did a magnificent job on R&R in Hawaii. Fort Derussey was an 1850 vintage fort the Army occupied on the far end of beautiful Waikiki Beach. No longer used as a fort, the land sported small cottages for vacationing soldiers. These cottages were reserved for enlisted men with families. I could see some children frolicking at the water's edge, and I could hear their happy screams over the noisy surf. We soldiers and our wives were then shown into an auditorium that was mostly a roof to keep out the sun. We were officially greeted by an Army chaplain who was a Catholic priest. As he spoke to us we couldn't help looking out onto the Waikiki tropical paradise and smelling that salt air brought to our nostrils by the gently wafting sea breezes. Capitalizing on the scene, and our joy at that moment, the chaplain gave us a welcoming speech. He thanked us for all we were going through in Vietnam. He had spent a year there and what bothered him the most was the apathetic, if not hostile, way he was greeted when he returned home. He wanted us to know that there were many thousands of people who appreciated what we had been going through, and he wanted to be the first to thank us for a job well done. He wished us a "heavenly time" in the islands, and he assured us the Army also wanted us to have a great time. As a result of his short speech, we were sent on our way feeling good about ourselves for the first time in a long while.

The Army had arranged fifty percent reductions in costs for restaurants, hotels, car rentals, and the like. This reduction allowed a much better vacation than we could have otherwise afforded, and we all took advantage of it. Dismissed from the open-air auditorium, Margy and I took a cab to the Waikiki beachside Halikulani Hotel. Margy had arranged a bungalow on the beach for us for that night. We ate, swam, laughed, and phoned Beth Ann, as well as our parents. That place was truly heaven on earth.

The next day we flew to the island of Kaui and the Hanalei Plantation. We ate at tables that were out-of-doors, and while small birds stole crumbs from our plates, gorgeous Hawaiian girls danced the hula! Margy and I had never experienced such a restful time together. The last night of my leave, we spent back at the Halikulani bungalow, but a pall hung over us that night. R&R was over. The long-awaited time passed so swiftly, we couldn't believe it. Long plane rides lay ahead for both of us the next morning, but our time together had been worth it. We would be back together in four short months. Knowing this goodbye was only for four months lessened the anxiety. The next morning, after a breakfast of delicious Hawaiian pineapple, Margy and I tearfully parted, going our separate ways. Boarding my plane, I took note that I really did feel rested and recovered. I was eternally grateful to the Army for providing me the opportunity of an R&R.

RETURN TO VIETNAM

If seeing Margy in Hawaii had been the zenith of my life, the return to Vietnam had to be the nadir! When my return plane's door opened to the air of Saigon, I gasped at the familiar heat and odor. The despair of the returning soldiers was palpable as we got off the plane onto that sizzling hot runway. Back at the Third Field Hospital, I changed back into my worn-in, comfortable jungle fatigues and those clumsy jungle boots. I didn't see Ron at all this time; he was on duty. I used his room to change and then left to catch a ride back to Tay Ninh. Luckily, I was able to hop on a C-140 jet-assisted prop plane that was flying directly to Tay Ninh.

Flying over the jungle near the Third Brigade base at Tay Ninh, I heard a click. The Air Force sergeant crew member put his finger through a new .51-caliber bullet hole in the side of the plane's fuselage. The large bullet had passed harmlessly out the other side of the plane, and, had it not been for the clicking sound it made, no one would have known that death barely missed us that day. Welcome home! After walking back from the airport carrying my wrinkled khaki uniform, I sat on my bunk to rest. Charlie Guess came and sat next to me. He eagerly asked me how my R&R had been. He was slated to go on his next month. Something came over me as I thought about that wonderful respite from which I had just returned, and I could hardly speak. I was surprised to find that I was very depressed now that it was over. Charlie really wanted to hear all about it, but the words just wouldn't come. I had a hard time speaking at all. Sensing my distress, Charlie left, saying he would ask me about it in the morning. I got undressed, got into my damp bunker bed, and slept away my jet lag. The next morning I felt a lot better, maybe even like my old self again. I told Charlie, and anyone else who would listen, great details about the beauties of R&R in Hawaii. Realizing I really did have a great time was good for me. Returning just naturally bummed me out! I was back in Tay Ninh, but I could look forward to spending only a few more weeks here until my transfer to the Third Field Hospital would come through. This was one of the first times I felt that my time was winding down, and I was slowly but inexorably becoming "short!"

Over the next few weeks, I decided life in Tay Ninh wasn't so bad after all. Outside of the danger, which I had to accept as par for the course, having to hump the boonies looking for Charley would have been a lot worse. This was my home, familiar and tolerable. A week had to pass for me to snap out of pining for my wife and things that couldn't be. At times like these, the new elation set in and I thought about getting short and finally going home. How peculiar that elation was able to settle in even though the war was getting worse. The local artillery unit was now firing all day, and that loud eight-incher seemed to fire over our heads all the time. The concussion from one of those shells actually knocked me off my above-ground bunk once as I napped one afternoon. After that monstrous round passed overhead, my ears rang for hours. Never having the warning the artillerymen enjoyed, I couldn't protect my ears by holding my hands over them. My hearing has never been the same, and the ringing ears persist to this day.

More and more "Doughnut Dollies" stayed in our area. These were "round eyed" American women who worked for the USO. They passed out doughnuts when they could, but mostly they were invaluable in raising the morale of the soldiers. Just seeing "back home girls" cheered my patients better than any medicine I could prescribe. These lovely young women visited our patients on a daily basis. The doughnut dollies suffered all the indignities of Army life I did, if not more. They lived in tents, ate Army chow and suffered from the unyielding heat as we all did. They always had a smile for the GIs and asked for nothing in return. They all deserved medals for their sacrifices, and they will always have my undying admiration for what they did.

A lot of oriental singing touring groups sponsored by the USO performed in Tay Ninh. They usually were very good at singing all the latest hits the music-loving GIs wanted to hear. Although most groups had some male performers who were very good in their own right, the very pretty and sexy girls were understandably the most appreciated, no matter what or how they sang. One night a group was performing near the brigade headquarters for a bunch of GIs on stand-down. Incoming rockets pummeled the area, scattering all the participants including the female singers. When the smoke cleared, the two beautiful women singers were the only wounded, and they were brought to our aid station for care. One of the female singers had a very minor frag wound of her arm, and I let an overly eager medic tend to her. The second woman was a different story. She was crying hysterically, so I tried to make a joke by asking her what infantry outfit she was with. No go, she was still crying, even more so having seen me. Her thumb was almost cut off through the outer joint, and she had a large fragmentation wound on her buttock. The buttock wound bothered her the most, not because it hurt, which I'm sure it did, but because she was worried about the scar it would leave. The metal fragment was protruding from the skin, signifying a superficial wound, and I assured her it would be easy to remove. She still was mostly worried about the scar and that another rocket would fall. I sedated her with morphine. The thumb wound responded to a few good sutures, looking and working as good as new. I debrided her buttock wound and dressed the wound unsutured as usual. She was absolutely horrified I hadn't closed the wound with stitches. She told me she was from Korea, and had dreams of one day going to the United States to continue her singing career. She felt if she had a huge scar on her buttock, her career would be over before it started. Another of my jokes failed when I suggested she needn't sing with her buttock. Managing a smile, she said her whole body was important to her and sometimes her buttocks would be modestly exposed in one of her best routines. I said I wished I had caught her act before she had been wounded. She must have been something! Now, she was smiling broadly, and I again assured her that in two or three days her wound could be closed and the scar wouldn't be bad at all. Off she went, limping slightly, back into her world and back into the inhospitable and frightening night. For a while, the USO had a hard time getting singing groups to perform in Tay Ninh.

Saigon City from the Newport Barracks

SAIGON

Near the end of April, having spent nine months with the 25th Infantry Division, my orders came through for me to be transferred to the Third Field Hospital in Saigon! I had confused emotions about leaving, not so much the danger of Tay Ninh, but of leaving Charlie Guess, Marty Bruggerman, and Hal Shields. We had worked very well together and I wished they could have come with me to my new post. I also was going to miss my other company officers and the medics I so admired. Charlie had received orders to report as a GMO in Ban Me Thuet in the central highlands. He wasn't very thrilled about his new assignment, knowing the danger there would probably be even more than he had experienced in Tay Ninh. The night before I was to leave for Saigon, we had a cookout with a case of the very finest "condemned" steaks and plenty of beer. After dinner, I was given a plaque of appreciation from Company D 25th Med. The heart-shaped plaque was made from ammo crate wood and beer can metal, all standard materials used by Vietnamese craftsmen of the time. I also received a cigarette box made from the beautiful wood of a local jungle tree magnificently carved with scenes of the Tay Ninh countryside. My Executive Officer then got up to speak. He presented me with the Combat Medic's Badge. He said in his speech that every member of Company D was going to receive the Combat Medic Badge because of the particularly hazardous duty the company had endured. Division Headquarters was aware that our company had lost three of its men during the first three months of 1969, and that we had received incoming almost every night during that same time period.

Continuing, the XO then presented me with the Bronze Star Medal! I was flabbergasted. Usually a doctor got the Army Commendation Medal for his serving in a combat unit, but the Bronze Star was something I didn't expect. Reading what the citation said, the XO brought tears to my eyes. After the speech, I was asked to say a few words, but I was barely able to speak. I first mumbled a prayer for our three fallen company members, but when I tried to talk after the prayer, I couldn't. At that point, I just waved goodbye, turned and walked away. Emotionally drained, I couldn't face them any more. I headed for the secluded safety of my hooch. As I sat down in the chair by the center table, I could hear the sounds of the men laughing, enjoying themselves. There were still a lot of steaks and beer left to devour and I was glad this would keep them occupied for a while. I needed some time alone for quiet reflection so I could digest all this and compose myself. Lying on my bunk, I read over the written citation on the Bronze Star. I wanted to be sure the citation said what my ears had heard. The emotions of that meeting rendered my ears and memory untrustworthy. Here is what it said:

"--for meritorious achievement from 1 March 1969 to 24 April 1969, while serving as Commanding Officer, Company D 25th Medical Battalion, 25th Infantry Division. His constancy under strain of enemy attack, his assiduous dedication to the care and treatment of patients, even at great personal risk, and the judicious leadership of his command resulted in an extraordinarily successful medical clearing operation. Captain Snider's devotion to duty is in keeping with the highest traditions of the military service and reflects great credit upon himself, his unit, the 25th Infantry Division, and the United States Army."

That night was one of the proudest moments of my life. I will always be thankful that I was able to serve as I did with Company D, 25th Medical Battalion, 25th Infantry Division.

Bright and early the next morning, having already said my goodbyes, I boarded a helicopter heading for Saigon and my new assignment at the Third Field Hospital. The jungle zooming by below soon gave way to streets and houses. We landed at Tan Son Nhut. Saigon seemed even busier than I had remembered. Jets were screaming and horns were honking. I sneaked past the ARVN guard at the gate, hoping to avoid getting shot, and hurried down the busy street to the Third Field Hospital.

My first assigned billet was a room in a three-bedroom house, five doors down the street from the hospital's front gate. I lived in that house for about two weeks. There were several other officers housed there but they were not doctors, nor in any way connected with the hospital. They were staying at the house on a temporary basis, as was I. The main thing I remember about that house was a rooster owned by a Vietnamese man who operated a farm in the city at the rear of the house. Here he raised chickens to be sold in the open markets that flourished on every street corner in Saigon. These markets had many booths and sold just about anything and everything you could imagine, including chickens.

The farmer's brassy rooster used to position himself right beneath my room each and every morning. He never missed one! The house had been built on cement blocks creating a three-foot crawl space between the dank earth and the first floor. At four o'clock each morning, long before the sun was to rise, the rooster began crow, perhaps to proclaim to all the hens that he was the toughest rooster around. His raucous crowing would keep up until I was wide awake and mad as hell. After many mornings of this Vietnamese rooster torture, I decided the bird had to die! Understand, I had tried all the preliminary steps, such as stamping on the floor, throwing stones at him from the alley, and threats to his owner. After all, killing was going on all over Vietnam, so my contribution to that theme would be one obnoxious, loud-mouthed rooster. I planned my ambush for the next morning. Being a city kid, I was amazed that the other house occupants weren't bothered in the least by that chicken! I set my alarm for three-thirty A.M. only to be greeted by a very hot Saigon night. I put on my steel helmet to protect my head from striking the floor joists in the dark. In olive drab boxer shorts, with dog tags dangling from my neck, and holding a flashlight, I began crawling around in the dark under the floor. Crawling was difficult since I had my .45 pistol in one hand and my GI flashlight in the other. Nonetheless I was determined and followed the crowing towards my prey. As I maneuvered along, sweating, under that floor that morning in Saigon, halfway around the world, I began to think, "What was I doing?" For the first time in my revenge-soaked mind I wondered where would my bullet end up even if I hit that bird? Surely it would pass through him and travel on. What would the farmer say after I showed him the assassinated body of his beloved rooster? What would the Vietnamese MPs do when they heard my

shot? Would they shoot at me? All my newly considered worries
became moot because the rooster saw me and easily scooted away
to lose himself in the crowd of the other chickens. I emerged from
under that house, resolved not to let a stupid rooster be the cause of
my death in Vietnam. Back in my room, I took a cold shower and
went back to bed much wiser for having thought it through. I imagined the rooster's cock-a-doodle-doing had a triumphant ring to it
from then on. The rooster had won, but I was transferred to new
quarters the next day. I was ashamed when I reflected later on just
how that rooster had moved me to consider such a dangerous step.

My new quarters were in the Newport Bachelor Officers' Quarters on the sixth floor, about two blocks away in the direction of the
airport. There weren't any chickens in sight. My roommate was
Captain Paul Arnold from Ohio, who worked in the Department of
Defense in downtown Saigon. Interestingly enough, his sister
worked there too. Like many civilians, Paul's sister had landed a
great-paying job with the DOD if she would work in Saigon. Paul
worked in the same section with his sister, and that was the only
way Paul's mother would have ever allowed her daughter to work in
Saigon. Paul was a very nice guy and considered his work in Saigon
was like a walk in the park. He was aware there was a war going on,
but he had no firsthand knowledge of it. Many soldiers working in
Saigon at that time were so far removed from any fighting, they actually enjoyed their tour in Vietnam. These soldiers worked for the
Embassy, the Department of Defense, one of the many supply de-
pots there, or some other cushy job that kept them in Saigon. Saigon
was called the "Paris of the Orient" for good reason. A modern city
with all the perks, Saigon flaunted a cosmopolitan atmosphere that
was hard to resist. Paul knew all the best places to eat in the city,
and, being a bachelor with a sister for an agent, he had a great social
life. There were hundreds of round-eyed girls working in Saigon
and plenty of things for young people to do. Paul became annoyed
at my reluctance to socialize, or to even eat out in restaurants. I'm
sure he thought I was crazy, but I didn't want to get killed eating a
steak or pick up some kind of intestinal parasite, hepatitis, or worse.
I just wanted to put in my three more months as safely as possible
and go home! Eventually I occasionally went out to eat and saw
some of the sights of Saigon with Paul, but I never completely lost
my uneasiness about it. Somehow, I felt I was betraying all those
grunts who were slugging it out with the enemy in a dark, damp

jungle, especially when I sat in some posh restaurant eating prime rib. I'd do my eating out when I got back to the States. Besides, I was no fun to be with; I still jumped when I heard the gears of a truck winding down to stop. Once, after hitting the dirt for some suspicious sound, Ron had to tell me, "Rick, that's just not incoming here in Saigon!" Try as I may, the instinctive reactions were too powerful for me to ignore. Saigon was too much for someone from Tay Ninh. I never became accustomed to life in the "Big City!"

The Third Field Hospital functioned like a large stateside hospital, nothing at all like the hospitals in the rest of Vietnam. I was assigned to work in the Emergency Room with Ron VanderMolen. There were four of us to cover the ER 24 hours a day, seven days a week, 24-7 as is said today. Two doctors at a time worked covering the busy hours from 0800 to 2000 hours, and just one of us worked the night shift from 2000-0800 the next morning. My duties as a physician in the ER were explained to me by Ron and the nurse in charge. I never had a formal briefing by the CO of the hospital and physician policies seemed loose. A lot of non-emergencies and many wounded were seen in the ER. There were five fully trained general surgeons, as well as orthopedic surgeons, a urologist, an ophthalmologist, an ear, nose and throat specialist, and a full compliment of internal medicine specialists and sub-specialists available in the hospital. Sidney Cohen was a fully trained obstetrician and gynecologist who also manned the ER with us. An Army obstetrician might seem unnecessary in Vietnam, but in Saigon, he served the many women who worked in various departments and agencies, as well as some of the wives of high ranking Vietnamese dignitaries. Delivering babies was a pleasant relief for him from all the wounded GIs he cared for.

Also working in the Third Field Hospital were anesthesiologists, radiologists and a pathologist. The latter was kept very busy running the blood bank program for our area, and he also did some laboratory work when necessary. Dialysis was available at the hospital and functioned very well when needed. Most renal failure patients were sent to Japan, but those patients needing dialysis acutely were able to have that process in the hospital. My duties were much simpler in Saigon than in Tay Ninh. Most of all, I had absolutely no non-medical Army command duties whatsoever. Details of Army command were no longer my bailiwick. All I had to do was to ex-

amine the wounded GIs and then summon the appropriate specialists to carry through the treatment. Orthopedics took care of anyone
with a fracture, and the fully trained general surgeons did most of
the debriding. Non-surgical problems were handled primarily by the
appropriate internal medicine specialists. Any soldier with a fever of
over 101 degrees Fahrenheit was admitted straight through to the
medical ward, where he was to be seen by the internist on call. Everything seemed streamlined. All the doctors were pleasant and helpful. The nursing staff was mostly female, which was unique, as men
were the nurses most everywhere else in the army facilities in Vietnam. Women nurses were a pleasure to work with, and they made
me feel like I was back in New Haven.

Ron and I were only partially trained surgeons and, as such,
were taken under the wings of several surgeons who wanted to
teach. Ron and I were eager to learn, and we got to do a lot of surgery during our stay at the Third Field Hospital. This duty was better than a residency and we reveled in it. The ophthalmologist and
one of the orthopedic surgeons were also interested in teaching, so
Ron and I got to do and see a lot with them to boot. We didn't have
a lot of contact with the internists because their work was very different than surgery.

The mess hall at the hospital was the best I had ever seen. The
food was real, not reconstituted as in the field. Sunday brunch was
something! Eggs done any way, bacon, sausage, pancakes, waffles
and even steaks were offered from early in the morning until late in
the afternoon. I gained back a lot of the weight I had lost in Tay
Ninh. Being in Saigon, there were precious few mosquitoes, and
screens were everywhere. With no mosquitoes to bite me, I saw no
reason to continue taking the malaria pills that caused me to have
weekly diarrhea. Stopping the malaria pills also helped me to gain
weight.

Other pluses of this duty station were the restaurant in the Massachusetts BOQ and the Circle 34 Officers' Club. Just about any
fare and drink were available at just about any time. I usually ate in
the restaurant for lunch, mainly cheeseburgers and French fries, but
substituting a grilled ham and cheese sandwich for the burger from
time to time. Officers were served in the chow line, but we had our
own dining room, which was pretty posh. There were upholstered
seats, cloth napkins, ice water, and air conditioning. I was used to
eating with sweat dripping into my food, but not here in Saigon.

My room on the sixth floor of the Newport BOQ was air-conditioned. This allowed the windows to stay closed keeping out the city sounds and the mosquitoes from the streets below. The front of the Newport BOQ looked out onto the soccer field and stadium, kitty-cornered across the street. Occasionally, I got to watch a game from the roof. The windows of my room looked out towards the Emergency Room of the hospital and an affluent neighborhood of comfortable houses owned by Vietnamese. Immediately across the street in front of my BOQ was a large, triangular-shaped field of shoulder-high elephant grass. Elephant grass, which can hide a human being very easily, grows all over Vietnam. This field was used by Vietnamese as a public bathroom. Men and women would walk into the grass to answer nature's call in relative privacy. The custom of using elephant grass fields as bathrooms helped explain the high incidence of infectious hepatitis in Vietnam. The drinking water was contaminated by this form of inadequate waste control. There were few facilities available for the Vietnamese people to use. Their credo must have been "any old port in a storm," which, in this case, was a field of elephant grass. The United States Public Health Department's contribution to the health of its citizens can be appreciated by visiting countries like Vietnam. Although the United States government tried to advance the public health concerns in Vietnam, this was a painfully slow process.

There was even an elevator in my BOQ, a convenience rarely seen outside Saigon. My room had a real bed, a bathroom with a shower, a dresser, a phone, and electric lights that worked from a switch on the wall. A maid came to clean and do laundry every day except Sunday. My clothes were always clean and pressed, including my underwear and socks. On the roof above the tenth floor were wire clotheslines for hanging laundry, as well as lounge chairs for tanning, reading, or both. The roof was a cool and breezy place to spend early evenings reading as long as the light would last. I really enjoyed the roof! All in all, Saigon was very good duty. I knew I was going to enjoy my new assignment.

From time to time, I would venture out into the city to do some sightseeing, either with Ron, Paul, or by myself. I quickly made a good number of friends at work or in the BOQ. One of my acquaintances was Colonel Knight. He was a "full bird colonel," i.e., he had an eagle as his insignia and was three ranks above me, a captain. Colonel Knight was a supply officer working long hours in a downtown office seeing that our soldiers got what they needed to carry on the war. At night, he would come home to the Newport BOQ. We usually ate together in the officer's' dining room and had long political discussions. He was one of those nice people who was genuinely interested in what other people were doing. Occasionally we would get a drink at the Circle 34 and continue our conversations there. He would always ask me about my family, which impressed me, and I tried to return the favor. We showed each other pictures of our families when we got new ones in the mail. His children were much older than my daughter. I enjoyed hearing about the problems of raising a family in the Army. He had graduated from West Point and was on the Army fast track for promotion. I surmised he was probably a genius at what he did as he was always meeting with bigwigs like General Westmoreland and the United States Ambassador to South Vietnam, Elsworth Bunker.

Colonel Knight came to my rescue once when I got entangled with a nasty major from my BOQ. Each night as the local bars emptied, streams of people would walk home to the BOQ past the hospital. I had just finished my evening shift in the ER, and as I was heading for my room in the Newport BOQ, I joined the flow of people walking by. I was blissfully puffing on my pipe, as I liked to do after finishing work. My mind was more than a million miles away from the other people as I sauntered along that pleasant night. The night was dark, and I failed to notice the black oak leaf insignia on the lapel of a man walking next to me. He remarked to me, "That's some pipe you have got there, mister!" I said something like, "Yes, thanks." He snorted back to me, "Don't you have any respect for a superior officer? Give me a salute right now and come to attention before you do it. Do you hear me?" Surprised by his sharp demands for unaccustomed Army etiquette, I did as he ordered, as best I could. Passersby, on their way home, were bumping into me, and no one was paying the least bit of attention to my unfortunate situation. "Sorry, Sir!" I said, "I didn't notice your rank in the poor light." "You didn't even look!" he snapped back, obviously irritated, and obviously intoxicated. He yelled at me some more, and then wrote down my name and where I worked in the hospital. He warned me that he was going to submit a formal complaint to my CO in the morning, and, if I ever passed him again, I'd better act more like an Army officer and salute, or he would have me court-martialed. "Yes, Sir!" I answered, and I turned to continue walking home. As fate would have it, he lived in the Newport BOQ too. Turning in unison, we both entered the main door of the building. I promptly ran up the stairs to avoid an elevator ride with that miserable so and so.

The next night I was telling the dinner table group the events of the night before. The major had been partially correct. I didn't give much of a hoot about the Army's mandatory etiquette, and neither did my colleagues at the table, as they scoffed at the major's demands. Like the others, I thought it was kind of a funny encounter and no big deal. Not so with Colonel Knight, who happened to be eating at the table also, and had heard the whole story. I was embarrassed I hadn't appreciated his being there. I should have checked who was sitting at the table before shooting off my big mouth. I presumed he would have sided with the major and would be disappointed with my sloppy attitude and conduct. The colonel asked me more details about what happened, which seemed to get him more worked up. I wished I had never mentioned the incident, but too late, the story was out. To my surprise, the colonel sided with me! "No one looks at rank walking on a dark street in the middle of the night!" he told me. "Chewing you out and making you stand at attention was way out of line. Officers should not treat other officers like that! I'll handle this." He was obviously very irritated with that major. I learned the colonel was the ranking officer in the BOQ and had a list of the men assigned to rooms therein. He was going to find out who harassed me, and he would "Take care of him!"

Several nights went by, and Colonel Knight didn't mention our conversation about the major at all. We talked about usual things, and I hoped my run-in with the major had been forgotten. After dinner several nights later, the colonel began to talk about the incident. He had found out the major's name. He knew him and had a long talk with him about me. The major apologized. He had had too much to drink that evening and was just trying to have "fun" with me. The colonel read this guy the riot act. He advised the major not to talk to me ever again, and he had better not try that kind of chicanery on any other officers. If he did, he would have to answer to him personally. Having told me of his meeting with the major in harsh tones and raised voice, the colonel then resumed his gentle composure and mild mannerisms. Wow, I never wanted to run afoul of Colonel Knight. He had quite a stern side to him, as did most high-ranking officers. His stern side seemed fair to me, however, and I admired the colonel for what he did on my behalf and in fairness. The Army was his life, and he clearly did not want the Army way of life to be a hiding place for bullies. For the next three months, the colonel and I remained friends, eating and talking together. He was a fine man and the Army was certainly a better organization because of him.

When I had been in Cu Chi many months earlier, I got to be friends with Warren Wheeler, a general medical officer. One day I saw him in Saigon, eating in the Massachusetts BOQ restaurant. Rekindling our old friendship, we did a lot of things together. He was working in downtown Saigon at a one-man walk-in medical clinic and lived in the Massachusetts BOQ. He was a bachelor and a very quiet man. He was from Alabama and had a light southern accent. Always a gentleman, he almost never swore or got angry. Warren was very intelligent, and he wanted to see some more of the South Pacific world we were in. Under his leadership we began to make plans to visit Australia before we left for the United States. This was the month of May and we would be leaving Vietnam in early August. There were three months left to plan a trip. We picked Australia as our primary target. The "Land Down Under" was what we both wanted to see, and we began to formulate plans to get there. Warren and I both had been on R&R, which everyone realized they were entitled to. Few knew, however, that during a year in Vietnam, leave was also possible.

Our commanding officers cut orders for us each to have seven-day leaves for early July. Now all we needed was transportation to Australia. This could be difficult, because we couldn't displace R&R soldiers from their plane seats to Sydney. If we applied two months in advance, we could make the arrangements, so that's exactly what we did. I had taken care of a soldier who worked in the travel allocation department at Tan Son Nhut. He had a bad case of venereal disease and was scared to death. Two weeks of antibiotic therapy resulted in a cure. My patient was so relieved, he personally got us on the plane to Sydney on the exact days we requested. All the good times I was to have in Australia, I owed to tetracycline!

The cardiologist at the hospital was a brassy, obese, and obnoxious man, Tony Casuli. I knew him at Fort Sam Houston back in Texas.

He stood out among that group of reserved men with his loud out-bursts about visiting "Boystown" in Nuevo Laredo, Mexico. He would yell to a friend while were marching, bragging about the good times he had with the prostitutes there. He acted like an over-grown juvenile delinquent out of the 1950s. At the time in Texas, I decided that I just didn't like this guy, and now, here he was again, in an important position at the hospital. From what I heard from his fellow internists, he was doing a very commendable job in his role as a heart specialist. Tony and I met and talked on several occa-sions, and I thought I had probably misjudged him back in San An-tonio. He no longer seemed to have a chip on his shoulder, and he was very comfortable in his job. I consulted with him on several patients I had seen in the ER and was impressed with his profes-sional demeanor and insight. There wasn't the slightest hint of the immature loudmouth I had seen at times in Texas.

Several weeks later though, I had an unfortunate confrontation with Tony. Any soldier with a fever over 101 was a straight-through admission to medicine, and I had such a patient that day. The ER doctors were not supposed to be responsible for a working diagno-sis. We were just to admit the patient to the Medical Service for the Medical Officer of the Day to see and diagnose. The soldier I admit-ted that day had a fever of 102 degrees and was complaining of a sore throat. He did have a very irritated throat so I took a culture before I admitted him to medicine. The culture results would be ready sooner for the doctor on the ward if I did one in the ER. The next morning Tony came down to the ER asking, "Where's Snider!" I said, "Here," and he walked over to me as I was standing by the stretcher that held the patient I had just been examining. Tony cupped one of his hands over my mouth and the other behind my neck. He shook my head back and forth while saying, "Why didn't you think of mononucleosis? Mono can present with a sore throat. You should have gotten a mono spot test yesterday and saved me a lot of work." Breaking his grasp on me, I stepped back, incredulous about the attack I had just experienced at Tony's hands. "How could a doctor do that to another doctor in the first place, wasn't that as-sault and battery?" I thought to myself. Besides, my job wasn't to examine that patient in any fashion. The patient was simply to be admitted to Tony, the MOD, and evaluated by him alone. The head nurse in the ER was shaking her head in total disbelief at what had just happened. I composed myself somewhat and then asked Tony to step into the nurse's empty office. After Tony and I entered, I closed and locked the door behind us. Very angry, I began shaking my finger at him and blurted out in the most threatening manner I could muster, "If you ever touch me again, I'm going to punch you in the nose. Who do you think you are, anyway?"

I'm sure I was cursing a blue streak, and I was relieved to see Tony's face pale a little. "Why are you getting so hot under the collar, anyway?" he responded. I reiterated my dislike of his throttling me, and he agreed not to do it again. Tony outweighed me by at least one hundred pounds and was much taller than I. My message seemed to get through, though. We each left that room, never to have any similar disagreeable encounters again. Actually, I avoided him like the plague. I think getting rid of the audience helped defuse Tony's reaction. He didn't have to save face without anyone around to watch.

Tony wasn't the only character around. Dr. Harold Shaw was a very tall and stocky surgeon from Mississippi. To me, he was an out-and-out megalomaniac. There was no doubt he was a gifted surgeon, but he just needed to grow up. A chest surgeon, he was smooth as silk when operating, but his demeanor out of the OR was a disgrace. He considered himself a supreme womanizer and would talk filth to any woman he chose. He felt above the rules of decency. Nurses were always reporting him for inappropriate behavior, but nothing ever seemed to come out of those complaints. One day, to my surprise, I saw the showgirl who had been wounded in Tay Ninh several weeks before! She was to have her wounds checked by the doctor in the ER, and I saw her for this. Evidently Harold had sutured her buttock wound after she returned from Tay Ninh. The wound that concerned her so much had healed nicely, and the scar was barely noticeable. I had her look with a mirror, and she was obviously pleased. As she was walking out of the ER, she ran into Harold Shaw coming in the waiting room. She was very pretty and he recognized her immediately. In a flash, he had lifted up her skirt to view his handiwork. Gasps came from the startled onlookers as her legs and underwear came into public view. The singer herself seemed stunned and could only smile nervously. When Harold finished inspecting her rear end he turned and walked away like nothing had happened. Harold was something, all right. He didn't seem to care a bit about other people's feelings, which is not a good characteristic for a physician. On surgical rounds he ignored the patient's questions and spoke only to the other surgeons. Once on rounds, a soldier, who had been wounded in the abdomen, was found to have a very low blood pressure just as our entourage came to his bedside. Harold listened to his lungs with a stethoscope he had rudely snatched out of the hands of a nearby doctor. Not hearing good breath sounds on one side he stated that someone missed a hemothorax. With a knife blade and no local anesthesia, he proceeded to place a chest tube on the side he suspected had blood. A painful procedure even with local anesthesia, Harold didn't use any at all as I recall! Moreover, he didn't respond to the patient's protestations. The group of rounding surgeons pleaded with him to stop, but Harold had the tube in place in an instant. He was callous, but he was an excellent, rapid surgeon. No blood was to be found in that soldier's chest. The patient went through that torture for no reason. A chest X-ray would have told us the same thing without any pain being inflicted on the soldier, but that would have taken a few moments, and Harold didn't want to wait. A young surgeon can learn a lot about what not to do and how not to act from a surgeon like Harold Shaw. I did.

There were many excellent surgeons there who were compassionate as well. These men did everything possible to reduce suffering, ease pain, and save lives rather than just time. Jim Guernsey was an academic surgeon from Stanford University and was a prime example of a kind and extremely gifted surgeon. The best surgeon I met there was Dr. Caesar Cardenas. Originally from the Philippines, he attended medical school in Manila but finished his surgical training in Cleveland. A general and thoracic surgeon, his knowledge and skill were remarkable. Unlike some, he was always available, and when he came to see a patient, he was calm, decisive, and very compassionate to the soldiers. I believe I learned more from Caesar than I had from anyone else. Watching how he worked was how I learned from him, not from formal teaching sessions. Caesar could formulate a plan of diagnosis and action quickly and precisely. As new data became available his plans would adjust accordingly. A favorite expression of his, as I remember, was, "Now, this changes everything!"

Caesar would often write letters to the families of soldiers telling them what he knew about their sons. That was above and beyond any regulation and was greatly appreciated by the families,

I'm sure. I saw him save many lives. He worked tirelessly, but he also knew when to give up. Two cases of civilian injuries come to mind when I recall Caesar. The first was a ten-year-old Vietnamese girl who had a large piece of metal casing sticking out from her posterior pelvis. This little Vietnamese girl was playing innocently when a shell exploded nearby, causing her injury. The metal piece was solidly fixed to her pelvic bones just above her rectum. She was wide-awake and in extreme pain. She couldn't or wouldn't move her legs, suggesting nerve damage. She had not lost much blood because the metal piece was acting like a cork, holding the blood inside the many severed vessels. Caesar examined her, and then the first thing he did was explain to the understandably frantic mother, in a very compassionate way, what he planned to do. He would have to take the little girl into the OR and remove the metal with her under general anesthesia. He explained he may not be able to stop the bleeding, but he planned to take every precaution possible. The mother gave her consent and, to my surprise, Caesar hugged her!

With a small tear in his eye, Caesar took that poor little girl to the operating room. There were many more wounded for me to see that day, which meant I couldn't go to the operating room with him. Caesar told me what had happened later that night. The girl had been given a general anesthetic, and Caesar went to work. When he removed the chunk of steel, she promptly bled profusely. The anesthesiologist had placed large IV lines before the metal was moved, and blood was administered before the metal piece was touched. Despite this pre-loading with blood, and six more additional units of blood, the girl died. I heard the screams of the mother when Caesar told her the bad news. I saw Caesar walk with the woman and her family down the covered outdoor corridor to the front of the hospital. Caesar took several days to bounce back from that case. He told me the huge fragment had just about cut the little girl in half. The iliac vessels, the ureters and much of her intestines were severed. He had clamped her aorta above the severed iliac vessels, but the vessels bled profusely anyway. I felt very sorry for Caesar; he took things very personally, which was probably the reason why I admired him. Caesar, in a reflective moment, told me that he had a great deal of empathy for the Vietnamese civilians because he had been a little boy in Manila during the Japanese occupation. That fact told me a lot concerning his understanding the nature of civilians caught in war.

The second case was similar. A young woman was in profound shock from a bullet wound through her lower abdomen. I opened her abdomen in the ER and clamped her aorta above the injury in hopes of stopping her bleeding. The blood I gave after the aorta was cross-clamped helped bring her blood pressure back towards normal, and she began to regain consciousness. I called for Caesar, and he came running. We took her straight to the OR, but we couldn't stop her bleeding. We gave her untold amounts of blood and clotting factors, but we never could control the blood loss. The high-powered bullet had pulverized her intestines, pelvic and back muscles. Several hours into the surgery, her young heart gave out and she died. If she ever meets Caesar in heaven, he can tell her he tried everything possible to save her, and with God as his judge, he will be right.

THE GENERAL AND THE BABY

Located in Saigon, the Third Field Hospital had a lot of dignitaries passing through in 1969, including a lot of high-ranking Army brass. The receiving area for wounded was in the paved lot next to the Emergency Room. Here were the familiar sawhorses ready to hold the stretchers. There were drains in the floor every few feet to receive the mud and blood washed from the wounded bodies. The area was covered with tin roofing and had fluorescent lights in rows overhead. At night, the lights, the insects, and the wounded GIs all accounted for a surrealistic scene. The struggle to save those severely wounded soldiers under that tin roof proceeded in an intense and grave fashion that was strangely quiet at times. Doctors, nurses, and medics all knew what to do and their efforts were pursued in hushed desperation without shouting or even raising their voices. A quiet scene like that said a lot about the consideration and the efficiency of the workers.

I worked on most of the wounded in this outside extension of the Emergency Room. Assisting in this outside arena were two of the best medics I had ever seen. One was Perez, a Puerto Rican native, whose first name I never knew. Everybody just called him "Perez!" He was nineteen, very good looking and he loved the ladies. While we were working, he would tell us all in great detail about his exploits with the women he had recently met. His prattle was never distracting and often helped ease the tenseness of the moment. His smile was infectious and his laugh comforting. He had a special way of helping the wounded GIs. He talked to each one like he knew them personally, and they responded as if speaking with an old friend. He had a heavy Spanish accent and was proud of his heritage. He loved to talk in Spanish with his fellow Puerto Ricans, and his gesticulations during those conversations were something to behold. His sidekick, and fellow medic, was a young man with the last name of Miller. I never knew his first name either, as Perez only called him "Meeler" so I, and everyone else, followed suit. "Meeler" was tall, prematurely balding, and very soft-spoken. He too had a way with the GIs and they responded well to him in kind. "Meeler" and Perez lent a certain lightness to this serious business. The nurses and doctors worked better when those two were on duty, and, providentially, they usually were working when the "fertilizer hit the ventilator."

When a wounded GI was brought in, he was usually covered with thick jungle mud and blood, obscuring his wounds. Perez or Miller would begin to hose the covering dirt and gore off the soldiers to allow an accurate inspection. To facilitate finding the offending wound, Perez would ask, "Where'd you get hit, soldier?" The reply was often, "Oh, about six clicks outta Trang Bang!" Perez would bristle and ask again in a harsher voice, "No, No! Where on your body? Dammit," his Puerto Rican accent being much more noticeable when he was irritated. The irony of that question with its answer as a map location, rather than an anatomical site of injury, always evoked laughs from the medical personnel in attendance, often to the confusion to the unsuspecting wounded soldier. When they understood what Perez was asking, the GIs would point to their wound, and Perez would clean that area first.

Often Perez would visit the wounded men he took care of in the ER after they had been treated. The wounded were kept on a surgical ward until their transfer to Japan could be arranged. Those wards were dismal and sad places where despair and pain reigned. Perez's visits, unsolicited and out of the blue, were cherished by those he saw. He would make them laugh with his stories and antics. He would often tell them he really didn't come to see their sorry asses, but he was just checking out the new nurses on duty. That Perez, he had a gift all right, and I learned a lot about interpersonal relations by watching him in action. He was remarkable. Everyone loved Perez. Nurses, doctors, high-ranking brass, and even the janitor had smiles for him as he passed by. He owned his world, and he loved his life.

It was only natural that I became very fond of Perez, and I tried to coincide my work schedule with his so I could enjoy his charismatic company. Understanding each other as we did, surgeon and medic, we worked very smoothly together, and I liked that. A good assistant can make all the difference in the world to a surgeon and, knowing this, I always sought to work with Miller and Perez. Soon, Perez, Miller, and I became an inseparable team, and their upbeat friendly outlooks rubbed off on me. The days flew by quickly and painlessly even with the war raging all around Saigon.

Often we would receive many wounded at one time. Calls would go out for help from the Emergency Room during those times of mass casualties. Doctors and nurses would rush in en masse, adding to an already confusing scene. Paradoxically, it was during such a mass casualty situation, that an amusing moment occurred, and rumors of my being rude to a three-star general began.

In the outdoor treatment area I caught a glimpse of a struggling GI, cursing a blue streak as his stretcher was being positioned on the awaiting sawhorses. This type of wild behavior usually marked the wounded man as being very seriously injured and in shock. I singled him out as my first priority that day and he was indeed in shock. His ashen face held dark eyes filled with terror as he cursed the enemy that had done this to him. Assessing his wounds and general poor condition, I opted for a shot of morphine. The drug would cause his low blood pressure to go even lower, but it would calm him enough to allow me to work. The morphine quickly gave him respite from the fear of the enemy that was frozen in his numbed brain, and he lay back on the stretcher, quiet now, but barely breathing. Not waiting for the corpsmen who began to cut away his clothes in order to find his wounds, I started a cut-down on one of his arm veins. To save his life, he needed blood rapidly and in large volumes. My first step was to locate a vein in his arm big enough to insert a large hose-like tube into it through which the lifesaving blood and fluids would easily flow.

Just as I made the cut over the upper forearm, the light with which I needed to see was repeatedly blocked. Shadows came over my surgical field at the most inopportune times, thwarting my efforts at performing the surgery this soldier so desperately needed. Glancing over my shoulder at my light source, I saw a portly man in a khaki uniform positioned right in front of my surgical light. Irritated, I said, "Please, get out of my damned light!" The man moved back slightly and then asked me what I was doing. More annoyed now, I answered curtly, "Trying to find a vein!" and added, "For God's sake, keep out of my light!" I heard Perez snicker in the background, and then I heard him explain to the person what I was doing.

The cut-down completed, I proudly began pumping several units of blood into my patient through the new big IV line. Color was slowly coming back into his ashen face, and the wounded GI began to speak coherently! As he began responding to the infused blood, I examined his wounds. Grenade fragments had fractured the main bones, the femurs, in both of his thighs. There were no other injuries. He was very salvageable, and was coming around from his previous frantic presentation nicely. I called for an orthopedist to assess him, and I continued to administer blood. His blood pressure stabilized. The orthopedist took my patient to the Operating Room for debridement of his wounds and fixation of his fractures.

I was washing my hands at the small sink in the treatment area when Perez came over to where I was standing. He stood there by me, laughing and acting silly. "Do you know what you just did?" he asked. "You told off a three-star general! You told him to get the hell out of your light!" Not remembering exactly all that happened, I was somewhat confused, so I asked him what he meant. "You told that three-star general to get back and to get out of your damned light, Doc. You should have seen him jump back! He turned pale and began to quiver a little. I'm telling you, it was something! A freaking three-star general, Wow!" Now I was getting the picture. Evidently, a visiting three-star general was looking over my shoulder, and I shouted to him to get out of my light. With a triumphant smile, I said to the nearly convulsing Perez, "Just goes to show you Perez, the real power in the Army belongs to the docs, man! Why, I can push a big three-star general around with my little finger." Perez got such a big kick out of that incident, he would tell and retell the story to whomever would listen, laughing about my cursing out "three-stars" and ridiculing the Army's rigid system of rank. I, on the other hand, was more careful in the future. From then on I would try to look before yelling. I never told Perez that, because I enjoyed listening to him rattle on about me. I guess it was flattering to hear the "No shit!" the story evoked from those who heard it. Perez would then point to me, and I would take a bow. Our mutual admiration was blossoming, and we became even more efficient working together.

In that same tin-roofed outdoor treatment area, something so horrible, and so unsettling happened to me that I will never be able to shake it from my consciousness. There is hardly a day when this specter doesn't haunt me, and hardly a night when I don't have the same terrible dream. Through the years I have found that a surgeon has a lot of nightmares, but this one beats all of mine.

I had been working the ten P.M. to eight A.M. shift for a week, and this night the work had been very light. At midnight, I had the luxury of falling sound asleep on a stretcher in the cool ER. About three A.M. Perez shook me awake. He was obviously very agitated. His face was pale, and he was sweating profusely. His Spanish accent was more noticeable, confirming his state of anxiety. "Come quick, Doc, there's a baby!" he said excitedly. His words dropped off with "baby." "Baby?" I asked, "What do you mean?" I rarely saw babies in the ER. "Come on Doc. Hurry! It's awful, man, just awful. Hurry, the kid is dying!" We ran through the door to the outdoor treatment area. There, in the dark and hot tropical night, spotlighted by the bright surgical lamp, was a tiny baby! As white as the sheet it was lying on, the little one was obviously in extremes. The baby looked oriental, but more Chinese than Vietnamese. His right leg was neatly amputated at mid-thigh, but there wasn't any active bleeding any more. While looking at that poor little pale infant and trying to collect my thoughts, the ambulance driver told me a rocket had hit the Cholon section of Saigon about an hour earlier. He was called there to help. The Vietnamese ambulances had taken all of the other wounded to the Vietnamese hospital, but he felt he should bring the baby here. The ambulance driver got another call and left. Cholon was the Chinese section of Saigon which explained why this child looked more Chinese than Vietnamese. I understood the Vietnamese had little love for the Chinese nationals who worked in Saigon, and ironically the NVA used Chinese Communist rockets to pelt Cholon. So here we were, with bugs flying into the lights, in the middle of the hot night, alone, in a struggle to save the life of the most innocent victim of war I had seen so far. I could not imagine anyone could be more innocent than a baby.

Perez snapped himself out of our momentary shared apoplexy by quickly opening a cut-down set, knowing that would jump-start me. During those few moments of gawking, I was trying to formulate my plan of action. To have any chance of survival at all, the baby would need blood right away! My guess was that the baby was about a year old and would have tiny veins, and a vein large enough to receive infused blood, would be the key to this child's recovery. Chubby babies like this one are the bane of a surgeon's existence, and I remembered what Dr. Willis J. Potts, a famous pediatric surgeon, had said about operating on infants: it often took longer to find a vein than to do the operation. That was in my mind that night as I started the search for a vein. I knew this was going to be next to impossible. The infant was groaning in agonal respirations, an indication that no more than a few moments of life remained. Only extreme youth allowed this child to survive this long! By this time, any older person with such a catastrophic injury would have died from blood loss!

Dr. Jim Guernsey was the surgeon on call for the ER that night, and I had asked Perez to call him at the onset. Knowing a back-up surgeon was on the way helped me a little, and I began the cut-down at the elbow on one arm. Having no luck in locating a usable vein, I tried on the other arm in several locations and then on the remaining ankle. The baby was drained of most of his blood and there wasn't any left in the tiny vessels to help me find them. The veins were made invisible without the blue-red blood in them to contrast with the surrounding pale tissues. By this time, I was frantic. The sweat was dripping off my face, and the insects had become intensely annoying. The futile cut-down procedures had taken only ten minutes, but, in those precious ten minutes, the baby's heart gave out. There were no more labored little breaths, no movement at all. The baby had died! The hot night now had a chill in it, and I shivered.

Jim Guernsey came down the lighted covered outdoor walkway and approached me, as Perez and I were standing in the light of the surgical lamp with the annoying bugs constantly circling around our heads. Jim looked at the dead baby, at Perez, and then at me. I knew by his face that he already had accurately assessed what had happened. The multiple extremity incisions displayed my frantic and unsuccessful efforts to find venous access. Jim studied the amputated thigh for a moment, and, looking up at me, asked in a very kind voice if he could show me something. He said he was thinking of what to do as he walked over from his quarters, and he wanted to show me what he had decided. Since the baby was dead, his instructions wouldn't help in this case but maybe would in a similar situation in the future. Using a surgical pick-up he quickly and cleverly found the transected vessels at the amputation site. He demonstrated how I could have placed a large catheter in this site and given blood through this severed vessel. Almost shaking, I told him that I had thought about that, but didn't choose to use this site because of the possibility of contaminating the IV line. Glaringly obvious to me now, at that point in the overall desperate situation, possible contamination of the IV site was a very small point! Words began to stick in my mouth. If only there had been more time to think. Later, as a practicing surgeon, I would also think treatment plans over as I walked into the ER to see a patient, just as Jim did that night. Perez had advised Jim the baby had an amputation in mid-thigh, so Jim was able to think over how to approach this problem on his walk from his quarters. Thinking things over on the way to the ER is a luxury the ER doctors themselves don't get to enjoy, because they come face to face with disaster abruptly. Jim assured me he didn't mean any criticism at all. He just wanted to point out this possibility to me. Then he left to walk back to his quarters, and I could feel my heart pounding in my chest.

Perez and I never even knew the baby's name, and I can't really remember whether it was a little boy or a girl. I don't recall having ever looked. What difference would that make? There were no family members or anybody present at all, just Perez and me with our dead little patient. The sight of that baby with the alabaster skin, lying on the dark stretcher in the middle of the night under the glaring lights and the circling bugs, has been indelibly etched into my brain. I still carry the mental picture with me. When I dream about that night, I awake thinking, "If only I had used that vein!" My emotions flare when I remember the Chinese baby died all alone. No mother, no father, just Perez and me. I imagine the eternal hour of horror that child endured as he bled to death that night. And for what? Death was delivered from an unseen and unknown enemy for no reason. What went wrong with the world that night? I think of the enemy soldier who fired that rocket that night. He should be told! He should be made to remember too! Words cannot accurately describe my confused state as I gazed upon that tiny corpse. I was horrified at the violence done to this completely innocent human being. I was severely disappointed in my surgical inability to save the child. Most of all, I was caught up in the recurring realization of the futility of war with its senseless loss of life. Perez and I baptized the tiny mutilated body in the hopes of possibly giving salvation. Despite the tenets of some religions, that child's soul had to be as pure as any soul could possibly be, and it should enjoy all of heaven's rewards by any standard. Just to be sure, though, we covered all bets with a little saline from the IV.

We left the baby in the cold morgue. The next morning, the body was gone. The disinterested clerk in the morgue told us a Vietnamese woman had come early in the morning, claimed the body, and took it for burial. No forms had been filled out, and no more information was available. The baby was just another nameless soul. A victim of war, a victim of man, its life was over!

Unable to shake what had happened from my mind, I was pretty low for a week or two. Perez was the one who helped me out of my doldrums. When he was sure I was ready for it, he asked me if I had been able to start the IV, and given the blood, would the baby have survived? After all, over an hour had passed since the injury and breathing was already agonal. I had to agree there probably would have been brain damage even if we had been able to restore reasonable blood pressure, and the odds were certainly against meaningful survival. Talking it through with Perez that day helped lessen my anguish and disgust. The fact that the baby probably would not have survived wasn't the whole point. I think the whole incident reflected my feelings on the futility of war and the meaningless daily loss of life that I was witnessing. To this day, when I pray in church on Sundays, I always ask God to care for that Chinese baby and my three men. Remembering is the only thing left for me to do.

AUSTRALIA

The day arrived when I was to leave for Australia. Warren and I said goodbye to the poor guys who had to stay behind, and we set out for the airport and our adventure. In no time we were flying at forty-five thousand feet, winging our way to the first stop, Darwin, Australia. Stretching my legs felt great and I walked around the small airport for the hour layover. The next step of the trip only took two hours, but our plane had to circle the Sydney airport because of a city ordinance forbidding planes to land before seven A.M., and the time was only six A.M. Wide awake and anxious to start our vacation, Warren and I used this time to plan our activities for the next week. I explained to Warren that I didn't want to hamper any plans he had to meet women. Being married, I planned on very sedate activities like sightseeing, visiting the world famous zoo in Sydney, and I wanted to visit some of the famous outback country I had read so much about. As I mentioned, Warren was a very quiet and undemanding man, and he assured me that the activities I had outlined were fine for him too. Warren said if the girl of his dreams came along, he would adjust his plans, but there were a lot of women back in Alabama, and a trip to Australia only came along once in a lifetime. In short, he planned to see all he could of this South Pacific country in the next week.

As we deplaned, the flight attendants sprayed us with insecticide, which was demeaning to say the least. I noted that the Australian soldiers were not sprayed, and that infuriated me. When I objected, the stewardess assured me that I was mistaken; all passengers were being sprayed regardless of their uniforms. Holding up the line of disembarkation for this minor problem quickly made me unpopular, so I swallowed my pride and moved on. Outside the airport building, the air was surprisingly cold. Having come from the hundred-degree heat of tropical Vietnam, the forty-degree weather in Sydney was very chilling. We hurried into the rental shop to stock up on warm civilian clothes to wear in this frigid place. Little did we realize that the temperatures in the Sydney area warmed up to about seventy degrees during the day, and the woolen clothes I selected soon became too warm. I adapted well, though, and actually relished the cool weather.

At the American Welcome Center we were given general instructions for "Yanks in Australia." Our GI predecessors in Sydney had tarnished the reputations of American soldiers on leave in this country. Consequently, we were asked not to wear our uniforms while on leave in Australia. Also, American GIs had such a high automobile accident rate, they were no longer allowed to rent automobiles. The unfamiliar "keep to the left" driving, coupled with alcohol, was a particularly dangerous combination. Disappointed about the latter, Warren and I took a cab to our hotel in downtown Sydney. Walking into the lobby, we were surprised to find that the hotel lobby was not heated. The woman who signed us in told me that few public buildings were heated in Sydney because it just didn't get that cold here. Despite the early hour of our arrival, we were allowed to go to our room where we showered, made phone calls home, and slept. Fortunately our room had a heater, and we got warm for the first time since coming to Australia.

I was famished when I finally awoke at 8 P.M., as was Warren. That night we ate in a restaurant that revolved around the top floor of the tallest building in Sydney. Our view of Sydney Harbor was breathtaking, and the Australian white wines were delicious. The dinner I had was a real treat and we drank steaming hot coffee with real cream while we planned the next day's activities. The wine helped me to sleep that night and by the next morning I was completely acclimatized to the new time zone and the cold. Fortified with a great breakfast, we set out exploring. I bought my wife a star sapphire ring and an opal pendant. I bought my daughter a koala bear made out of kangaroo fur with a wind-up music box inside that played "Waltzing Matilda." We took a trip around the huge Sydney bay on a spacious tour boat that we practically had all to ourselves, followed by a sunny afternoon in the wonderful Sydney Zoo. The next day we went to the outback on a bus tour. The "Three Sisters Wilderness" was breathtaking, and then we rode mine cars through abandoned mines in Katoomba. One night we went to a waterfront diner where we ate lobster and drank Australian Riesling wines.

Waiting for a bus back to town after that meal, we realized, too late and to our surprise, we were waiting on the wrong side of the street. The last bus had left, and we had to cough up the money for cab fare back to our hotel.

Every place we went people said, "You must be Yanks." I learned to say, "Good day mate!" with a perfect Australian accent. I loved Australia, but the trip only made me more homesick for America. One evening, we saw Barbra Streisand in "Funny Girl" and that really made me long for home and to hear a New York accent. Sometimes our being Yanks stood out like a sore thumb. My worst faux pas was asking, "Where are the chairs?" in a white-tiled stand-up pub in downtown Sydney. We got a snarling, "You must be Yanks!" in retort and we were advised that Aussies enjoy their pints standing and leaning against the chest-high shelves that lined the walls. The humiliation at the derisive laughter my exchange with the bartender evoked was salved by the delicious brew I sipped that night. The dark ales and beers of Australia, Ireland and England were truly to be savored, and "almost like eatin'" indeed! We lounged on the grass of Victoria Cross Park and delighted at the elementary school children as they frolicked in their Eton coats with straw hats pinned to their coats by blue and white striped ribbons. A senior registrar, equivalent to America's resident, gave us a grand tour in The University Hospital of Sydney. This was a treat for us to see modern civilian medicine once again.

That Australian trip had been a marvelous opportunity for me and I vowed to revisit it with my family someday. Refreshed by the rest and sated with the memories of good food and drink, I was resolved to finish out my remaining six weeks in Vietnam with a renewed determination. The smell of Saigon as the plane door opened was disheartening to my new resolve, but I returned to my job smiling broadly.

In Sydney, Australia

THE LAST DAYS IN SAIGON
AND
FATHER SULLIVAN

My remaining time in Vietnam marched on. An American man walked on the moon that month, and I had another gut-wrenching experience on the earth. I admitted about my one-hundredth GI to the medical service for a fever of over 101. I did not examine him in any great detail, confident the patient would be examined and diagnosed by the Medical Officer of the Day who was responsible for these patients on the wards. I understood the nurse on the ward who received this patient would notify the MOD another "fever of unknown origin" was there for him to see. With this particular soldier, that may not have been exactly what happened.

Several days later, I was notified by the Chief of the Medical Staff that my presence was requested at an upcoming morbidity and mortality conference. Not having any idea why my presence was needed, I attended the morning conference the next day. There, I found out the soldier I had admitted had died! I heard that his diagnosis was pseudomonas pseudomallei pneumonia which was a pneumonia caused by a very virulent bacteria found in Vietnam. I had heard of this type of pneumonia, but never saw a case until now. After the case had been presented in detail, the whole audience looked at me and I knew my face turned red. The Chief of Staff asked me why I hadn't examined this patient and possibly ordered a chest X-ray? Surprised at his question, I was almost speechless. I wondered if he knew about the policy of admitting patients with a fever of 101? Answering his inquiry, I sputtered out that as I understood my duties, I was to admit any American soldier with a temperature over 101 as a fever of undetermined origin (FUO), and that his care would be automatically transferred to the MOD. The embarrassment and humiliation I initially felt turned to anger as I listened to an internist whom I had never seen before state there was no such policy. He didn't understand why I had been so derelict in my duties and not even ordered a chest X-ray!

"Now hold on a minute, here!" I said in the firmest voice I could muster. "Just what is the policy?" The chief of staff, an orthopedic surgeon, responded that he wasn't familiar with that policy, but he promised to meet with the ER people to find out which policies were in effect. I felt blind-sided! Why hadn't someone inquired about the policy before? I knew that I alone had admitted many such patients in the past. Did I get a "bum steer" from the others when I arrived, and why spring this on me with out any warning? I left that meeting very ill at ease, but I wanted some answers.

When I composed myself, I asked the charge nurse in the ER about the policy and if she knew about that patient. I was very relieved to hear that she agreed the policy was as I described, and that the ER doctors were not expected to do any type of work-up on patients who had to be admitted in any case. The MOD and the ward clearly were to initiate care. She went on that my patient was rumored not to have been seen at all on the day I admitted him. By the next morning, the patient was very ill with the rare and often fatal condition. Most of the GIs admitted with FUOs were not seriously ill, and perhaps the doctor on call was not called, or didn't respond. From that day on, I felt my character had been unfairly challenged, but I got over it. I did talk with the MOD personally from then on whenever I admitted a FUO with a temperature over 101.

Third Field had an excellent priest in Father Sullivan. He held a Mass each Sunday at ten A.M. in the hospital chapel. Father Sullivan was very well liked, and his Masses were crowded with Catholics from Saigon as well as the hospital. His homilies were what most Catholics wanted to hear, not boring and mercifully short. The highlight of his Masses had to be the folk singing. Folk Masses were fairly new, one of the better innovations of the 60's. To me, they were more enjoyable than the stuffy, old-fashioned services that made me feel left out. The guitarist at Father Sullivan's Masses was very talented. Not only did he play the guitar masterfully, he sang all the songs in an infectious manner that invited everyone to join in. The best song had to be a very upbeat version of the "Our Father!" I was a very shy singer of songs, but the guitarist made me feel like I was in a Broadway musical. The guitarist also acted as an altar boy and even took up the collection at just the right time. I thought he must have been studying to be a priest and got drafted.

During my last week in Vietnam, the Circle 34 held a going-away party for Father Sullivan. He was being transferred to another chaplain's spot up north. Being very popular, and known to take a sip of whiskey once in a while, Father Sullivan's going away party was to be held at night with a live band. I went to his party, and enjoyed all the speeches, especially Father Sullivan's farewell address. His speech was poignant, well thought out, and very well delivered. After he finished his speech, I invited him over to my large table for a drink. The band resumed playing, having been interrupted by the speech making, and there was a different female singer on stage now. I told Father Sullivan how much I enjoyed his masses and how good I thought the guitarist was. Father Sullivan agreed he was exceptional, a good assistant and a very talented musician. I asked if his assistant were going to be a priest. Looking surprised, Father Sullivan said, "Gosh, no! My assistant is an Orthodox Jew and had been a Rabbinical student for a while!" Evidently chaplain's assistants had to embrace ecumenism because of their limited numbers. Up to that moment, I had no idea anyone other than a Catholic could sing the songs and function as an altar boy as well as that young man did.

Father Sullivan took his leave from my table and went from table to table to say his goodbyes. He said he felt things were going to get "out of hand soon," and he wanted to be ready to depart the Circle 34. At the time, I had no idea what he meant by "getting out of hand," but I soon did. The new woman singer was a stripper! She began to bump and grind to the hoots and hollers of the audience, while the good Father hurriedly rushed from table to table talking to his old friends. When the stripper was down to just her top and bottom, Father Sullivan waved goodbye to the boisterous crowd and exited to pleas for him to stay for the end. There was no stopping this properly modest priest, and he was out of the club as well as my life for good. The stripper finished her act by removing all she was wearing, but that process took another fifteen minutes. I had never seen a strip dance, and when this one was over, I remarked to Ron, "Now I have seen everything!" and left in the footsteps of the priest.

My head was reeling with the echoes of the shouting and from the strong drinks. Sitting alone in my room on the side of my bed I realized, although I had been joking with Ron, I HAD seen everything Vietnam had to show, and I was going home in a few days. With nine or fewer days left in country, I was now properly referred to as a "One Digit Midget," and that made me grin from ear to ear. The next day I was relieved from work, and I spent the hours readying for the trip home.

GOING HOME

That grand day came at last, the day of days! I was loaded into the back of a quarter-ton truck with my duffel bag. Ron VanderMolen and several lucky others also finished with their tours in Vietnam were loaded with me, packing us all in like sardines. I didn't mind, I was going to DEROS the hell out of here. I had entered Vietnam at one end of the Long Binh base, and now I was to leave from the other end. At one time, I had been told that my tour would be shortened by ten days from a full year to 355 days, but my ten-day "drop" didn't materialize. I had already been in Vietnam for 363 days; tomorrow would be 364! I prayed to get out the next day. The rumor was that we would. When I arrived at the DEROS camp in Long Binh, Warren Wheeler was already there. The processing out took an hour or so, and everything was in order for my departure. The camp was full of giddy soldiers excited about going home. I had my picture taken by a famous sign pole that had direction arrows pointing to cities around the world, such as Los Angeles, New York, Dallas and even Newark! With nothing else to do but wait, I sat around with a bunch of officers, shooting the breeze. Warren entertained us all with an imitation of LBJ's famous "Why Vietnam" speech. Warren was perfect, imitating LBJ to the nth degree. The laughs of the soldiers spurred Warren on for another paragraph or two. I never realized this quiet man could command so much attention from so many. His timing and mannerisms were very funny, and he became the toast of the replacement depot that day.

With nothing else for us to do the rest of day 363, we found the beer hall the Army had so thoughtfully placed nearby, and we all drank a few. We shared a table with a very drunk major from the Big Red One Division. Ron had served with First Division, and they naturally began to talk about old times. Suddenly the major stood

up, overturning his chair with a crash, and he began a drunken tirade. He praised his old division with tears in his eyes, but then he
started to demean all the other divisions in Vietnam, one by one.
Ron and I got out just in time. Drunken tempers began to flare and a
fight quickly broke out. I didn't want to get hurt in a beer hall on my
last day. Ron and I hid in our temporary barracks for the rest of the
afternoon. In the evening we were ordered to take a shower at this
time or go home the way we were. About three hundred men
traipsed to the showers at one end of the camp, wrapped in towels,
and wearing flip-flops. That night, as I tried to sleep, I thought I
heard incoming. Several others were awake and looking around
also. We all agreed that we were just nervous, and that couldn't
have been incoming here; not in safe Long Binh. I tried to sleep, but
the sounds of three hundred GIs snoring kept me awake for a long
time. Knowing that I could sleep on the plane, I relived most of past
year in my mind and was finally able to fall asleep thinking about
my wife and my daughter.

At breakfast the next morning, a sergeant announced that our
plane was on time and this was the last meal we would enjoy in
country. Cheers rang out, and everyone made a mad dash back to
the barracks to get ready to leave. I put my duffel bag on the baggage cart while holding onto my shaving kit. I queued up to board
our "Freedom Bird." A sergeant at the bottom of the portable stairs
stopped me and told me my sideburns were too long and I would
have to go back to the barracks to shave them off. I tried to argue,
but he wasn't even listening. Ron told me he would save me a seat,
and I started back. Passing a mud puddle, I thought for a second,
then bent over, moistened my sideburns with the muddy water. I
pulled my safety razor from my dopp kit and shaved my sideburns
by feel. I turned and ran the few steps to the stairs. There were
cheers for my ingenuity as I showed the sergeant my shortened
sideburns, and, laughing, he waved me aboard. I settled in my seat
next to Ron and awaited our trip back to the "World!"

"Don't kiss the tires!" The phrase went around our plane as we
began to taxi down the runway in preparation for take off. I heard
that once a returning GI was so happy to get back to the United
States, that, when he got off his plane, he kissed the tires of the
plane that had brought him home. Sadly, the tires skidding on touch
down, had heated to the melting point, causing his lips to stick when
he kissed the tires. Some said his lips had to be cut loose from the

tires! Obviously, this was a rumor, but it seemed like good advice. I wasn't going to kiss those tires, and that was for sure!

The twenty-four-hour hour flight from Long Binh to Los Angeles dragged at times. At LAX, I boarded a flight to Newark where Margy and Beth Ann would be waiting. After waiting an hour in line to use the phone, I called Margy and told her that I was coming into Newark, my airline, my flight number, and my estimated time of arrival. I remember that we both chuckled during our conversation, we were so excited. My seat for the flight was in coach, but after being airborne for a while, a stewardess invited me to move up to First Class. The stewardess had a brother in Vietnam, and since the plane wasn't full, she invited to move forward. I moved up and enjoyed a great meal, but soon fell asleep only to wake up as the plane landed at Newark Airport.

From the dimly lit corridor, I spied two of the most beautiful people in the whole world. Margy was wearing the muumuu she had bought in Honolulu and had dressed Beth in a miniature matching outfit. Running over to them, and picking them up, I kissed them over and over again. My war was over, and I felt like crying. I prayed there would be nothing but joy and peace from now on.

EPILOGUE

As a child on Long Island, New York, my father took my sister, brother and me to see the parade our town, West Hempstead, was having for the returning veterans of World War Two. He made us hold our hands over our hearts as the American flag came by and I remember him telling us how proud he was to be an American. Writing to my parents from Vietnam, I remember telling my dad that I would never have a parade like the one we saw in 1945 for the Vietnam War, and I thought that wasn't right. When I pulled into my dad's driveway in Montclair, New Jersey, for the first visit with my parents on returning from Vietnam, I saw what my father had done to make me feel better about my war. Strung across the front yard was one of my mother's bed sheets with large black letters proclaiming, "Welcome Home, Captain Snider, We Are Proud of You!" My world was becoming right.

REFLECTIONS

Looking back on my Vietnam experience from the vantage point of over thirty-five years of marriage and four grown children, there is no doubt my time in that long-ago war profoundly affected my very essence. The memories have not dimmed with time. The memories of my three dead men, the Chinese baby, and all those who died on both sides have become indelible, and they still ache. Several years ago I visited "The Wall" in Washington, D.C., and the names of my three men are inscribed on the black granite of that awe-inspiring monument. The names on that wall are a fitting tribute to the memories of the men they represent. Just seeing the names of my and all the other men on "The Wall" has helped immeasurably. I know their names will be seen for centuries to come. The memories of the Chinese baby and all the other ghosts of war dead will fade with me. There can be no memorials for all of them, which is sad.

Any war is a waste, and there is nothing unique about the war in Vietnam. No war is better than any other especially if you have to die in it. I can't help thinking about the Rebel soldiers in the Civil War. Did they die for nothing? Does anyone who gets killed in a war ever die for anything? Only a few wars in the history of man left the world a better place. As far as Vietnam is concerned, I don't blame anybody for his or her feelings and actions. Those against the war felt they had valid points, including the likes of Jane Fonda and Bill Clinton. The election of an alleged draft evader to President of the United States saddened me, but such is life after war.

Twelve years after the war was over for me, a mother asked me if I thought her son, who was killed in 1968 in Vietnam, had given his life for nothing. Her anguish was evident, and I tried to find an answer that might ease her suffering. No soldier ever really wants to "give up" his life. Everyone wants to live. Soldiers fight for their buddies, sometimes dying in their company, but they never fight for political issues. The important thing has to be if a soldier did his job, not whether his war was a "good one." I quoted that mother a line from a poem I happened to remember. The name of the poem is "My Son," and the lines are as follows:

> "It matters not where some men live,
> if my dear son his life must give;
> God's test of manhood is I know,
> not will he come, but did he go."

The mother's son did his duty out of simple obedience.

There is still some notion that eighteen-year-old men had a choice about being drafted and going to Vietnam. That is totally erroneous. Not to go was to give up one's citizenship forever, and few wanted to do that. Most of us felt we had no choice, and we didn't. Also, most of us felt the Vietnam War wasn't any more unjust than any other war, and we realized the justness of the war had nothing to do with doing our duty. Decisions about the war were made by our government, and this wasn't the first time a government sold young men down the river.

I was filled with admiration for our fighting forces doing their jobs with little griping and a great deal of courage. The men sent to Vietnam were models of the American soldier tradition and should eternally be remembered as such. The unappreciated Vietnam veteran is wholly undeserving of the negative mantra he is still forced to shoulder. I saw America's sons in action firsthand, and I was proud to be one of them. Remember what they did, and, most of all, remember those who died there. Far away and all alone, they missed their loved ones terribly when they died. Those who died in Vietnam deserve unflagging remembrance. That's all they wanted, for us to think about them from time to time after they were gone.

GLOSSARY

11 Bravo – the MOS of the grunt

Ao-Dai – Vietnamese women's formal wear consisting of a long white shirt with tails to the knees, and black slacks

APC – Armored Personnel Carrier

ARVN – Army of the Republic of Vietnam. South Vietnamese regulars known as "Marvin the Arvin"

Bac Si – Chinese literally meaning "barefoot doctor," a village person who tended his fellow villagers medically, generally meaning "Doctor"

Charley – sobriquet given to enemy soldiers derived from "Victor Charley" in the army alphabet; short for Viet Cong soldiers but also stood for the North Vietnam Army soldiers

CID – the Military's Central Intelligence Division

COs – conscientious objectors or commanding officers

Dai Wi – Vietnamese for Captain

debride – to cut away all non-viable or infected tissue in a wound

dee dee mau – Vietnamese for get (the Hell) out of here

DEROS – Date Estimated Return from Overseas. The long-awaited day to go home

DOD – Department of Defense

DPC – Delayed Primary Closure

EM – Enlisted Men

FUO – Fever of Unknown Origin

GMOs – General Medical Officers as opposed to Specialists

grunt – Army slang for the rifleman

hooch – Japanese word for quarters or house

JATO – Jet-Assisted TakeOff

KIA – Killed in Action

LRPs – Long Range Patrol. Units made up of tough soldiers who
   stay under cover in the jungles and observe enemy activities
materiel – the supplies of war
MOS – Military Occupation Speciality
MP – Military Police
NCO – Non-Commissioned Officers, i.e., sergeants
NCOIC – the Non-Commissioned Officer In Charge
NPDs – nighttime defensive positions taken by soldiers on patrol
NVA – North Vietnamese Army regulars
PSP – standard military interlocking Perforated Steel Plates
punji sticks – sharpened bamboo sticks placed in the bottom of a
   concealed pit. The tips of these sticks were often covered with
   human excrement to hasten infection in the hapless victim
RPG – rocket propelled grenades, a much-feared Chinese Commu-
   nist bazooka-like weapon
RTO – soldier who was the patrol's Radio-Telephone Operator
T&TGSW – Through and Through GunShot Wound
VC – Viet Cong, Victor Charley, or Charley-the enemy
WIA – Wounded in Action

INDEX